THE
BRITISH
AND
CYPRUS

T0323117

THE BRITISH AND CYPRUS

AN OUTPOST OF EMPIRE TO SOVEREIGN BASES, 1878–1974

MARK SIMMONS

In Memory of my Father
Albert Frederick Thomas Simmons (Tommy) Royal Navy
and my friends
Albert James Ley, Royal Marines and L.E. (Robbie) Robins Royal Air
Force,
all of which served on Cyprus.

With the archways full of camels
And my ears of crying zithers
How can I resolve the cipher
Of your occidental heart?
How can I against the City's
Syrian tongue and Grecian doors
Seek a bed to reassemble
the jigsaw of your western love?

'Port of Famagusta', Laurie Lee, Cyprus 1939

Cover illustrations. Front, top: Author's collection; *bottom*: *Illustrated London News*. *Back*: Author's collection.

First published 2015
Reprinted 2021

The History Press
97 St George's Place, Cheltenham,
Gloucestershire, GL50 3QB
www.thehistorypress.co.uk

British Library Cataloguing in Publication Data.
A catalogue record for this book is available from the British Library.

ISBN 978 0 7509 6070 0

Typesetting and origination by The History Press
Printed in Great Britain by TJ Books Limited, Padstow, Cornwall

Contents

Acknowledgements

A book like this is an oral history of the British involvement with the island of Cyprus, a special place to many peoples and races down the ages, and to the British to this day – be they servicemen, ex-pats, or tourists – and could not have been written without a great deal of help.

I owe a huge debt to many people who, with great kindness, have made available valuable original material in the form of diaries and letters.

The Royal Navy, because Cyprus has no real natural harbour and never became a fleet base, had little direct contact with the island. However I am grateful to the late Tom Simmons, my father, for his yarns about 1947. And also Corporal T.A. Hannant RM for the exploits of HMS *Hermes* in 1974.

My own Corps, the Royal Marines, came up with a wealth of information. Brian F. Clark (Bomber), the secretary of the 45 Commando '*Baker Troop*' association, spent most of a winter's afternoon relating his experiences in Cyprus and Suez during the 1950s. He even gave me a copy of the Troop Journal, which was invaluable and largely instrumental in persuading me to write the book.

Thanks also to the late OC Baker Troop Major F.A.T. Halliday, and troop members Colin Ireland, Sergeant Derek Wilson, George Ferguson and John Cooper. The Troop Journal is in the RM Museum soon to be located in Portsmouth Historic Dockyard. It is now available as a Royal Marines Historical Society publication, *Cyprus Crisis 1955–1956*.

Colonel Tim Wilson also gave much information on the deployment to Cyprus of 40 Commando in 1955 as did Fred Hayhurst, and to all my 'oppos' in the 40 Commando association who shared their yarns with me.

Spike Hughes wrote from Spain about his time in Support Troop 45 Commando and Operation Lucky Alphonse also featured in *A Fighting Retreat*, by Robin Neillands, another former Royal Marine. The stories of Marine David Henderson, 45 Commando, and Captain A.W.C. Wallace RM, came from Britain's Small Wars website.

The story of Arnold Hadwin I came across in *The Light Blue Lanyard*, the story of 40 Commando RM by Major J.C. Beadle, which was first published in the *Lincolnshire Evening Despatch*.

Former soldiers were just as helpful. Twin brothers Richard and Mike Chamberlain did their National Service with the Royal Corps of Signals and left a vivid picture of Cyprus just prior to the EOKA troubles, through the paper *Cyprus Today*.

Charles Butt, who served with the Intelligence Corps Field Security Section, sent me a wealth of information and helped with some searching questions about the EOKA period. It was Charles who directed me to the British Empire and Commonwealth Museum.

The British Empire and Commonwealth Museum also supplied me with oral history tapes for R.W. Virant, Royal Corps of Transport, and Lieutenant Colonel Wilde, Royal Engineers.

Gary Spencer served with Royal Army Medical Corps during the 1974 troubles helping Cypriot refugees in the Athna Forest Camp. John Johnson, 4th Royal Tank Regiment, served with the UN.

Colonel Colin Robinson did several tours of duty in Cyprus, in particular in the early months of 1964 with the 16th Parachute Brigade.

Hugh Grant, another Para who served in Cyprus during the last few months of the EOKA troubles, wrote *A Game of Soldiers*, another gem. As was *Airborne to Suez*, the memoirs of Sandy Cavenagh, Medical Officer of 3 Para, the early chapters of which cover his time on Cyprus.

Gordon Burt, another member of the Parachute Regiment, came from the archives of the Imperial War Museum as did the fascinating story of Major W.C. (Harry) Harrison, Royal Army Ordnance Corps, who was seconded to the Cyprus police as the Government explosives expert.

Auberon Waugh's memoirs *Will This Do?* told of his National Service with the Royal Horse Guards, and his description of the Guenyeli massacre was graphic.

The story of the Ashiotis Incident from the late Alan (Gunner) Riley came from his oppo Dave Cranston, both ex-Royal Ulster Rifles, through the *Britains-small-Wars* website.

The Royal Air Force has had a long association with Cyprus. Squadron Leader Norman E. Rose and Squadron Leader Colin A. Pomeroy gave a grandstand view of the 1974 invasion. Geoff Bridgman for the 1980s. Raymond A. Ferguson for his yarns as a regular airman toward the end of the EOKA troubles. Thanks to the late Group Captain L.E. (Robbie) Robins, AEDL, for his thoughts about Cyprus during various visits and supplying illustrations, free use of his extensive library and his general hospitality.

Vyv Walters for his view of Cyprus in the last twelve months before the 1974 invasion. And Robert Gregory for his nine-day rides around Cyprus on a motorbike in 1942.

Jack Taylor, former Royal Marine and policeman, served with the Cyprus police through much of the EOKA troubles, his memoirs *A Copper in Kypriou* being another rare find.

Civilians were, perhaps, understandably not so forthcoming. However, the British Empire and Commonwealth Museum oral tapes library supplied me with the memories of Mr Lennard, a Colonial District Officer, who arrived on Cyprus with his family two weeks after the first EOKA bomb attack. His wife Mary-Pat's views on civilian life at the time were helpful. Thanks to Mrs Hazel Fowdrey, wife of Doctor Alan Fowdrey, for a wartime picture, and Faith Lloyd, who served with the Red Cross in Palestine and Cyprus 1949–51, and Sheila Mullins for her thoughts on teaching Greek Cypriot children at Bermondsey Primary School and her visits to Cyprus, and to Jan Bradley for her memories of the 1974 invasion.

The Imperial War Museum supplied the diary of Mrs Sommerville, a service wife who was a contemporary of the murdered Catherine Cutliffe. Thanks to the late Edward Woodward OBE and John Parker.

Museum personnel were most helpful: Doctor Gareth Griffiths, Director of the British Empire and Commonwealth Museum, and Mary Ingoldby, the oral history co-ordinator. Sadly the British Empire and Commonwealth Museum closed in 2008 and was wound up in some controversy in 2012. Thanks also to Stephen Walton, archivist at the Imperial War Museum.

Thanks to M.G. Little, archivist Royal Marines Museum, and Y.H. Kennedy at the Historical Records Office Royal Marines.

James Crowan, reader services at the Public Records Office who steered me in the direction of HMS *Comet* and *Charity*, and Kate Tildesley from the Ministry of Defence Naval Historical branch who helped with the above.

Many publications were helpful: Captain A.G. Newing at *The Globe and Laurel*, journal of the Royal Marines; the editor of *Pegasus*, journal of the Parachute Regiment; the editor of *RAF News* and the RAF Association; *NESA News* publication of the National Ex-Services Association; Gill Fraser at *Cyprus Today*; the editor of *Soldier* magazine and the *Legion* magazine, and *Britain's Small Wars* website; and *The Thin Red Line*, the regimental magazine of the Argyll and Sutherland Highlanders.

Some more rare books were helpful: Suha Faiz's memories of an *Unknown Cyprus Turk* recommended to me by the Green Book Shop, Kyrenia, Northern Cyprus.

My local second-hand bookshop, Bookends of Fowey, obtained for me *The Memoirs of General Grivas*, edited by Charles Foley, and Foley's own *Island in Revolt*.

Lawrence Durrell's *Bitter Lemons of Cyprus* was another insight into the EOKA period. Colin Thubron's *Journey into Cyprus* gives a memorable picture of the island prior to the invasion and division of 1974, and I can sympathise with his blistered feet; mine too have suffered on Cyprus. Also Penelope Tremayne's, *Below the Tide*, gave a great insight into living in Greek Cypriot villages during the troubles.

To Shaun Barrington, my commissioning editor at The History Press, for continued support, and to John Sherress, fellow author, always a good proving ground.

And to Margaret, my dear wife who too has suffered from blisters on Cyprus. And proofread most things I have written, and typed and edited so many things. To all these I am grateful and to those that lack of space prevented an account from being included, their view was important in the overall story. Many thanks to all.

Glossary

Attila	Turkish Army operation code name for 1974 invasion of Cyprus
Black Mak	Soldiers' slang for Archbishop Makarios
Camp K	British detention camp near Nicosia used for EOKA suspects
CFBS	Cyprus Forces Broadcasting Service
Clear Lower Deck	Situation Report to all ranks Royal Navy and Royal Marines
Dighenis	George Grivas's code name. Mythical figure in Cyprus history and mythology
Enosis	Political union of mother Greece and Cyprus
EOKA	National Organisation of Cypriot Fighters
EOKA-B	Second coming of above (1974)
GNG	Greek National Guard. Cypriot Army with Greek mainland officers
GPMG	General Purpose Machine Gun
Green Line	United Nations buffer zone between North and South Cyprus, policed by UN troops
GUZ	Naval slang for Plymouth, Devon. Believed to come from the First World War identification letters for the port

KOYLI	King's Own Yorkshire Light Infantry
LCVP	Landing Craft Vehicle and Personnel
Mason–Dixon Line	Dividing Nicosia between Turks and Greeks. Taken from the line that divided the slave states from the free in the USA
Murder Mile	Lendra Street, Nicosia
MMG	Medium Machine Gun (Vickers)
NATO	North Atlantic Treaty Organisation
Oxi Day	28 October Greek celebrations over the defeat of the Italians in the Second World War
Q Patrols	Police vehicle patrols in towns
RUR	Royal Ulster Rifles
Sangar	Small sandbagged defensive gun position
SBA	British Sovereign Base Area
SLR	Self-Loading Rifle
TMT	Turkish terrorist group
TRNC	Turkish Republic of Northern Cyprus
Uhi	Remote area of landscape
UNFICYP	United Nations Force in Cyprus
Volkan	Turkish counter-terrorist organisation that pre-dates TMT
Xhi	Greek right-wing resistance group during the Second World War

List of Abbreviations

The following abbreviations have been used in the notes, which appear at the end of each chapter.

ADM-(PRO)	Admiralty – National Archives (Public Records Office)
CIA	Central Intelligence Agency USA
(DEFE)-(PRO)	Defence Office
FCO-(PRO)	Foreign and Commonwealth Office
KV-(PRO)	Security Service Files
WO-(PRO)	War Office
BECM/Oral Tape	British Empire and Commonwealth Museum/Oral Tape
ITA	Interview with the author
IWM	Imperial War Museum
LTA	Letter to the author

INTRODUCTION

Kolossi Castle 1974 and 1992

On the night of 19 July 1974 an RAF Nimrod XV241, from No. 203 Squadron, in the maritime reconnaissance role, took off from Luqa Airbase Malta. It climbed into a starlit night sky turning east, its objective the island of Cyprus just over 1,000 miles away.

XV241 co-pilot Colin Pomeroy was initially disappointed at missing the Annual Summer Ball in the Officers' Mess that night but was about to see history in the making. Colin recalls the approach to Cyprus:

> Some 150 miles out we could clearly see from the flight deck, fires burning out of control on the Troodos Mountains and soon we were down at low level off Kyrenia above the grey invasion fleet. Although we were scanned by search and fire control radars, not one anti-aircraft gun pointed upwards at us, which was most comforting, but we made a point of neither flying directly over or towards any of the Turkish Warships.[1]

On that same July day the Commando Carrier HMS *Hermes* with 41 Commando Royal Marines embarked, arriving off the southern shore of Cyprus. Hermes had arrived off Malta, home then for 41 Commando, three days earlier after a deployment to the USA and Canada. However, the declining situation on Cyprus had required the diversion to the island for an 'indefinite period'. On 21 July the main body of the Commando were flown off *Hermes* into the Eastern Sovereign Base Area of Dhekelia.[2]

Two thousand, three hundred airline miles to the north-west the advance party of 40 Commando Royal Marines, the United Kingdom Land Forces Spearhead Unit for July, had left Seaton Barracks, Plymouth, for RAF Lyneham and air transport to Cyprus to reinforce the garrison. Nobody knew quite what to expect. Yours truly, a young Marine Commando then fresh from training, would be in the next wave.

All this activity was the result of the Turkish invasion of 20 July, an event that many on Cyprus and in Greece to this day blame on the British. To them it was the fruition of nearly 100 years of misguided rule, and involvement with the island, by Britain.

In 1992 I returned to Cyprus for the first time since the invasion of 1974. Yet nearly twenty years on it all looked so different. From Kolossi Castle's sandstone battlements I tried and largely failed to locate the old position I and my fellow Marines had occupied. The Vehicle Check Point (VCP) had been on the north side of the Episkopi–Akrotiri SBA.

It had been within sight of the castle which was just outside the base area. The original Crusader castle was built in 1210, more than likely by the order of the Knights of St John of Jerusalem, otherwise known as the Hospitallers. The order lives on today with its headquarters at Valletta, Malta. However, the castle passed between the two great orders, the Hospitallers and the Templars, over the years until the latter were indicted for heresy. Some say the present castle dates from 1454 built on the ruins of the original.

The keep is over 70ft high, and in the east side is a panel bearing the coat of arms of the Lusignans. Here abouts the knights cultivated vines that produced Commandaria, one of the oldest wines that are still drunk. Thick and sweet, more like a fortified wine, 'it was famous throughout European Christendom, and fuddled successive Plantagenet Kings'.[3] On the south side of the sugar factory there is an inscription saying the building was repaired in 1591 when Murad was the Pasha of Cyprus. The Englishman Fynes Moryson, who passed this way in 1596, commented on the cultivation of sugar-cane and the use of the mills. By 1900 the Scotsman Cecil Duncan Hay, with his family, lived on the Kolossi estate in a house attached to the keep. He planted the cypress trees that are now taller than the keep, while the family used one of the huge castle rooms as a badminton court.[4]

Somewhere nearby sandbags had been filled to build the sangar. Our task was to regulate the flow of traffic in and out of the SBA, which included members of the Greek National Guard and the Greek Cypriot Defence Force, Turkish and Greek Cypriot refugees. For in the face of the Turkish invasion, people flooded into the British Bases, mainly Turkish Cypriots to Episkopi-Akrotiri, Greek Cypriots to Dhekelia and foreign nationals and tourists to both.

The invasion was the result of a mainland Greek plot, by the Military Junta then in power in Athens, to bring about Enosis, the union of Cyprus with Greece, by deposing the Cypriot President Archbishop Makarios. Makarios had once been a champion of Enosis but had come to realise it could never work given the volatile mix on Cyprus and the stance of Turkey. Enosis was not a new idea even in the 1950s. Indeed at the start of British rule in 1878 the Bishop of Kition, welcoming Sir Garnet Wolseley landing at Larnaca, raised the subject, hoping Cyprus could in time be 'united with Mother Greece, with which it is naturally connected'.[5] The only concrete result of the 1974 plot was the invasion by Turkey and the division of the island along the Green Line; thus the Greeks had really scored an own-goal.

I walked along the Akrotiri road half hoping to find the sangar, or even a rotting sandbag or discarded entrenching tool. Off-duty time had been passed reading or listening to the forces radio. There had been tense night patrols amid the plantations to 'dominate the ground' and stop arms smuggling through the base area. Once we put out a 'contact' report over the radio when a donkey jumped us. The Greek National Guard fired on us across the border. They thought we were Turkish paratroops was one yarn we were told, while another was that we had taken an offensive stance with our observation posts overlooking the SBA boundary. A Marine from A Company was wounded in another encounter, but in this case fire was returned, wounding one of the Greek National Guard who later died.

A little disappointed with Kolossi Castle and my memory, I took the road north toward the distant dark Troodos Mountains. The road climbs gently through a white rocky landscape. The thin white-grey soil is ideal vine country and vineyards are dotted everywhere across the terraced ground. The villages around here are known as the 'Commandaria Villages', after the wine favoured by the Crusaders.

At Pano Kivides I stopped, *pano* means above or higher. The village, once Turkish, is abandoned. You have to drive down a bumpy lane even to get to it. The only noise came from a lizard that scurried away at my approach. The buildings were eerie and the village had a Pompeii-like quality. But now the houses were only frequented by the odd roving goatherd. For its people village ties were stronger than national or religious belief. The fact that more Greeks were displaced and moved south to the Turks who went north is a statistic bad enough in its own way but it cannot tell the tragic story of every village, family and person.

In 1974 there were atrocities on both sides. Within the SBA was safety, but outside was different. East of Limassol at the mixed village of Tokhni an EOKA-B gang murdered all the Turkish men over the age of 16. That village even today has a haunted atmosphere.

EOKA had been formed by Archbishop Makarios, General George Grivas and others; in 1953 its sole aim was union with Greece by force. EOKA means 'National Organisation of Cypriot Fighters' (in Greek transliteration *Ethniki Organosis Kyprion Agoniston*). In 1971, Grivas returned to Cyprus in secret, disguised as a priest, to organise the EOKA-B, meaning EOKA number two or the second, with the blessing and backing of the colonels in Athens. Grivas died in January 1974 before the July coup against his old ally Makarios. Nicos Sampson led the EOKA-B during the coup and Turkish invasion and usurped presidential power, however only holding the post for eight days. He was a former murder group leader in the 1950s terrorist campaign and was known as the 'chief executioner on Ledra Street'. He became 'vilified by many, admired by few'. He would have his photo taken with one foot atop the corpse of a Turkish Cypriot he'd killed. Under his leadership EOKA-B killed more Greek opponents than Turks, and buried many of the former in unmarked graves. Afterward he tried to plead he had been forced into the office by the Greek Junta;

however he quickly resigned. With the return of Makarios he was tried for treason, found guilty and sentenced to twenty years in prison.[6]

Some 300 Turks were murdered at Tokhni and some villages near Famagusta, and it is believed some 2,000 Greek Cypriots disappeared in Turkish hands during the same period, some being deported to Turkey for interrogation.

The nature of the Greek Cypriot has changed. The events of 1974 are partly responsible. The loss of Kyrenia and Famagusta, the best resorts, resulted in panic building in the south and an overemphasis on tourism. Over half the population are now involved in the trade; they say Cypriots dream of 'hotels and taxis'. The youngsters dream of leaving the island; at 8 years of age they start to learn English.

From Pano Kivides I headed for Malia where I turned south again toward the sea. The run toward the coastal road passes the Sanctuary of Aphrodite, set amid orange groves on rising ground enjoying a cool breeze from the sea, sometimes known as Old Paphos. It was once one of the most popular places of pilgrimage in the ancient world right up to Roman times. In its heyday the temple would have dominated the seaward approach to the south coast. I wonder what stories its few remaining ancient stones could tell witnesses to over 2,000 years of history, and what they would say of the British.

'Cyprus should be Greek there is no doubt about it,' Michael, one of the locals told me near Pissouri Bay where I had gone in search of food. But Michael was not as local as all that, for his tall frame, fair skin and blonde hair betrayed his background: Athenian by birth, Cypriot by marriage.

'I was a paratrooper in 1974 ready to come and fight for Cyprus. But you English let us down. Not you personally, it was your weak politicians,' he hastily added. For '*philoxenia*', the law of hospitality, would not allow an insult to a stranger. I pointed out the Greeks had broken the tripartite agreement of 1959 and had given the Turks the legal right to intervene. And from the north coast Cyprus was only 40 miles from Turkey. Surely the geographic position of the island made it as history had demonstrated a crossroads of the Middle East rather than just another Greek Island.

'You English,' he said smiling, 'history for a Greek goes back through his family hundreds of years. And the Turk,' he said, contorting his face as

if there was a bad odour in the air, 'have been about only a few years compared to us. Did you know [I did not at the time] the whole of the Middle
East was Christian for centuries before the Turk who are just Mongol
barbarians my friend. Goodbye English,' said Michael as we parted. 'Do
not worry about the history it is hard enough for us.'

Surely Michael, it seemed, was guilty of a familiar misconception
Penelope Tremayne had identified so well: 'Cypriots are Greeks, but
Greeks are not Cypriots.'[7] However, his words did put a thought in my
mind: had we the British, as Michael had hinted, somehow betrayed the
legacy of Hellenism with our actions on Cyprus, and in a way betrayed
our own roots?

Patrick Leigh Fermor came across the same question in his travels in
the Peloponnese, that England had let the Greeks down and even more
somehow turned Turk against Greek on Cyprus. He wrote in 1958:

> The conviction that its emergence 'inter-communal fighting on Cyprus'
> was fostered by Great Britain to bring in outside support to an otherwise
> untenable case has done more than anything else to embitter the problem
> in Greece.[8]

I crossed again into the SBA near Paramali, another Turkish village
deserted now, except occasionally for squaddies on exercise. Its mosque
and Muslim cemetery are identified by a sign asking people to respect
its sanctity.

Near the entrance to the Sanctuary of Apollo I was pulled in at a Ministry
of Defence VCP manned by MOD (Ministry of Defence) police who were
locals working for the British. How things have changed. Badly I tried to
explain I had seen Frankie Howerd entertain the troops here at the Greek
theatre overlooking the sea in 1974, with a pop group, the name of which
escapes me. But the police were more interested in my passport and driving
licence and probably thought another 'rambling mad weighty John who
has been in the sun too long'. Greek Cypriots tend to call all Englishmen
John. But they smiled and nodded and said, 'Have a nice evening.'

I was soon back at Kolossi Castle again. The cicadas were tuning up
for the night. I recalled a Turkish family we had helped at the VCP; why

they stuck in my mind I don't know. They had arrived in a grey battered Austin A55 crammed with the entire family, from gran to babes in arms, the roof packed high with pathetic possessions tied on through the doors. One of the back tyres was flat, and the engine was badly overheating. When the ignition was switched off the engine, so hot, ran on and on with pre-ignition, then at last shuddered as if dying before finally stopping. I remember giving Spangle sweets to the children from our ration packs. We had changed the wheel on the old Austin for them, using a bottle jack from our own Land Rover, refilled the radiator and sent them on to the tented refugee camp in the SBA. It was the air of fear about them that stuck in my mind. Fear that we would not let them into the SBA and they would be at the mercy of the EOKA-B. Where they are now or even who they were I have no idea. They are surely in the north of the island having gone through the melting pot of history.

The deployment of 40 Commando Royal Marines to Cyprus in 1974 was unusual. The Commando was the spearhead unit in July and was flown out to reinforce the western SBA. On 20 July the advance party left Seaton Barracks, Plymouth, by road, for RAF Lyneham and Fairford and flew to Akrotiri where it came under the command of HQ 19 Airportable Brigade. The Commando's main task, with 1st Royal Scots, the resident battalion in Akrotiri, to maintain the security of the SBA.

Although the Commando changed company positions several times during its first deployment the general pattern of operations was the same. The border of the whole SBA was covered by a line of overt OPS, sand-bagged sangars and a series of VCP check points and road blocks.

After three weeks the situation seemed to have stabilised and the Commando was released and started to fly back to the UK. However, after two days the flight back was cancelled, with half the unit still in Cyprus, the rest back in Plymouth, some of whom had already gone on leave. However, the recall system was used again and the vast majority returned to Plymouth and then to Cyprus, to be greeted with. 'Well did you enjoy your weekend leave in Guz?', Guz being naval slang for Plymouth.

The recall was the result of the Turkish Army resuming its offensive on 14 August. What has been called Phase 2 of the Attila operation.

The Commando resumed its duties in the western SBA, and also helped in constructing refugee camps and clearing service married quarters and hirings in Limassol outside the SBA which had been the subject of some looting. It also helped with requests from the UN. It was in this same general area 40 Commando was deployed in 1955–56.

Notes

1. LTA, Squadron Leader C.A. Pomeroy, 10/6/2000
2. *Globe and Laurel*, Journal of the Royal Marines, August 1974
3. Colin Thubron, *Journey into Cyprus*, p. 151
4. Dr Ekaterinich Aristidou, *Kolossi Castle through the Ages*, pp. 43–4, and Tabitha Morgan, *Sweet and Bitter Island*, p. 57
5. Sir Harry Luke, *Cyprus*, p. 174
6. *Daily Telegraph*, 11/5/2000 and *The Guardian*, 21/5/2001 and David Matthews, *The Cyprus Tapes*, p. 7, 'Annie Barrett telephoned from Kyrenia and called him "The butcher of Ledra Street"'.
7. Penelope Tremayne, *Below the Tide War and Peace in Cyprus*, p. 10
8. Patrick Leigh Fermor, *Mani: Travels in the Southern Peloponnese*, p. 210

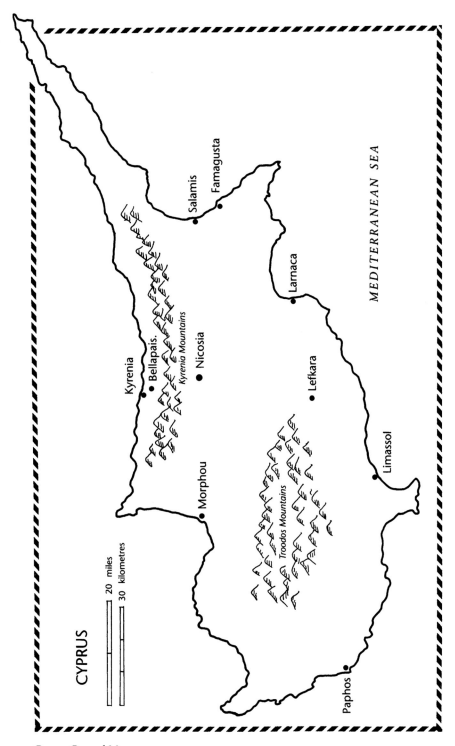

Cyprus General Map

1

THE EARLY
YEARS

Benjamin Disraeli came back with Lord Salisbury from the Congress of Berlin in 1878 claiming 'peace with honour'; they also had Cyprus in their pocket.

On 13 June 1878 the Congress of Berlin had convened to try to make sense of the Treaty of San Stefano, signed three months earlier after the fourth war of the nineteenth century between Russia and Turkey. Most delegates' thoughts were on Russia's further encroachment on Turkey's European frontiers; no one thought much of the Middle East and even less of Cyprus. However, the senior British negotiator, the ambassador in Constantinople, Sir Henry Layard, had already done a secret deal for *Perfidious Albion*; on 4 June a 'convention of defensive alliance' was signed between Great Britain and the Ottoman Empire. So the Sultan Abdul Hamid II ceded the island of Cyprus 'to be occupied and administered by England'. The role of Cyprus in this was to become Britain's forward base to support Turkey against any further Russian aggression. Although the island was never suitable as a fleet base, Britain was willing to support the Ottoman Empire as a buffer against Russian designs on India.[1]

On 12 July 1878 Vice Admiral Lord John Hay hoisted the Union Flag in Nicosia and assumed the temporary administration of Cyprus from Bessim Pasha, its last Turkish governor. Ten days later Lieutenant General Sir Garnet (later Field Marshal Viscount) Wolseley landed at Larnaca with a force of British and Indian troops and took over the Government as the first British High Commissioner.

Then the only road on the island connected Nicosia and Larnaca but was in a poor state of repair. The British troops marched the 30 miles or so along this road from Larnaca, which partly crossed the Mesaoria Plain, a flat featureless cauldron of heat and dust to the south of the Kyrenia Mountains. Even in the 1950s Lawrence Durrell saw camel caravans crossing the 'brittle and arid soils' of the Mesaoria, more like a desert in summer.[2]

The locals must surely have thought how mad the British were to move about in the summer heat in red coats. Indeed one of the first, if not the first, squaddie to die on Cyprus lies buried in the English cemetery at Kyrenia. His tombstone reads:

> Number 141 Sergeant Samuel McGaw, VC, 42nd Royal Highlanders died on the line of march to camp Chiftlik Pasha of heat apoplexy, 22 July 1878. Aged 40 years.[3]

McGaw from Kirkmichael in Ayrshire had won his VC in the Ashanti War on 21 January 1874 at the battle of Amouful where the then lance sergeant had 'led his section through the bush in a most excellent manner and continued to do so throughout the day, although badly wounded early in the engagement'.[4]

Five years after his death the grave site at Chiftlik, where he had been laid to rest, was to be levelled so his remains were disinterred under the direction of Captain Scott-Stevenson, Commissioner of Kyrenia. This was reported in the *Cyprus Herald* of 17 June:

> The remains were carefully placed in a shell and conveyed to Kyrenia; on the 12th inst. Captain Scott-Stevenson in the full uniform of the Black Watch followed the remains of this gallant soldier to the little cemetery above Kyrenia and laid them beside those of his comrades who died there. The shell was covered with the British Flag and carried on the shoulders of six Turkish Zaptiehs. After the internment Mrs Scott-Stevenson decorated the grave with wreaths of passion flower and jasmine. A suitable monument will be erected by the desire of the officers of the Black Watch.[5]

The city of Nicosia in 1878 was still largely confined within the Venetian walls of the town, a little over 2 miles in circumference, in a circle, with eleven equidistant great heart-shaped bastions. The original Crusader walls had been much longer but the Venetians had destroyed these to make the defence line shorter. When the Union Flag was raised over the city in July 1878 it was not the first occupation of the island by troops from the misty shores of *Albion* that had taken place over 600 years before.

Richard I Coeur de Lion, the Crusader king known as 'the Lionheart', conquered Cyprus in 1191 in a three-month campaign and established there a base of operations for the Christian forces in the east. Richard sailed for the Holy Land during the Third Crusade 1189–92. His fleet of 200 ships left Messina, Sicily, on 10 April but heavy storms forced them to seek shelter. Most went to Rhodes, but four were blown toward Cyprus, two being wrecked on the coast near Limassol. One of them carried the king's fiancée, Berengaria, and his sister Joan, but this ship, although battered, managed to anchor off the coast.

The ruler of Cyprus, Isaac Komnenos, ordered his men to capture the shipwrecked survivors. Isaac had no liking for the Latins and had an understanding with Saladin to deny his ports to the Crusaders. He attempted to lure Joan and Berengaria ashore hoping to hold them to ransom; when that failed, he withheld fresh water.

On 6 May Richard arrived at Limassol with the bulk of his fleet. He soon demanded the release of his people. Isaac rejected the demand following which the Crusader army landed, occupying Limassol. Three days later the two men met at Kolossi to try to settle things peacefully. It was agreed that Richard should abandon Cyprus while Isaac, for his part, would support the Crusaders financially and with men, and the island would help provision the army. But as soon as Isaac realised Richard's force was small he reneged on the deal and demanded the Crusaders leave Cyprus or face battle. Isaac's actions were not that uncommon for the times but had he known Richard better he might have come down on the side of caution.

Angered by Isaac's treachery Richard landed his army and advanced toward Kolossi village where the enemy were camped. In the battle Isaac's forces were defeated and he fled to Nicosia. Richard returned to Limassol, where on 12 May he married Berengaria in the Chapel of St George in Limassol Castle. At the same ceremony Berengaria was crowned Queen of England, and Richard, rather prematurely, was crowned King of Cyprus. While in Limassol, Richard met the deposed King of Jerusalem, Guy de Lusignan, and the two became allies.

Richard of legend, a brave, chivalrous knight and fearless soldier, was, as far as we know, in reality somewhat different. He was a good soldier, but also boorish, sadistic and greedy. Richard I was crowned in England at Westminster on 3 September 1189 and immediately set about raising money for the Crusades. He sold castles, manors, privileges, public offices, even towns and is said to have remarked: 'I would sell London, if I could find anyone rich enough to buy it.'[6]

The campaign Richard undertook to conquer Cyprus was short and decisive. He marched east along the south coast from Limassol to Kiti near the Salt Lake and from there across country to Famagusta, which fell without a fight. Then he turned west toward Nicosia. Richard ran into Isaac's main forces at Tremethousha, midway between Nicosia and Famagusta. After a fierce but brief fight, Isaac's force was overwhelmed. Guy de Lusignan, commanding the fleet, captured the castle of Kyrenia from the sea and imprisoned Isaac's family, who had been sent there for safety. Guy passed east along the coast to the castle of Kantara where he found Isaac and captured him.

Kantara is the best preserved of the three castles that dominate the Kyrenian mountain range, the others being Buffavento and St Hilarion. All were later largely dismantled to various degrees by the Venetians. From Kantara's walls 2,000ft above the sea one can see both coasts of the Karpas Peninsula, Famagusta Bay, and even the Turkish coast. Given the remoteness of these castles, Richard's campaign to subdue the island in a month is impressive.

At the Apostolos Andreas Monastery that lies 4 miles from the tip of the Karpas Peninsula, later called the Pan Handle by British troops, Isaac was brought before Richard, whom he begged not to be put in irons. Richard agreed and had him put into silver chains and taken to Palestine, where he died in squalor in the dungeons of Castle Margat near Tripoli in 1195.

Richard's enforcement of the feudal laws of conquest upset the locals straight away when he took half their land and gave it to his knights. On 5 June he sailed for Syria, leaving a garrison to hold the island. However, it soon became obvious after a Cypriot revolt that Richard did not have enough men to hold Cyprus. So rather than take men from other fronts he used another favourite tactic of his and sold the island. He sold Cyprus to the Knights Templar who paid 40,000 gold bezants as a deposit while the balance of 60,000 would be paid yearly by instalments. So Cyprus, Richard hoped, would become a nice little earner.[7]

The Templars had equal trouble with the locals and they sold Cyprus on to Guy de Lusignan, Richard's old friend. With better treatment of the locals it was the beginning of a long Frankish line, who would rule Cyprus for 300 years. One local, the hermit Neophytos in a letter '*Concerning the Misfortunes of the land of Cyprus*', did comment on the first English occupation. He had no love for Isaac, 'who utterly despoiled the land'. And as for Richard, he was no better: 'the English King, the wretch, landed in Cyprus and found it a nursing mother. The wicked wretch achieved nought against his fellow-wretch Saladin but achieved this only, that he sold our country to the Latins.' As for the Hospitallers, Templars, and other Franks, their 'bandying' of the island did it few favours.[8]

———

In July 1878 Sir Garnet Wolseley set up his first camp a mile west of Nicosia on what was thought as the traditional place of King Richard's encampment. A prefabricated wooden military bungalow on its way to Ceylon was diverted at Port Said and became the first Government House on the same site.

Wolseley appeared to have had a burning dislike of foreigners, hardly a good attitude for the British governor, especially in a new land. He wrote in his diary for 16 August 1878: 'What poor fools we English travellers are and how our open purse is made to bleed by the scheming villainy of all foreigners. I don't like foreigners I am glad to say.'[9]

On the 18 August he went to the official blessing of the Union Jack in the cathedral in Nicosia, where he found the clergy to be 'dirty greasy priests'. Also it was a long service which did not improve Wolseley's humour:

> at last the Abbot stepped forward and took the British Jack from the table where it had been lying while these incantations were being gone through and incense being burnt over it. As if our flag required any purification – and opened and fastened it to the halliards and it was hauled up amidst loud 'Zita's' from the ugly crowds. Cheers were given for the Queen and, the ceremony over, went back to breakfast.[10]

This should have been an honour to have the flag blessed in this manner and shows Wolseley at his worst. He did in general dislike all priests, Anglican's just as much. However, he quickly identified that Turkey had financially ruined Cyprus:

> He (being the Sultan) takes all the plums out of the island, throws upon us the responsibility of governing it well, which means large expenditures, while he reserves to himself the power to sell three-quarters of the whole area of the island and insists on our paying him a large sum annually as a rent for the estate he has ruined.

By September 1878 he was informing Lord Salisbury that the £103,000 the Grand Vizier expected annually for Cyprus was 'simply ridiculous to think of paying such a sum'. But if this was reduced to '£100,000 we should do very well here as long as nothing was charged against us for Military expenses'.[11] In fact, the British garrison had been suffering considerably and was causing Wolseley some concern. On 17 August he wrote:

> The thermometer in our camp stood at 110 degrees FAH, in our hospital morgue. What must it be like in a bell-tent? A bell-tent is next to useless here. The west winds are most trying. We have now about 18 per cent of the Europeans in hospital with fever. Which is not however of a very bad description. One of the sappers, here in hospital shows signs of typhoid his tongue being black and foul.[12]

At the time many theories were put forward on the causes of the camp fever. But it was not until 1898 that Sir Ronald Ross identified the malaria-carrying mosquito as the culprit, which bred in their millions in the marshes surrounding the coasts, particularly around Larnaca and Famagusta. It would not be until 1948 that the marshes were drained and Cyprus was declared free of malaria. Wolseley did have the sense to move most of his troops to camps on higher ground where the winds were fresher and away from Nicosia: 'for I am sure if we remained in it we should all suffer; it is one great cess-pit into which the filth of centuries has been poured'.[13] Queen Victoria even took a personal interest in the welfare of the troops suggesting sending the men to sea for a cruise to improve their health.

Locusts had plagued Cyprus for centuries before the British arrived. In 1355 the Italian Villani wrote:

At that time the locusts were so abundant in the isle of Cyprus that they covered all the fields to the height of one-quarter braccio and ate everything green on the earth and so destroyed [the farmer's] labour that there was no fruit to be had in that year.[14]

In 1590, Tomaso Porcacchi of Venice wrote of his visit:

Cyprus suffers yet another plague, that now and then a certain insect infests it. About every third year if the seasons are dry, they grow slowly in the likeness of locusts, and in March being now winged and as thick as a finger, with long legs, they begin to fly. At once they come down like hail from heaven, eat everything voraciously and are driven before the wind in such huge flights that they seem dense clouds.[15]

A hundred years later the Dutch traveller Cornelis Van Bruyn on the island observed the locusts around Famagusta '… were like a dark cloud through which the sun's rays could scarcely pierce'.[16] Hamilton Lang, the British Consul in Cyprus, wrote in 1870 that Mehmed Said Pasha had virtually managed to wipe out the locusts with the help of Richard Mattei. Mattei was an Italian who had settled in Cyprus where he owned a prosperous and well-run farm. Garnet Wolseley had met him in 1878; he likened him to Count Fosco in Wilkie Collins's *The Woman in White* but felt the wine from his farm was amongst the best on the island.

Wolseley was glad to have him on his unofficial council, and to use his experience in using traps to eradicate the locusts, which sadly had returned due to Government negligence in the past five years.[17] And so the traps were soon in use again. Lieutenant Donnisthorpe Donne of the Royal Sussex Regiment serving with the Cyprus police in the spring of 1882 was on trap inspection duty:

> The Locust campaign was now fairly well started and these pestivorous insects were now appearing in alarming quantities and every day increasing in size and developing their destructive qualities. I was ordered out again on the 21st March by the Commissioner on a round of inspection embracing all the traps in the Nicosia District which took me a week riding round. Throughout the Mesaoria plains stretching from the Carpas to Morfu on the North, there were altogether in use upwards of 140 miles of traps and screens! This astonishing length will give some idea of the work in hand.
>
> The screens were of canvas bound with oilcloth at the top and about 3 ft high, the oilcloth over which the animals could not crawl obliging them to crawl along the canvas until they happened into the pits prepared for their reception. These pits were dug at right angles to the screens at intervals of about 20 yards, being likewise lined with zinc, preventing the locusts from climbing out again.
>
> In whatever direction the locusts appeared to be advancing therefore, were the traps and screens erected to intercept them. In this manner vast multitudes were destroyed. In Timbo, Morgo, and Piroi the locusts were passing the Larnaca road in countless myriads filling the traps to overflowing. The streams were all full of them: the country was all black with them, such an extraordinary sight did they present.[18]

This elaborate military-like operation did work in a few years eradicating the pest from the island, with the help of the Desert Locust Surveys in Africa, and without any pesticides.

In October 1878, a young Lieutenant of Engineers Herbert Kitchener, later Field Marshal Earl Kitchener of Khartoum, arrived on Cyprus.

His cousin Thomas Cobbald MP used his sway with Lord Salisbury to obtain for Herbert the job to survey the island. Kitchener was instructed to produce a detailed ordnance survey map at one inch to the mile, with larger scale where necessary.

Kitchener found Wolseley encamped in a monastery garden near Nicosia. Writing to his sister Millie he found Wolseley 'agreeable and pleasant', though his manner and that of his staff was not to his liking and he hoped to have 'very little to do with them'. Kitchener, for the time, was not a typical empire builder, for later he wrote: 'It is just what I expected; the English have come with English ideas in everything and a scorn for native habits or knowledge of the country.'[19]

Kitchener soon argued with Wolseley, who himself was under pressure from the Treasury over the expense of the survey. Instead of a detailed map Kitchener was ordered just to chart the land instead. In May the survey team was recalled to Nicosia and returned to England; years later Wolseley would admit that abandoning the survey was short-sighted.

In 1879 Major General Sir Robert Biddulph became High Commissioner and put his weight behind completion of the survey. Kitchener returned to Nicosia in March 1880; by June the survey was going well. He found the legacy of the Turkish system had left Cyprus in 'a thoroughly exhausted and ruined condition'.[20] During that second tour Kitchener enjoyed the experience of many squaddies on the island. While working in the Troodos Mountains a brigand took a shot at him but missed. In 1882 he left Cyprus a captain. His map of Cyprus was published in April 1885.

The celebrated writer Rider Haggard visited Cyprus twice in the nineteenth century and recorded his 1899 visit first in serialised form in the *Queen* from 5 January to 29 June 1901, and then in his book *A Winter Pilgrimage: in Palestine, Italy, and Cyprus in 1900*, published in October 1901 by Longman. He considered that: 'With a little more care and capital she might again become what she was of old, the Garden of the Mediterranean, a land of corn wine and in fact as well as figuratively a mine of wealth.'[21]

Haggard spent many days exploring the Roman ruins of ancient Salamis on the east coast. He had an idea to set a novel in the city. Salamis was once the native city of Barnabas, who was to become the Patron Saint of Cyprus. Barnabas was a scribe by trade and is said to have made a copy of St Matthew's Gospel, which traditionally was placed on his breast by his cousin John Mark when in due course he was martyred in his native city and buried in a rock tomb nearby. The tomb and Gospel were discovered in 478 and the manuscript was presented to the Byzantine Emperor Zeno; to this is due the independence of the Church of Cyprus and its high position in the Orthodox world.

Salamis had a large Jewish community in ancient times until a revolt in AD 115 when a quarter of a million inhabitants died and the Romans expelled all the Jews from Cyprus. A few miles north of Salamis and about a mile inland amid good farmland lies the village of Trikomo, where on 23 May 1898 was born one George Grivas. He was the fourth of six children, four of whom were girls, born into a well-to-do family, his father a prosperous cereal merchant, with a large house of twelve rooms, and a big garden full of fruit trees.

As a young boy, George was fascinated by paintings of the saints in the twelfth-century village church of the Blessed Virgin Mary. Today Trikomo is more like a ghost village, yet with a curiously large memorial raised by the Turks to the events of 1974. The church has been vandalised, its walls are covered in graffiti, while nearby a new mosque is being built. All this seems over the top, as half the houses appear abandoned and falling down, and if more evidence was required, they do not have the obligatory satellite dish confirming occupation; thus one gets the impression, perhaps in error, of an attempt to obliterate the memory of Grivas.

Sir Harry Luke first went to Cyprus in the spring of 1908; he would come to know his 'enchanted island' through all its glories and pain in the course of fifty years. However, an incident during his first visit prepared him well for the future. Cyprus, at that time, was being administered by Britain while still under the suzerainty of Sultan Hamid II. One night the 24-year-old Harry was invited to dine with the king's Advocate and his wife; however, an 'anxious note' arrived at the last minute from the hostess cancelling the dinner party. An incident had taken place in the kitchen whereby the kitchen-boy had tried to slit the throat of the cook, who was by this time losing 'his life-blood on the kitchen table, where should have lain not he but the saddle of lamb'. What was the cause of this attempted murder? A crime of passion? The result of a love triangle, perhaps? No, nothing that simple. Rather an argument over which bishop should fill the vacant seat of the archbishopric of Cyprus.[22] For a decade since the death of Archbishop Sophronics II in 1900 the Greek Cypriot population, who elected their bishops, was split into two bitterly hostile camps, one in support of Bishop Cyril of Kition (Larnaca) and the other for Bishop Cyril of Kyrenia, both contending for the vacant ecclesiastical throne. It was not until 1910 that the rift was eventually healed when Cyril of Kition prevailed.

As we have seen, the Emperor Zeno in 478 had confirmed the independence of the Cyprus Church as one of the oldest constituent bodies of the Holy Orthodox Eastern Church. Although small, the Cyprus Church, in the pecking order of Orthodoxy, comes before that of Russia or Greece. With independence came political power from the Emperor for the Archbishop of Cyprus, for all to see, in the cape of Imperial purple and the sceptre to replace the pastoral staff. Thus the Archbishop was political leader as much as spiritual and had to wear two hats that could and did conflict. However, they had been put there and given these privileges by a Byzantine monarch and had no legacy from any Hellenistic period.

In the thirty years between the British arrival and the visit of Harry Luke, Cyprus had been transformed. Railways and roads criss-crossed the island, and many of the wadis, raging torrents in winter, had been bridged. From 1911 a company ran motor vehicles between the main towns carrying mail. By the end of the First World War, from a situation of no post offices in 1878, there were sixty-five main offices and 196 mail stations. Government buildings, court-houses, hospitals and even prisons had sprung up.

In 1843 the British Consular Agent reported of Famagusta that it was a town of squalor in terminal decline and was inhabited 'by a miserable population of 500 Turks of both sexes'. Within a few years of British arrival its harbour was dredged, its docks restored and it was open again to ocean-going traffic.[23] Today Famagusta appears in decline again, its great sandstone Venetian monuments full of rubbish and crumbling away into the sand. The harbour is only used by the odd ferry from Turkey.

Entering the citadel below a large relief of the Lion of St Mark you can make your way up onto the battlements, what Lawrence Durrell called the 'grass grown turrets of Othello's tower'.[24] Famagusta was the setting for William Shakespeare's great tragic tale of Othello and Desdemona. From your vantage point your gaze sweeps across the harbour and city walls of palm-shrouded sandstone to the south and the ghostly quarter of Varosha, deserted now, part of the dead zone between north and south, hardly now the 'prince of walled cities' Colin Thubron saw in 1972.[25]

On the whole Cyprus had prospered under British rule, belying the criticism put forward of poor material progress. Especially so given the legacy of Ottoman rule in the shape of the 'Tribute', which many Cypriots still cite as a grievance against Britain. The 'Tribute' was the Turkish condition for British occupation of Cyprus. Basically, Britain would ensure the Sultan's Government did not suffer financially for ceding Cyprus to Britain. The figure was based on the average difference between the island's revenue and expenditure in its last five years of Ottoman rule.

Turkey spent nothing on Cyprus and took what it could; the figure came out at £92,799 a year, the sum being debited annually to the island's revenue, together with 4,166,220 okes of salt [unit of measurement].[26] None of the 'Tribute' found its way into the Turkish exchequer. Rather it was retained by Britain to pay Turkish debts, mostly to British and French bond-holders, for Turkey had been in default on some loans since 1855.

Winston Churchill as Under-Secretary of State for the Colonial Office visited the island in 1907 and found the situation a disgrace:

> But the fact stares me none the less in the face that we have no right whatever, except by force majeure, to take a penny from Cyprus tribute to relieve us from our own just obligations, however unfortunately contracted. There is scarcely any spectacle more detestable than the oppression of a small community by a great power for the purpose of pecuniary profit; and that is, in fact, the spectacle which our financial treatment of Cyprus at this moment indisputably presents. It is, in my opinion, quite unworthy of Great Britain, and altogether out of accordance with the whole principles of our colonial policy, in every part of the world, to exact tribute by force from any of the possessions or territories administered under the crown.[27]

Sir Charles Orr was a captain when posted to Cyprus in 1911 as Chief Secretary to the island and saw Churchill's aim achieved:

> An end was put however to the absurd situation [of the Tribute] when, in 1907, the Imperial Government decided to ask Parliament to vote a fixed annual sum of £50,000 as grant-in-aid of Cyprus revenues; and although this was at first limited to a period of three years, it has continued ever since.[28]

Captain Orr saw it as in the 'circumstances' hardly 'a matter of surprise that the payment of the "tribute" from Cyprus revenue has been a subject of burning dissatisfaction amongst Cypriot people ever since the British occupation'. The large annual payment had 'paralysed progress, and left barely sufficient funds to keep the administrative machinery in working order, whilst allowing little for such vital purposes as education, road construction agriculture, and re-afforestation'.[29]

For many years the island's revenue remained small; by 1908 it exceeded £300,000. By 1959, the last full year of British administration, it had risen to £23 million, which included an HMG Exchequer grant of £5.8 million.

For decades agriculture remained painfully primitive, even under Britain. Much was done by the Forestry Department in reforestation after the island's trees had been ravaged for centuries to supply timber for shipbuilding and fuel. There is no doubt that under British rule Cypriots were better off than had they remained with Turkey, or for that matter even if they had joined Greece.

Notes

1. Sir Harry Luke, *Cyprus*, pp. 85–6, 'Now let us revert …', and C.W.J. Orr, *Cyprus under British Rule*, pp. 35–7, 'In 1878, whilst the Berlin Conference was still sitting …'
2. Lawrence Durrell, *Bitter Lemons of Cyprus*, p. 143
3. The English cemetery, Kyrenia
4. Citation of the Victoria Cross
5. *Cyprus Herald*, 17/6/1883
6. John Matthews and Bob Stewart, *Warriors of Christendom*, p. 85
7. Luke, *Cyprus*, p. 39
8. Ibid., pp. 40–1
9. Garnet Wolseley, *Journal Cyprus 1878*, p. 49

10. Ibid., pp. 51–2
11. Ibid., p. 90
12. Ibid., p. 51
13. Ibid., p. 87
14. Oliver Burch, *The Infidel Sea*, p. 224
15. Wolseley, *Journal Cyprus 1878*, p. 178
16. Ibid., p. 178
17. Ibid., p. 64
18. Ibid., p. 182
19. Horatio Herbert Kitchener, Notes from Cyprus, *Blackwood's Edinburgh Magazine*
20. Ibid.
21. Peter Berresford Ellis, H. Rider Haggard, pp. 159–60, 'Rider had decided to visit Cyprus …', and H. Rider Haggard, *A Winter Pilgrimage in Palestine, Italy, and Cyprus in 1900*
22. Luke, *Cyprus*, p. 17
23. Ibid., pp. 129–30
24. Durrell, *Bitter Lemons of Cyprus*, p. 162
25. Colin Thubron, *Journey into Cyprus*, p. 203
26. Jan Morris, *Pax Britannica*, p. 41
27. FCO-(PRO) 67/241/41397H and John Reddaway, *Burdened with Cyprus*, p. 31, 'The one truly disgraceful blot …'
28. Sir Charles Orr, *Cyprus under British Rule*, p. 62
29. Ibid., p. 48

2

THE FIRST
WORLD WAR

The year before the outbreak of the First World War the *Handbook of Cyprus* 1913 edition described, since 1878, the British had brought forth 'a golden age of equity, prosperity, and security':

> The future of the island should be a bright one, if only the Cypriot will whole-heartedly and energetically extend to the administration the co-operation which is so sorely needed and so constantly solicited. Financially, the country finds itself for the first time for many centuries on a secure and certain basis. The revenue tends to rise from year to year; and this increase is not due to additional taxation, but to the greater prosperity of the people themselves.[1]

The 'secure and certain basis' for Cyprus along with the rest of Europe was about to be shattered. However, prior to this, Britain had been concerned over the island's defence. In 1912, the Imperial Defence Committee identified a possible threat from the Austro-Hungarian Empire. The garrison on Cyprus was tiny, consisting of one company of infantry, 100 men, and 750 men of the island's police and some small detachments of Army administrative staff. It was estimated an invading force of only 8,000 men could take the island.

Britain was looking for allies in the Mediterranean. During the London conference of 1912 after the First Balkan War, Lloyd George, then Chancellor with Winston Churchill, in a secret meeting proposed to the

Greek Prime Minister Eleutherios Venizelos that Cyprus be ceded to Greece in return for a naval base on Cephalonia. Venizelos seemed keen on the idea suggesting British sovereignty of Argostoli, the main port of Cephalonia. However, the idea was quickly scuppered by the Colonial Office and War Office who were unwilling to surrender Cyprus to Greece. While the island was only a British protectorate sovereignty at that time remaining with the Ottoman Empire. Friendly relations with Turkey had soured over the years but they were not yet at war.[2]

News of the outbreak of war reached the Cyprus Government while they were high in the Troodos Mountains on their annual summer retreat away from the baking heat of Nicosia. Hamilton John Goold-Adams was High Commissioner at the time, a title that would later be changed to governor. Communication was slow; it took ten days before he contacted the Colonial Office to acknowledge news of the outbreak of war, and then he was more concerned with the imminent return of the island's Chief Secretary Charles Orr who had been away and whom he clearly disliked, finding him 'highly strung'.[3]

When on 8 August 1914 Britain and her Empire went to war with Germany there was no certainty Turkey would join the war on the German side. The country was 'the sick man of Europe' and in no real condition to fight. But its Government was in the hands of the 'Young Turks', a bizarre collection of revolutionaries and opportunists who had murdered the Sultan's son-in-law, hanging him from a public gibbet in Istanbul, to show where the real power lay behind the throne in 1914. They eagerly played the great powers off against each other, finally coming down on the German side when Britain withheld two battleships under construction in British dockyards for Turkey, and Germany replaced them albeit with inferior ships. On 5 November Turkey entered the war and Britain annulled the treaty of 1878 and annexed Cyprus. In October Goold-Adams was still at his Troodos Mountain retreat. The Colonial Office was not impressed, concluding 'he cannot be depended on for energetic action in an emergency'.[4]

It was left to Harry Luke to announce to the leading Turkish Cypriots the annexation of the island to Britain and the cutting of the 400-year link to the Ottoman Empire. Those Turkish Cypriots born on the island would now be regarded as British subjects along with the Greek Cypriots. While those not born on the island had a year to leave, if they did not, 'within the said period of one year will on the expiration of the said period be British subjects', so the declaration by the king in Council read.[5] At the same time, to ensure the Suez Canal remained totally under British control, Britain disposed of the Egyptian Government and annexed Egypt.

In early 1915 Britain her Empire and France set out on the ill-fated Dardanelles Campaign, which would be fought virtually within sight of historic Troy. Britain offered Cyprus to Greece thinking she would need little incentive to join with the Allies in this new Trojan War.

Sir Edward Grey, the Foreign Secretary, felt the handing over of Cyprus to Greece for immediate war aid was a good idea. However, Lord Kitchener did not, feeling they should retain the island in the war against the Turks. Prime Minister Herbert Asquith listened to the arguments in Cabinet on 20 January 1915:

> We had a long talk about the Balkans and Greece and how to bring them in. Grey is anxious to be able to dangle before the Greeks Cyprus as a lure. It is not worth much to us, indeed nothing …[6]

On the 16 October 1915 the offer of Cyprus to Greece was made, although it would not become Greek until the war was over, provided Athens would join the Allies against the Central Powers straight away. The same telegram was sent twice on the same day. The British were even in favour of recruiting the Archbishop of Cyprus to plead their cause in Athens. However, the offer was turned down by King Constantine who had succeeded to the throne in 1913. His prime minister, the Cretan-born Eleutherios Venizelos, was in favour of the Allied cause, but the king was under the pressure of bedroom diplomacy, his queen being the kaiser's sister. Venizelos did manage, before his Government fell, to make the port of Murdos on Lemons Island available to the Allies to use as a forward base and fleet anchorage.

On Cyprus the 'combative' Archbishop Cyril II had been quick to seize the opportunity of November 1914 and had told the High Commissioner Goold-Adams: 'Our satisfaction at the annexation of the island to Great Britain. For we consider this event as a stage from which it may the more easily return to the arms of its Mother Greece.'[7]

A year later Goold-Adams met the Archbishop again, who was to be disappointed in his assumption, for the official communiqué informed the local population that Greece had turned down the offer of Cyprus for joining the allied fight and finished with: '... the Greek Cypriots would doubtless now recognise in the fullest manner their obligations as British Subjects.'[8]

British strategy in the Middle East and in the Gallipoli campaign turned Cyprus into a communication, Military Intelligence and stationing hub and the island became a source of supplies. From November 1916 onwards Turkish prisoners of war from various fronts were transferred to Cyprus, over 10,000 being held in POW camps near Larnaca. Meanwhile wounded and sick Allied servicemen were sent to hospitals and convalescent homes in the Troodos Mountains.

The island contributed much-needed supplies to the war effort. The British, who had done much to restore the island's forests after decades of Ottoman neglect, now decimated them to provide timber for the war effort, while 13,000 muleteers and 7,000 mules left the island for service in Macedonia and Egypt. Much of this was supervised by the New High Commissioner Sir John Eugene Clauson, who took office in January 1915. Clauson was a good choice by the Colonial Office to replace Goold-Adams. He had a fine military record. Early in his army career he had designed a pontoon bridge which later went into use with the Army. He had served on the Committee of Imperial Defence. He also knew Cyprus well, having been Chief Secretary on the island from 1906 to 1911. His clear thinking and plain 'despatches read admirably'.[9]

However, Clauson soon clashed with officials of Military Intelligence. He felt there was no real threat of espionage on the island. SIS in Alexandria was responsible for reviewing intelligence on Cyprus. They soon became concerned about the large movement of aliens to the island. People displaced by the war arrived on the island, mainly Christians and Jews fleeing the Ottoman Empire and the likely conscription into the Turkish Army. Also German submarines were known to approach the coast, Clauson was soon reporting to London: 'The High Commissioner is far too lenient in his dealings with the Austrians and Germans in Cyprus, and that they are allowed to wander about practically without restraint.'[10]

In 1917 the Eastern Mediterranean Special Intelligence Bureau [EMSIB] set up a small counter-espionage unit on Cyprus, based in Nicosia. They uncovered some minor activities. Turkish Cypriots were aiding Turkish POWs to escape, while others were raising money for the Turkish Army. Some arrests were made, but when it came to court they were released on the grounds of lack of evidence.

Clauson did have a better working relationship with the Naval Intelligence Service on the island. Mainly because their security concerns were more clearly definable; coastal depots were placed under armed guard, and an island-wide telephone system was set up to report submarine sightings that could quickly be reported to NIS and from them by wireless to patrol ships.

In August 1917 an attempt by EMSIB was made to put Cyprus under military control due to 'undesirable activities of the enemy'.[11] Clauson was quick to defuse the situation, sighting Scott's criticism of his administration lying behind the request. The Colonial Office backed their man and Captain Scott was recalled from Cyprus and at Clauson's suggestion, Captain Mervyn, a former police commissioner in Nicosia, was appointed to supervise intelligence work on the island.

Finally, late in 1917, EMSIB had to admit:

There appeared to be no definite enemy organisation in the island, although there were evidently many potential enemies among the population. Both Greeks and Turks were said to ignore the benefits which British rule had bought them … in the opinion of the intelligence officer the only danger in the island itself was the fact that the mildness of the Proclamation under Martial Law gave scope for a smart enemy agent.[However] The intelligence officer was doubtful as to whether any of the local suspects were worthy of a place in the printed Black List of EMSIB.[12]

A week after the guns of the Great War fell silent Clauson asked for six weeks leave to be spent on Cyprus on the grounds he was exhausted. Throughout his time in office he had been suffering from pulmonary tuberculosis. He died at Government House on 31 December 1918, aged 52. He was laid to rest in the Anglican cemetery in Nicosia. His grave is now hidden at the back of the cemetery, marked by a horizontal stone of white marble. The inscription says he died in the service of his country.[13]

The story of Cyprus and the First World War does not end there, for the island was at the centre of some discussions at the great Paris Peace Conference of 1919. During the war Lloyd George and Venizelos had kept in touch, the former insisting together they had plotted the overthrow of King Constantine. Venizelos was one of the stars of the Peace Conference; President Woodrow Wilson called him the 'biggest man he met' with unbounded enthusiasm; he was even compared by some to Pericles. He held dinner tables spellbound with stories of life in the Cretan Mountains as a guerrilla, of how he had taught himself English by reading *The Times* with a rifle resting on his knees.[14]

Lloyd George encouraged Venizelos in Greek claims, no doubt including Cyprus. The latter was not overly interested in the island. If Britain wanted to hand it over that would be good, and Greece would always let Britain use bases there. If Britain wanted to keep it, well that was understandable. However, the Foreign Office under Lord George Curzon, the War Office and the Colonial Office were strongly against Lloyd George's offer. On 5 August 1920, Curzon made it clear to Venizelos that Cyprus would remain part of the British Empire.[15]

Notes

1. *Handbook of Cyprus 1913*, pp. 30–1 and Reddaway, Burdened with Cyprus, p. 36, 'An early edition of the handbook …'
2. Panagiotis Dimitrakis, *Military Intelligence in Cyprus*, p. 12
3. FCO-(PRO) 67/173, 28/8/1914, and Tabitha Morgan, *Sweet and Bitter Island*, p. 67, 'This was where Goold-Adams …'
4. Ibid., 67/174 31/8/1914 and Morgan, p. 70, 'Finally Goold-Adams addressed …'
5. Sir Charles Orr, *Cyprus under British Rule*, pp. 172–3, 'On November 5, 1914 …'
6. Dimitrakis, p. 16, 'In the international diplomatic arena …'
7. Sir Harry Luke, *Cyprus*, p. 89, 'After the annexation …'
8. Ibid., p. 89, 'His Excellency the High Commissioner …'
9. FCO-(PRO) 67/180 and Morgan p. 77, 'Goold-Adams successor …'
10. KV-(PRO) 1/18, pp. 2–6
11. Ibid., p. 32
12. Ibid., pp. 26–7 and Dimitrakis, p. 15
13. Morgan, p. 94
14. Macmillan Margaret, *Peacemakers*, p. 361
15. Dimitrakis, p. 17

3

CROWN COLONY:
THE INTERWAR YEARS

In the field of education the British did miss a golden opportunity to influence the local population by not teaching English and Empire values widely. In the early years the Government stated that the island was only under lease. Freya Stark wrote during the Second World War:

> I believe that when the history of the British Empire comes to be written, the reasons for its difficulties and perhaps eventual fall will be found in its never having really bothered about education … In Cyprus we never bothered to see that English was taught![1]

The result was that Greece supplied Greek Cypriot schools with teachers who at the time were largely ebullient with Greek Nationalism in an extreme form. Even the teaching syllabus came from the Ministry of Education in Athens.

Penelope Tremayne, while working for the Red Cross in remote Cypriot villages during the troubles of the 1950s, came across this problem. To her amazement she learnt that some civil servant at the Education Department 'had the brilliant idea of importing, direct from Athens, text books for the Greek Cypriot schools'. She went on to describe them in some detail:

They are slightly Victorian in tone, rather elevated and full of pale blue pictures; packed with piety and dramatic patriotism.

A page opened at random shows two crossed muskets, and the piece that follows tells of the glories of the war of liberation. As the book is not compiled for Cypriots, it does not mention that Cyprus took no part in this glorious struggle. Over the whole of another page the Greek flag is printed, with, superimposed on it a six verse poem of devotion.

She was bewildered that such a thing had been allowed to happen, and this mistake had directly fuelled the terrorist campaign.

At that moment, thousands of school children throughout Cyprus sat at their desks with the same pages, or at one of the many others devoted to the same subject, learning at the expense of the British Government that the blue and white flag was that of their Motherland. And at the same time squads of soldiers were pounding up and down the mountain sides on a variety of unenviable jobs, including the tearing down of this same emblem from the roofs of the schools where it fluttered. How on earth were the Cypriots to make sense of it all?[2]

The young George Grivas attended these mainland Greek-run schools before and during the First World War. He found the school 'firmly disciplined' and wrongdoers 'could count on a beating with a raspberry cane' but he liked his studies, 'in which the glories of Greek history always took first place. I was particularly fascinated by the legends of Dighenis Akritas, the half-mythical guardian of the frontiers of Alexander's Empire.'

Grivas would use the name Dighenis as his code name during the EOKA troubles. Some sources say Dighenis was a folk-hero, a kind of Robin Hood, who took part in battles to repel the Saracens. Myth says the small offshore islands and rocks around the coast of Cyprus were hurled there by the arms of this giant god-like warrior. At 11, Grivas went to the Pancyprian Gymnasium in Nicosia, a secondary school. Grivas noted 'it was staffed by teachers from Greece who brought fresh fervour to our nationalism. At that time Greece was winning one victory after another in the Balkan Wars and popular feeling toward the crusade for a greater Greece ran high.'[3]

There were some private British schools on Cyprus. Suha Faiz, a Turkish Cypriot who served in the Colonial Service and later married an English woman, went to just such a school. 'Just about the time of our return from England (1930) two English girls, they couldn't have been more than in their mid twenties, opened a small school in Kyrenia run on Froebel lines.' (Froebel, a German educationist, evolved a new system using instructive play.) Faiz was five when he started school. The school had once been a private house, 'almost fronting onto the main road into Kyrenia, with a large garden at the back'. The school was close to the sea and the Crusader Castle. 'There were only around a dozen of us at the school, and apart from one or two English, we were all Turkish.'[4]

—✦—

The relationship between Greeks and Turks on Cyprus, although painted rosy by some commentators, is rather different when examined.

After the Turkish conquest of 1571, there was an initial period of Greek joy at the escape as they saw it from the tyranny of the Venetians. But the new conquest introduced into Cyprus a large number of Ottoman Turks. The original settlers were mostly soldiers but over the years these were supplemented by Turkish immigration from Anatolia and Rumelia, something that had not happened on this scale under previous occupa-tions. Relations with their new Greek neighbours were, as Sir Harry Luke put it, 'if not, intimate, were on the whole quite amicable.'[5]

The Turks restored the Orthodox Church to its place of dominance on Cyprus and with it the Archbishops had their office restored for the first time in 300 years. By the seventeenth and eighteenth centuries the Archbishops wielded great power in many ways greater than the Turkish Pasha, or so they thought. By the nineteenth century the bishops were virtually ruling Cyprus through control of its finances. But things changed dramatically in 1821 for on 21 March Germanos, Bishop of Patras, on the Peloponnesian Greek mainland, raised the flag of revolt in the monastery of Agia Lavra near Kalavrita. The War of Independence against Ottoman rule had begun.

The Turkish Governor of Cyprus, Kuchuk Mehmed, acted with speed against the Orthodox Church on the island to forestall any trouble, which at the time was unlikely, in his action being backed by the Grand Vizier.

In July he arrested the Archbishop and the bishops of the principal towns together with some leading Greek citizens. Archbishop Kyprianos and three other bishops were humiliated and tortured by having saddles put on their backs and bits thrust into their mouths, breaking their teeth, before the Archbishop was hanged and the bishops beheaded and the citizens were despatched by the Janissaries.

Going to these lengths proves relations between Greek and Turk were anything but good even before the revolt on the mainland began, and at this stage it reached its lowest point until the civil war of the 1960s on the island.

—∿∿∿—

Even after the Greek Prime Minister Venizelos had accepted the view of the British, at the Paris Peace Conference, that they wished to retain Cyprus, the Greek Cypriot community still sent delegates to London spending months there hoping for an audience with Lloyd George, knowing he had been sympathetic to their wish of union with Greece. Finally in October 1920 they were told by Leo Amery, the Under-Secretary of State for the Colonies, that no change was contemplated in the island's position. Even Lloyd George had come to accept the War Office arguments:

> The potential strategic importance of Cyprus is great; both from a naval and from an air point of view … Though the island possesses no adequate harbour at present, the Admiralty state that an excellent base for submarines and destroyers could be made at Famagusta … While the possession of the island by Greece could hardly be considered a menace to the British Empire, the danger of its falling into the hands of a stronger Power cannot be wholly disregarded.[6]

Under the 1923 Treaty of Lausanne Turkey relinquished her claim to Cyprus. On 1 May 1925 Charles Hart-Davis, the Commissioner for Nicosia, announced before an expectant crowd gathered before the law courts in Konak Square Nicosia, bedecked in Union flags, that Cyprus was now a Crown Colony. The High Commissioner Malcolm Stevenson, who had held the post for some six years, would now be known as the governor.

The change in the island's status heralded much-needed reforms to the outdated Ottoman institutions. The power of the *sharia* courts over domestic matters in the Turkish Cypriot community was greatly reduced. In fairness to the British administration, similar changes had already taken place in Turkey, where, in the context of Atatürk's sweeping modernisation programme, both *sharia* courts and the caliphate had been abolished.[7] It was hoped the island's new status and reforms would encourage a wave of 'commercial settlers' and investors to Cyprus, and these new people would show the Cypriots 'the proper way of English life'. A rather arrogant view but typical of the time.[8]

In November 1926 Ronald Storrs became Governor of Cyprus. He was not in the usual mould of empire builder, and felt he had already reached the climax of his career as Governor of Jerusalem for he felt 'there is no promotion after Jerusalem'.[9] However, in 1926 he was appointed Governor of Cyprus. It was not a happy position for him: he disliked many of his British subordinates and their narrow adherence to the Imperial Line, and he found the Greeks, in particular those preaching Enosis, to be deceitful. Storrs did his best; he presided sympathetically over the Legislative Council, and encouraged tourism and archaeology. He got more money for agricultural research, but even so he found the 'island was habitually on the edge of chaos'.[10] In 1928 he had a nervous breakdown; when he returned the next year he found little had changed.

The night of the riot in 1931 he had been preparing Christmas presents and cards for his staff:

> when a crowd of several thousand people stormed the gates of Government House, shouting 'Enosis, Enosis.' They broke all the front windows, and threw burning sticks into the house. The riot act was read in English and in Greek, and a volley was fired by the police, but by the time the crowd had dispersed into the night the house was in flames.[11]

The Faiz family, of Turkish Cypriots, were at the forefront of events in 1931. In October Suha, the youngest son, saw the arrival of British troops. They came into Kyrenia in vehicles he had never seen before:

These have wheels like an ordinary motor car, but are completely covered like a tin box on wheels. Our teachers tell us that these are 'armoured cars' with soldiers inside. The Greeks have been rioting, and last night burned down the Governor's house in Nicosia, however, he is safe, and now that the soldiers are here we are alright.[12]

Suha's father, an inspector of the Cyprus police, was in charge of the constables sent to Government House when the mob attacked it. He got the governor, Sir Ronald Storrs, away escaping in the dark across a dry wadi at the back of the old military bungalow as it went up in flames. The young Turkish Cypriot Inspector was awarded the King's Police Medal for gallantry.

Storrs lost many of his prized possessions in the flames: his Steinway piano and his mother's violin and his collection of books and letters. He left Cyprus a disillusioned man and wrote, 'as for the things that went in Cyprus, perhaps they were taken because I cared for them too much …'[13]

The Greek Cypriots had been expounding the cause of Enosis from the first arrival of the British on the island. They assumed that Britain would allow Enosis for had she not ceded the Ionian Islands to Greece to mark the emergence of a New Greek Kingdom in 1862.

Had not the Royal Navy (in fact a combined fleet with French and Russian ships) annihilated a Turkish Egyptian Fleet in Navarino Bay, ensuring the birth of an independent Greece in 1827? The truth was Cyprus had never been part of the modern Greek state and the British saw it differently. She had been part of the Ancient Greek world during the Classical Hellenic period and the following Hellenistic period, but so had Sicily and large parts of southern Italy and parts of what is now Asian Turkey. The Phoenicians, who came from Syria, if we were to follow chronological order, would have a prior claim to the island.

The Greek Cypriot people today are the children of the Byzantine world out of which grew the Orthodox Church. The Church that has used the glories of ancient Greece for its own ends, which is the same Church that was so virulent in its passion to destroy anything it could have of the ancient Hellenic pagan world in its early days. Sir Harry Luke points out:

It would be wrong to doubt the intense Greek consciousness of the Greek Cypriots of today, but it would be equally mistaken to suppose that this consciousness has always manifested itself in a politically nationalistic form. Before 1832 there was no clamour for Enosis none could arise seeing that it was already there in the sense that the Greeks of Greece and those of Cyprus shared the same (Ottoman) nationality.[14]

—∿∿—

In 1931 Britain had troubles at home. Sterling had been forced off the gold standard and the pound had suffered 30 per cent devaluation against the dollar. The unemployed had taken to the streets against the Government's austerity programme, while servicemen had found their pay cut by as much as 25 per cent. Perhaps most disturbing was the mutiny of the Atlantic Fleet at Invergordon on the Cromarty Firth. In the Empire Gandhi was demanding independence for India.

The day after the burning of Government House, Storrs requested military aid from Egypt. The Royal Navy cruisers *London* and *Shropshire* soon arrived off the coast. The former landed shore parties of Royal Marines and sailors at Larnaca to protect Government establishments. They were met by unruly crowds who stoned them. The leaders of the revolt were confined in *London* and *Shropshire*, where they were treated well, and plied with food and drink. 'A few stiff whiskies helped steady the nerves of those still a little shocked at being hauled from their beds in the wee small hours.'[15]

A company of the King's Regiment was ready to fly in from Palestine. Infantry detachments based on the Troodos area moved to Nicosia, while a company of the Royal Welch Fusiliers deployed in the city. Demonstrations spread to Famagusta and other towns. However, by 28 October the revolt was put down with force. The bishops of Kyrenia and Kition were arrested and the Greek Consul-General Alexandros Kyrou deported. Other Greek Cypriot leaders were held in British warships and later deported for life. The revolt cost the lives of six Greek Cypriots and thirty wounded. The British suffered no casualties and the Turkish Cypriots remained quiet.

Grivas says that 'fierce reprisals' were taken against the Greek Cypriots after the riots of 1931. The Legislative Council, which Storrs had encouraged, was abolished and flying the Greek flag was banned. British actions were strict but not fierce compared to Turkish actions only 100 years before.[16]

The Greek prime minister, Eleutherios Venizelos, a friend of Britain, summed up his position and that of Greece: '... the Hellenic Government could not interfere in a question which was an internal affair of Great Britain. There was no Cyprus question between the British and Greek Governments.'[17] Venizelos died in 1936 and thus ended the Greek policy of support for Britain over Cyprus. Future Greek Governments would offer increasing support to Greek Cypriot aspirations for Enosis.[18]

Laurie Lee came to Cyprus in 1938. He had already walked out one midsummer's morning across Spain and into that country's civil war. In November he set out via Italy and Greece with his fiddle to earn a living. He spent that winter before the war in Cyprus; as he says, he knew nothing about the island, he just 'turned up'. After a stormy crossing from Athens, Lee arrived in Limassol in December. It was raining. For much of his first visit he stayed in Famagusta; five years later he would publish the poem 'Port of Famagusta' where he wrote about its 'occidental heart' and 'Syrian tongue and Grecian doors' and its 'jigsaw of your western love'.

Lee had Christmas lunch with a Greek tailor, Polichronos, and his family who had befriended the affable English man. The Greeks treated him with 'amazing courtesy'. He went with Picton, 'a cheerful old English man with a white beard', to the English Church, and 'bellowed carols with the sun streaming through the windows': 'Here were gathered the crumpled sandy faces of my compatriots and the service echoed with the rhythmic phrase of the "virgin's womb".'

A few days later he went into Famagusta's famed red light district 'looking for a whore' and there was a big selection. His girl had a 'dark smile' and her 'skin was rough'. When he left she waved goodbye from the door. In the moonlight he found 'the city walls were majestic and the eucalyptus trees amazingly fragile and lovely as I went back to the hotel'.[19]

Suha Faiz and his elder brother returned to Cyprus in the summer of 1939 for a holiday from school in England that was planned to last a month. However, in September once again Britain and Germany went to war:

My immediate reaction was youthful excitement that I was going to stay indefinitely in Cyprus. Father and Mother must have been desperately worried, whether to accept that all their plans and expense, so far on an English education for their children must be abandoned or whether they should try and get us back to England ...[20]

Suha's father was then Superintendent of Police in charge of Larnaca district and also, for a period, responsible for the adjoining district of Famagusta while the British Superintendent was on leave. Suha continues:

In Larnaca we lived in the official house allocated to the Superintendent, a typical Public Works Dept Building, solid and roomy, with the usual veranda running all round. It was not far from the palm and cypress shrouded Hala Sultan Mosque on the edge of the Salt Lake. 'An important shrine of Islam' being the tomb of the Prophet Mohammed's aunt Umm Haram.

I can see now how busy and preoccupied father must have been during the weeks while war was looming. What with preparations for all the civil defence wartime controls must have filled his time and mind.[21]

On one of his father's tours of inspection he took Suha with him to the Karpas Peninsula:

This I recall as quite an expedition with some hair-raising roads. I was struck, and impressed, that Father seemed to know individually every policeman he came across even outside the police stations, notably as we were not in his own district but at the far end of Famagusta district.[22]

Suha's parents did send the boys back to England. They got to Britain just weeks before the German Blitzkrieg on the Low Countries and France. Within a year Suha's father, in his early 40s, was dead. He died of cirrhosis of the liver, although not, as is more common today, brought on by over-use of alcohol, for he was an observing Muslim. Rather in his case it was the result of malaria, caught in his youth which had been incubating and attacking his liver.

Malaria was another of the plagues to afflict Cyprus, affecting whole communities. Many youngsters who had the disease died while others who survived were disabled for life or like Suha's father died young. It would be another Turkish Cypriot, Mehmet Aziz, who would eradicate the disease-carrying mosquito from the island.

In the late 1930s Cyprus was often discussed by the British Chiefs of Staff. However, they were generally not in favour of developing the island as a military base, preferring to foster good relations with Benito Mussolini and Fascist Italy. Prime Minister Neville Chamberlain was certainly against the idea. In April 1938 the Committee of Imperial Defence concluded: 'It was unnecessary to proceed with the idea of developing a base at Cyprus.'[23]

Notes

1. Stark Freya, *Dust in the Lion's Paw*, p. 233
2. Penelope Tremayne, *Below the Tide*, pp. 106–107, 'It seems that …'
3. Charles Foley (ed.), *The Memoirs of General Grivas*, pp. 2–3, 'The village school …'
4. Faiz Suha, *Recollections and Reflections of an Unknown Cyprus Turk*, pp. 27–8
5. Sir Harry Luke, *Cyprus*, p. 79, 'The conquest of 1571 …'
6. David Lloyd George, *The Truth about the Peace Treaties*, pp. 1238–39, and Dimitrakis Panagiotis, *Military Intelligence in Cyprus*, p. 18
7. Tabitha Morgan, *Sweet and Bitter Island*, p. 104
8. Ibid., p. 104, 'With the previous uncertainty …'
9. Jan Morris, *Farewell the Trumpets*, p. 392, 'Storrs approach to these problems …'
10. Ibid., p. 393, 'Alas for Ronald Storrs …'
11. Ibid., p. 394, 'One night in 1931 …'
12. Faiz, p. 31, 'We have been told …'
13. Morris, p. 394, 'He was not a strong man …'
14. Luke, p. 176
15. Iain Ballantyne, *HMS London*, p. 60, 'At Larnaca …'
16. Foley, *General Grivas*, p. 12, 'Throughout the first half …'
17. Luke, p. 185, 'After the short sharp …'
18. Dimitrakis, p. 21, 'In Athens, the administration …'
19. Grove Valerie, *Laurie Lee: The Well-Loved Stranger*, pp. 112–13, 'Among painted fishing boats …'
20. Faiz, p. 59, 'It was the summer of 1939 …'
21. Ibid., p. 60, 'Father was then …'
22. Ibid., p. 61, 'On one of father's tours …'
23. FO-(PRO) 371/2236 and Dimitrakis p. 22, 'In his turn …'

4

THE SECOND
WORLD WAR

The view of the Axis threat to Cyprus by the British had changed by
1939; the Cypriot Regiment was founded that year. However, to start with
few recruits joined from either the Greek or Turkish communities; only
once the Italians invaded Greece in October 1940 did Greek Cypriots
join Commonwealth units in large numbers. In 1941 6,000 would fight
against the Germans in Greece.

For a time it had been thought that Famagusta might be developed
as a naval base. But after the signing of the Anglo-Egyptian treaty this
changed to Alexandria, for the distance from Egypt to Cyprus of over
300 miles, according to the official history:

> meant that no matter what provision was made at Cyprus it would still
> be necessary to use Alexandria as an advanced operational base, and it
> would have to be defended. The protection and control of the Suez
> Canal depended upon our power to defend Egypt, so that any develop-
> ment of Cyprus would add to, and not lessen the tasks of the army and
> air force.[1]

Right from the start of the war the Greek Cypriots again started lobby-
ing for Enosis. Some Foreign Office diplomats did think ceding Cyprus to
Greece might be wise. However, the Colonial Office was strongly against it

terming the island 'a strategic colony'.[2] German radio propaganda broadcasts also tried to stoke the embers of Enosis. In March 1940 they claimed:

> Discontent in Cyprus is constantly increasing. On 9 March 1940 a general strike took place. This strike followed a series of local strikes. Dissatisfaction on the island is caused by the fact that the prices of commodities of prime importance have risen since the outbreak of the war by 25 per cent.
>
> ... the people of Cyprus think that this situation [of peasants starving due to no income from exports] has to cease once and for all; they hope that Germany will come out of this war victorious; they know that such a German victory would mean their own union with their Greek Fatherland.[3]

As the Phoney War progressed France became interested in Cyprus as an advance base for aircraft on seaward patrols, especially towards the Italian Dodecanese Islands, and for giving depth to the air defences of Beirut. The British, on the other hand, did not wish Cyprus to grow into a defensive commitment involving forces that could ill be spared. They agreed, however, that the airfields at Nicosia and Larnaca should be improved and that refuelling and rearming facilities should be made available to the French.[4]

By the end of spring 1941 Cyprus was largely encircled by Axis-occupied territories. The next target could well be Cyprus. The island had already been bombed by the Italian Air Force, the Regia Aeronautica, in September 1940. In May 1941 the Italians bombed Nicosia Airfield, and later in the month German and Italian aircraft from the Dodecanese islands attacked. Little damage was done, though two civilians were killed. There was little that could be done in defence. Cyprus had no anti-aircraft guns and only two obsolete fighter aircraft.[5]

General Archibald Wavell, C-in-C Middle East, had little to spare for Cyprus but decided the 7th Australian Division's Cavalry Regiment should be sent to the island. Wavell apologised to the Governor William Denis Battershill that it was an Australian unit, not knowing Battershill was married to an Australian, who responded, 'I've been married to an Australian for 25 years. What's a regiment.'[6] However, the Imperial Defence Committee were more concerned with Syria and conceded that 'no additions' could be made to the 'garrison of that island, its task was to make sure that the enemy did not gain possession of Cyprus without a fight'.[7]

Along with the Australians was a battalion of the Sherwood Foresters. The Royal Navy based some of HMS *Illustrious*'s aircraft there after the carrier was badly damaged on convoy duties around Malta. The Royal Australian Air Force had some Hurricane fighters on the island. The Australian Cavalry Regiment went into camp near Famagusta and then en masse went for a night on the town. According to the Regimental Bulletin after being granted leave they headed:

… straight for the night-spots of Famagusta. This sortie was to have grave short-term consequences for the physical well-being of the diggers. Over-indulgence in the local brews had a devastating effect on even the most hardened and impervious drinker.

It was not more than two hours before the first survivors returned staggering to the encampment, much the worse for wear, and the rest of the night was spent by those on duty retrieving sodden wrecks from all over the town. Every man on the Regimental pay-sheet was accounted for in fact next day on parade, we were 13 over strength! At a subsequent Court of Enquiry, it was proved beyond reasonable doubt that no blame was attachable to any member of the Regiment for the events that occurred on the night of 5 May 1941 in the port of Famagusta. Evidence proved conclusively that the real culprit-the real fifth columnist-the true snake in the grass as: The rough red wine of the country-Kamandaria!

Shortly after this the Australians moved to Athasiassa camp close to Nicosia. On the route of march they received a riotus welcome moving through Famagusta; 'The street was veritably packed with the good citizens and yeomen cheering and shouting.' The female population was also prominent in the crowd. 'From balconies protruding above the narrow street, the young virgins of the district waved gaily coloured table cloths at us while downstairs their less prudent sisters showered us with flowers.' Having recovered from their first introduction to the local alcoholic beverages the gifts of 'bottles of wine and ouzo' was welcome. By the time they reached the centre of town 'the whole ruddy caboodle came to a grinding halt and we were entirely hemmed in by the mob'.[8]

The column had been halted by the local bishop who wanted to bless them. The CO, Lieutenant Colonel Logan, agreed he had little option and the men were told to 'pay attention to divine service'. The crowd became silent:

> Holy water was liberally sprinkled upon the leading tank which aptly, was named 'Cascade' in honour of a popular Tasmania brew. The saintly old Father Xmas Bishop with the long white beard kissed The Goon (Colonel Logan, the Regiment's CO) on both cheeks and said that was the best he could do for us at such short notice. The crowd went berserk. Greek, Turkish, Cypriot, Lebanese, Egyptian, Spanish, Syrian, Palestinian, Maltese and even Italian flags were waved furiously amidst innumerable Union Jacks and the flag of Famagusta Rovers Soccer Club.[9]

The regiment's armour, fifteen Vickers MK VIA and B tanks, were obsolete, as were the four 2-pounder anti-tank guns. As the Australians arrived British troops were preparing to evacuate Crete.

On Cyprus many non-Cypriots began leaving the island. Battershill's office organised the evacuation. Polish and Jewish refugees were the first to go; last were the dependants of Government officials. As the foreign nationals were leaving Cypriot women and children took to the road after the governor asked them to return to their villages; 5,000 left Nicosia alone.

About this time Freya Stark arrived on the island curiously on a Greek Navy corvette from Beirut. She was on leave from her Foreign Office job in Cairo:

> Cyprus was full of troops in expectation of a second Crete, English women were nearly all evacuated–a discrimination inside the boundaries of the empire which naturally did us no good with the Cypriots, but spread a beautiful solitude and peace over the island.[10]

Battershill had been determined that all British dependants must go including some who worked for the Red Cross. Shipping took them to South Africa via Port Said. By 13 June 1941 he was able to report the last evacuees, 164 British women and children had left. *The Times* reported 'the island is stripped for war and prepared for all eventualities'.[11]

Doctor Alan Fawdrey and his wife Hazel were in Cyprus in 1941 and left for South Africa, but not before he was to have a direct effect on the health of the Cypriot people. His wife Hazel tells the story:

When we were in Cyprus in 1941 Alan noticed there were quite a few children with bulging tummies and were anaemic. And so he tried to find out what was the matter with them. He discovered their spleens were enlarged but it was not malarial and in due course he found out what was the matter with them. They had a hereditary illness called 'Cooley's Anaemia' today called Thalassemia. Cyprus was the only part of the Empire that had this disability and he became quite famous for working on it for fifty years with his peers and the Thalassemia Society.[12]

Thalassemia is sometimes called Mediterranean Anaemia, an abnormality of the red blood cells and bone marrow, with enlargement of the spleen.

The garrison of Cyprus was designated '7th Infantry Division' in an attempt to deceive the Axis powers, complete with wooden tanks, fake gun positions and bogus signals traffic. The Australians' main role, along with other troops, was to reinforce the deception by vigorous roaming about the island; they called it 'showing the flag'. Air raids on the island in this period did increase.

Following the fall of Crete air raids by the Luftwaffe and the Regina Aeronautica increased. The Vichy French Air Force flying Glenn Martin bombers out of Syria also joined the battle, at one stage executing a raid on the airfield just as the British ground crews were lining up for their mess. The raid caused many serious casualties amongst the ground staff. A number of Australians were injured in these attacks. In order to simulate the brigade size group, patrols of light tanks, machine-gun carriers and trucks of the regiment roamed far and wide over the island. The normal headdress of black beret with the small collar-badge size 'Rising Sun' was often substituted for the Australian slouch hat or steel helmet to make it appear as though there was a large force on the island. The ruse would of course, have not fooled anyone, let alone the locals.[13]

Freya Stark saw some of the defences that were constructed for the anticipated invasion:

Flat places were dotted with small earth cones, like nails on the soles of mountain boots, to deter airborne landings, and a fierce controversy raged as to whether they did not make things too easy for the enemy when once the landings had taken place. In this dilemma some ground was fortified and some not, and paratroop invaders could shelter behind the cones after landing on the open ground beside them; our fair-minded loss of the advantages of both sides seemed secure.[14]

In July 1941 General Claude Auchinleck replaced Wavell as C-in-C Middle East. The Vichy French forces had been defeated in Operation Exporter against the French in Syria, lasting five weeks.[15] Thus he was able to reinforce Cyprus. Three battalions of the Durham Light Infantry arrived by sea by fast ships from Alexandria. 'The operation started on July 18th and continued until the end of the month, a division of troops, units of the Royal Air Force, with mechanical transport and stores, being carried to the island in cruisers, destroyers, and the fast minelayers *Abdiel* and *Latona*.'[16]

The troops were quickly unloaded at Famagusta, and taken to airfields at Nicosia or Lakatamia where they were issued with entrenching tools and they dug in. Troops were in a state of high alert; one company was ready at short notice to move to Paphos, the port closest to Axis-occupied Crete. Cypriots were also employed on the defences, 20,000 being retained 'on attractive wages'.[17]

The proposed invasion of Cyprus from the German point of view presented great problems; unlike Crete it lay outside the range of effective German fighter support. Hitler had become affected with a distrust of airborne operations in general. General Kurt Student, commander of the German Airborne forces, wrote: 'After Crete I proposed that we should make an attack upon Cyprus in order to make a jumping-off ground for an attack on the Suez Canal. But Hitler rejected it because of the losses we had received on Crete.' The Fuhrer's eyes were firmly fixed to the east and Russia.[18]

Of course, it was not all rushing about and frantic activity, even for the troops on Cyprus, and certainly not for Freya Stark:

I had to promise the tired Navy that under no circumstances would I ask to be evacuated, and now, after safe arrival, I convalesced beside water so limpid, so transparent, so green near shore and variegated-like the leaves of those hothouse plants-with such patterns of sunlight on its submerged sands that the sight of it alone made one forget all trouble.[19]

In 1942 Robert Gregory of the RAF came by a roundabout route to Cyprus. He left the UK in February for Singapore but Malaya soon fell to the Japanese. 'We sailed all the way around Africa and did not get off until we arrived in Egypt in April.' By May he was on Cyprus with HQ 259 Wing. Robert was detached to the Army and became a mail man delivering post on a Norton 500cc motor bike:

It took nine days to cover the island; it was like paradise riding around in shorts all day. We often took part in scrambles and races against the Army but usually lost'. However in October Robert left Cyprus for North Africa 'and went back to the real war.[20]

Freya Stark found solitude in the village of Prodromos high in the Troodos Mountains, where she loaned a cottage: 'vines grew around the house, and pinewoods and browsing goats climbed up to minor Olympus.' The population of the village was small, only 400, apart from a friend in the Yorkshire Hussars who 'gave me a ride in one of his Crusader tanks'. She saw few people spending 'a month of solitude'.[21]

Charles Foley, who would later edit the *Times of Cyprus*, first visited the island in 1943. On arriving at his hotel in Nicosia he was soon hoping 'that my first visit to Cyprus would be my last'. It was very hot, he could get no water from the pipes for a bath and 'my knees refused to fit under the marble wash-stand and there was nowhere else to set up the type-writer' and 'the tea was mildewed'.[22]

Foley, a well-known newspaper correspondent, was soon besieged by people to discuss the Cyprus problem, something of which he was totally ignorant. He was soon told Gladstone had hoped to see Cyprus become a Greek Island. And Churchill had said: 'It is right and natural for Cyprus to belong to Greece, the Cypriots patriotic devotion to what they call their motherland is an ideal to be cherished.' But Cyprus in 1943 was a backwater, whatever Churchill had said in 1907.

A few days later Foley was able to raise the question of Cyprus with a Government Minister when he got a lift in a plane from Algiers to the UK. The Minister was Harold Macmillan. After a long conversation covering the war Foley asked him about Cyprus, which Foley says had a queer effect on Macmillan: 'Cyprus, h'm, how did Disraeli describe it to Queen Victoria? "The Key to western Asia?" I dare say he was wearing his suit of Imperial spangles at the time.' With that Macmillan fell asleep.[23]

By late 1943 the garrison of Cyprus had grown to 10,500 troops: 1,500 British, mainly artillery and RAF; 6,000 Indian Infantry; and 3,000 Cypriots. The 25th Army Corps Headquarters was another deception, and was merely a 'skeleton HQ'. Churchill did enquire about troops and aircraft for his Dodecanese Campaign.[24]

Operation Accolade, a full-scale attack on Rhodes and Karpathos, and occupation of other Aegean islands, was to take advantage of the collapse of Fascist Italy. However, Cyprus was of limited use to the RAF, being outside the range of single-engined fighter aircraft; only the British Beaufighter and the American P-38 Lightnings had the range. The operation would be a disaster, the last British defeat of the Second World War.[25]

Cyprus did become a training base. SOE had wanted to train guerrillas on the island, first on the eve of the expected German Invasion and later to send agents into occupied Greece and her islands.

In July 1942 Geoff Chapman, a forestry worker and fluent Greek speaker, was summoned to SOE headquarters in Cairo. He was taken to Force 133, the city's branch of SOE. There he had lengthy interviews about 'Cyprus' and his 'career', and he was recruited as a Special Agent, with the rank of major and responsibility for resistance on Cyprus.[26] Yet even by that time the danger to Cyprus had passed. SOE worked hard to maintain fear of the Germans with the local population. But even they could see, with Axis defeats in North Africa against Rommel's Afrika Corps, the tide had turned.

Relations between servicemen and locals on Cyprus were not always good; riots and street brawls were common in areas where Cypriots and servicemen mixed. On New Year's Day 1944, RAF personnel were involved in fights with some locals. SOE reported concerns about this,

that 'British troops' act 'superior and do not treat Cypriots properly …';
however, it was felt 'pro-Axis' elements were at work fostering ill-will
between the two groups.[27] SOE feelers extended into many factors of life
on the island:

> at Engomi village near Nicosia, a Greek-Cypriot teacher openly spoke
> against the Allies in his classes. SOE planned to ask the colonial administra-
> tion to remove him to a distant village, since Engomi provided Cypriot
> labourers for the military bases, he could be a bad influence on these
> already agitated workers.[28]

By this time Greek Cypriot trade unionists and members of the
Progressive Party of Working People (AKEL), the Cypriot Communist
Party, were identified as the main security threat on the island, rather
than the Abwehr, German Military Intelligence, or the SD, secret service
branch of the SS. SOE thought that all AKEL members were ready to
take up arms against the colonial Government:

> There is a lot of talk down here of 'the day of the civil revolution' which
> will occur as soon as only a token force of the British and Indians is left
> in Cyprus. The Cyprus Volunteer Force is mentioned as a potential revo-
> lutionary force. A superior leader of AKEL told me lately that even if the
> armed riots were ultimately doomed to failure, they would bring Cyprus
> into the public eye, that to allay censure from the USA and the sentimental
> British Public, Whitehall would grant sweeping reforms.[29]

However, support for AKEL did not grow significantly on the island.
Partly due to the in-fighting between the Communist EAM-ELAS
and the pro-republican EDES on mainland Greece, which after the war
would degenerate into civil war.

In March 1944 trade unionists and the AKEL organised a strike by
Government labourers that lasted twenty-three days, holding up work
at Government workshops and on RAF airfields. The Church of Cyprus,
AKEL, the trade unions, and the National Party of Cyprus, strange bed fel-
lows, now called for Enosis union of Cyprus with Greece. A general strike

was planned for 28 August 1944 which the AKEL hoped would develop into open revolt, with members of the Cyprus Regiment and Volunteer Force joining them. The British learnt of the plan and simply banned the demonstration and deployed forces to avert any uprising. The governor, Sir Charles Woolley, was pessimistic about the future, feeling 'a particular dangerous period will occur when the return of the Cyprus troops, many of whom are fanatical followers of AKEL, takes place …'[30]

On the same day Woolley wrote his report, 31 March 1945, infantry weapons were stolen from a Cyprus Volunteer depot – eight Bren guns and fifty-eight rifles, along with thousands of rounds of ammunition. By mid-April much had been recovered in the garden of a leading AKEL member. Several AKEL members along with CVF soldiers were arrested.

Smuggling of small arms became rife on the island. In mid-April 1945 the Government released the full official text on the law of trafficking and the possession of arms. The 1945 Regulations stated: 'Anyone caught stealing, receiving or otherwise being illegally in possession of weapons of the Armed Forces or police, could henceforth be sentenced to prison for life and in any case for not less than seven years.'[31] However, a short amnesty was granted: if arms were surrendered to the police within fifteen days, no action would be taken.

In October 1945 mutiny broke out within the Cyprus Regiment in Famagusta. The regiment had become a problem for the Colonial Government, wondering what to do with them. The war was over. Naturally the Cypriot soldiers wished to return to civilian life. Their record was good: 37,000 had fought for the Allies and they had suffered over 3,000 casualties. The Cyprus Regiment served under the Colonial Constitution and not the British Army. When it was revealed they might be sent to Palestine to help the British Army, mutiny broke out with demonstrations by their families. Indian troops were brought in to restore order. One Cypriot sergeant was killed and four others wounded. Other minor mutinies took place in Italy and North Africa while AKEL continued to agitate for self-determination.

Through the good offices of the Welfare Department of the Colonial Office, Suha Faiz got back to Cyprus after the war to visit his mother. He joined a ship returning Italian prisoners of war home. After unloading the Italians at Naples the ship went on to Egypt:

From Port Said I got a deck passage on a schooner bound for Cyprus. We disembarked at Limassol by small boats there was not anything like a quayside only a jetty. By chance the collector of customs was yet another uncle. I didn't know him from Adam but, from my passport details, a policeman, having known my father, made the family connection.

A taxi was summoned and Suha was soon on his way home to see his mother in Nicosia. He found Cyprus a land of plenty after the rationing of wartime Britain, stopping for lunch at a roadside cafe of 'delicious meat, rice, potatoes, vegetables, and fruit in abundance'. His elder brother had joined the British forces like thousands of other Cypriots. He became a sub-lieutenant in the Royal Naval Reserve and took part in the D-Day landings.

But even this world of plenty and a sense of 'paradise attained' did not delude him for he felt 'there was a serpent in that Eden'.[32]

Notes

1. I.S.O. Playfair, *The Mediterranean and Middle East*, Vol. 1, p. 9, 'Now that Italy …'
2. Panagiotis Dimitrakis, *Military Intelligence in Cyprus*, pp. 23–4, 'Right from the start …'
3. Medium-wave broadcast from Breslau in 'Greek for Greece' 18/3/1940. FCO-(PRO) 323/1737/8 and Dimitrakis, p. 25
4. Playfair, p. 27, 'The French were anxious …'
5. Dimitrakis, pp. 25–6, 'By spring 1941 …'
6. Paul D. Handel, *Australian Armour in Cyprus*, p. 2
7. I.S.O. Playfair, *The Mediterranean and Middle East*, Vol. 2, pp. 203–4, 'The reply to this …'
8. Handel, p. 2
9. Ibid., p. 3
10. Freya Stark, *Dust in the Lion's Paw*, p. 136
11. *The Times* 18/6/1941 and Tabitha Morgan, *Sweet and Bitter Island*, p. 165
12. BMCH Oral Tape 277 Mrs Hazel Fawdrey.
13. Handel, p. 7
14. Stark, p. 136
15. Playfair, Vol. 2, p. 205
16. Admiral of the Fleet Andrew Cunningham, *A Sailor's Odyssey*, pp. 402–3, 'After the end of the Syrian campaign …'
17. Morgan, p. 170, 'Cypriots too …'
18. Christopher Buckley, *Greece and Crete 1941*, p. 323, 'There was a direct consequence …'

19. Stark, p. 136
20. LTA, Robert Gregory RAF 15/7/2000
21. Stark, pp. 137–8, 'Except for Sim Feversham …'
22. Charles Foley, *Island in Revolt*, p. 6, 'This time I meant …'
23. Ibid., p. 10, 'The Minister was …'
24. Dimitrakis, pp. 37–8
25. Anthony Rogers, *Churchill's Folly: Leros and the Aegean*, p. 28, 'It was recommended …'
26. Morgan, pp. 183–4, 'In the first week …'
27. Dimitrakis, p. 47, 'Meanwhile, crime, riots …'
28. Ibid., p. 49, 'Colonial office officials …'
29. KV-(PRO) Report of SOE Commander 14/6/1943, p. 2, HS 3/118 and Dimitrakis, p. 50, 'There was some anxiety …'
30. George Horton Kelling, *Countdown to Rebellion*, p. 109
31. Dimitrakis, p. 51
32. Suha Faiz, *Recollections and Reflections of an Unknown Cyprus Turk*, pp. 76–7, 'the ship decanted me …'

5

THE GATHERING STORM 1947–1954

In 1946 Clement Attlee's post-war Labour Government looked at the future of Cyprus within the British Empire. Foreign Secretary Ernest Bevin initially favoured Cyprus being given to Greece in return for bases in Greece, her islands and on Cyprus. After all, he argued, Greece was a loyal ally. However, the General Staff was against the plan, indicating the island's position in the Middle East with the looming Cold War was vital. It was a similar position to that Britain had faced in 1915 when for internal reasons Greece had not accepted the offer. In 1946 the precarious situation in Greece and the danger of civil war changed Bevin's position. In November of that year fighting broke out between Greek troops and Communist rebels in Macedonia. In December Bevin told the Greek ambassador in London that it was 'senseless to hand Cyprus to Greece if that country was on the point of going communist'.[1]

Clamours for independence had been growing within Britain's Empire months before the guns fell silent at the end of the Second World War. Trouble flared first in India between 1945–47, then with Palestine 1945–48, and in Egypt in 1946. The Palestine situation brought Cyprus right into the front line.

In Palestine the British found themselves trapped between two warring factions, the Arabs and a large but rapidly expanding Jewish minority. However, the British Mandate in Palestine had been fixed for twenty-five years and was due to run out in 1948.

Before the Second World War the rise of Hitler had aggravated the problem in Palestine as Jews flooded out of Europe. In the last years of the 1930s Jewish settlers were reaching Palestine at the rate of a thousand a week.

In 1946 a steady stream of run-down vessels of all shapes and sizes, loaded to overflowing with people, began to arrive in Palestine hoping to flood the country with illegal immigrants. The vast majority of these people had never seen the country before and were mainly the poor survivors of Hitler's death camps. These vessels were intercepted at sea by the Royal Navy and brought into Palestine, where the passengers, often in an appalling state, were off-loaded and transhipped to internment camps in Cyprus.

The crews of the Royal Navy destroyers and light cruisers had the unenviable task of boarding these ships where more often than not they received a hostile reception. Some boarding parties were met with steam hoses, fire bombs, shots, and attacks by groups of men and women armed with axes and bars. Often the destroyers were lower in the water than the steamers so nets were rigged over the decks to stop all manner of missiles, although there was no protection against the buckets of human waste tipped over boarding parties. A number of sailors and immigrants were killed in these high seas encounters.

Ordinary Seaman Tom Simmons from the destroyer HMS *Chivalrous* was on these patrols when the ship visited Cyprus in November 1947 and he missed the ship's sailing:

> I went to the RAF Hospital in Nicosia with an able seaman. I think he had fallen. It must have been an injury. I'll tell you why, because we had a sick bay attendant and if it had been appendicitis or something like that, he would have gone. I went with him really as company and to carry his kit.
>
> When I left Famagusta for the hospital there were four destroyers in the bay. When I got back they had all gone. One of the biggest refugee ships had been spotted trying to get to Palestine. That's when I always remember I got through on the phone to the Naval Attaché in Nicosia. In the course of the conversation I said to him. 'But I've got the middle watch tonight'.
>
> 'Good Lord' he said 'no one's indispensable.'

Of course he was right, you see, the ship would have sailed even if the captain had not been there.

The destroyers followed the steamers out of sight plotting them on radar and then closed on them before they reached territorial waters and then boarded.

'It hardly seemed fair considering their state and what they had been through' said Tom. 'But there we are, we had a job to do and as usual we were in the middle.'[2]

In September 1948, 40 Commando RM arrived on Cyprus by sea from Malta disembarking at Famagusta and deploying to Dhekelia Camp, which was then a series of wooden huts, which was close to the Jewish internment camp at Xylotymbou. The huts occupied by the internees were contained in fenced compounds. 40 Commando relieved a battalion of the Light Infantry and assumed duties for guarding some 8,000 Jews, who had been turned back by Navy patrols while attempting to enter Palestine illegally. Much of the Commando was able to take part in training and enjoyed the islands recreational facilities. Arnold Hadwin OBE, a National Service Marine, enjoyed the light-hearted atmosphere and recalls the birth of Prince Charles.

Arnold and his oppo had been on a scheme when they descended to the west of the Kyrenian Mountains into a village. It was a Monday in November and he was surprised 'to find all the School Children shouting and waving flags and the whole population excited to the point of non-alcoholic inebriation'. Arnold and Tom his oppo had been on a Commando initiative test and away from contact with the outside world for several days:

'At first Tom and I thought Enosis had been declared in our absence. And when we were surrounded by the entire populace and hustled into the local hostelry we just thought it was their way of saying all was forgiven'. The Greek Cypriots were dumbfounded the two Marines did not know.

'Elizabeth-she has a son' Tom asked them 'Who's Elizabeth?'

The entire village staged a party that went on into the next day and the two Marines were the centre of attention:

They gave us a hero's welcome; nothing was too good for us. You would have thought we'd had a hand in it. Our closest drinking buddy was the village policeman. I will never forget the day after Prince Charles was born. Nor will I ever forget reading in a newspaper some years later that our drinking companion had been gunned down by EOKA terrorists.

Soldiers and Commandos guarded the internment camps where the Jewish refugees were taken on arrival in Cyprus. St David's, west of Nicosia, was one such camp, which today lies within the UN Buffer Zone between north and south. It is said you can still see a faded painting on the officers' living quarter's wall. There's a map of Cyprus and the surrounding countries, a man stands on the European shore in tattered clothing wearing the Star of David on his coat; he is reaching out to a young girl in Cyprus, who is in a tented camp behind barbed wire. There are some Hebrew letters but too faded now to read, but the picture tells its own story.[3]

Thomas (Bing) Crosbie served with 40 Commando from 1947–50 in the Mediterranean part of which was spent on Cyprus; he joined the unit when he was just 18. 'On leaving Palestine we spent an agreeable period of about a year on Malta before moving to Cyprus', where he helped guard camps of illegal Jewish immigrants; he recalls the one at Xylotymbou about 10 miles from Larnaca:

It was just like you see in POW camps of World War Two. Towers on the corners and bends, one man in those little watch towers in the daylight hours. We did two hour watches, sometimes patrolling between them and around the camp all night long. This went on for about nine months. The winter months were damn cold that year … The men and women in the camp were treated very well by us and we often talked to them through the barbed wire fences. They got plenty of food delivered into the camp … They were getting fed better than we were.

When patrolling we often found places where the captives had managed to escape through the wire … Of course we didn't use dogs to patrol around the camps and though we had searchlights they were not powerful enough and often in the wrong place. I think the inmates more or less came and went as they pleased, for a run ashore in Larnaca or Nicosia.

How many escaped to get a boat to Israel, God only knows. When we did catch anyone getting through the wire at night they were just kept in cells overnight and released back into the camp next day. So they certainly were not mistreated in any way.

After a few months some illegals began to be released to proceed to Israel. They took their meagre belongings with them. One incident I remember well because I lost out through it, when checking some luggage. On one lorry I became suspicious of one large wooden crate. So I had a look at it and decided that there were too many gaps in the planking, there seemed to be something loose inside. So I told the officer supervising the checking that I thought there was a person inside the crate. He ordered me to push it off the back of the lorry and I refused, it was a good five feet to the ground, if there was anybody in there they could be hurt. The officer ordered me again, and again I refused telling him there was somebody inside the crate. He ordered me down from the lorry and sent someone else to push it off. There was a young woman in the crate luckily she was not hurt too badly. I was put on a charge for refusing a direct order and lost my newly won lance corporals stripes. I was confined to barracks for a while. I think the CO really agreed with my stance but in those days refusing a direct order was just not cricket old boy.[4]

By the end of 1948 all the Jews in detention camps had been released, after the British withdrawal from Palestine after which the state of Israel was declared.

Mrs Faith Lloyd-Phillips, wife of a district commissioner in the Colonial Service, arrived on Cyprus in 1950, after they had been in Palestine during the last years of British rule:

I loved Cyprus. When we arrived they were writing things on the walls but no more than that. I think they began to realise when you start killing people the Government might do something. You see terrorism today has all stemmed from Palestine. Well that's my view. You see the Cypriots just copied the Jews.

Faith's husband was blown up in the attack by the stern gang on the King David Hotel in Jerusalem which was being used by the British;

ninety-one people were killed and forty-five badly injured. Her husband escaped with cuts and bruises. However, there is no evidence to suggest EOKA were much influenced by events in Palestine. Faith continues:

> My husband was District Commissioner for Nicosia and we had a lovely house there. We lived in the Turkish quarter only because that's where the house was. It wasn't a Turkish house but a PWD house.
>
> We had friends on both sides and Greek and Turkish servants. I preferred the Turks, I rather like Muslims, and I had preferred the Arabs to the Jews in Palestine.[5]

George Grivas was well versed in irregular warfare before the Second World War. He had fought against Turkish guerrillas in the mountains behind Smyrna today Izmir, while in the Greek Army, and had suffered defeat against the inspired leadership of Mustafa Kemal who would later become Ataturk. It was here he had his 'first taste of guerrilla warfare and began to realise its possibilities'.[6]

During the Second World War Grivas fought in the Greek Army against the Italians and later the Germans. In Athens, during the occupation, he formed resistance groups known as the Xhi which he called his 'private army', a nationalistic right-wing group who appear to have spent as much time fighting the Communist Greek Resistance as they did the Germans. As far as the Communists were concerned Grivas wrote: '... their only purpose was to seize power as soon as the Germans left. Meanwhile they collaborated with the occupiers and worked against the Nationalist forces.' Winston Churchill had shared this view of the Communists in Greece, that they were only interested in power after German defeat. Grivas also felt the exiled Greek Government in Cairo gave him no support, and the British, for a long time, were used by the Communists. There would be a similar recurring theme in his EOKA campaign, of a lack of support from allies bordering on a conspiracy against him.[7]

The Greek Civil War started in places before the German withdrawal had begun but really blew up in September 1944. Grivas was in the thick of the fighting in Athens. British troops were soon on the same streets trying in vain to separate the warring factions. At one stage Grivas, with a small force, was surrounded by the Communists in Thyssion, a district below the hill of the Acropolis; here he was rescued by the timely arrival of two British tanks. A ceasefire was organised and Grivas withdrew his men to a police station. Later again he had to be evacuated by British troops, of whom 120 were killed in Athens trying to stop the fighting.

In May 1948, Grivas, by now pensioned off by the Army, was scratching around for something to do. He met Christodolous Papadopoulos who was a lawyer and a member of the Cyprus Ethnarchy, the church council, but had, like Grivas, lived in Athens for years. Papadopoulos agreed to go to Cyprus to find out how serious the people were about Enosis. On his return he told Grivas that passions for Enosis were high. Grivas tried to get official backing from the Greek Government for an Enosis campaign but although he got favourable support in some quarters in private, he got none in public and no practical help.

It was not until May 1951 that a group of men met at the Tsitsas Cafe in Athens. Grivas was present with George Stratos, a former Greek War Minister, and three exiled members of the Ethnarchy Council. The outcome of the meeting, says Grivas, 'was a proposal that I should undertake the leadership of an armed struggle to throw the British out of Cyprus'.[8]

On 5 July Grivas, with his wife, returned to Cyprus. This was his first visit to his homeland in twenty years; they stayed with his brother Michael, who was a doctor, in Nicosia. This visit was mainly to study the terrain and people. Among the people he found '… little but scepticism toward the idea of a rising against the British'.[9]

Grivas soon met Archbishop Makarios, whom he had met previously in Athens in 1946, to whom he outlined his plans, but he found him 'reserved and sceptical'. They had another meeting before Grivas returned to Greece but again the Archbishop appeared to have 'grave doubts'. However, Grivas seemed to have none. He felt a campaign could be waged by small guerrilla teams in the mountains, and by terrorists in the towns against Government civil and military targets.[10]

Born in 1913, Archbishop Makarios was a completely different character to the single-minded Grivas. Makarios came from a near-mythical romantic background. Like his father, Makarios – whose family name was Mouskos – had been a shepherd in his youth, living a solitary life for months on end with the sheep. He was entered for the priesthood at Kykko Monastery on Cyprus which lies high in the Troodos range of mountains. The Kykko was rich and powerful within the Orthodox world and had a miracle-working icon, said to have been painted by St Luke.

Makarios, handsome and elegant, was a brilliant student, going to Athens, and then America attending Boston University. In 1950 he became Archbishop at the age of 37, the youngest bishop ever elected to the post. An astute politician, he favoured a more diplomatic approach to obtain Enosis, but was willing to use Grivas if required.

In July 1952 a secret meeting of the Liberation Committee took place in Athens, with Archbishop Makarios in the chair: present were George Stratos; the Loizides brothers; General Papadopoulos; Colonel Alexopoulous, both former comrades in arms to Grivas; and three lawyers. Grivas outlined his plan of campaign. Makarios immediately poured cold water on it saying: 'Not fifty men will be found to follow you.' Grivas responded that he was sure the Cypriots with good leadership would follow him.[11]

In October Grivas again returned to Cyprus; he was on the island for five months. During this visit he secretly recruited a small circle of trusted aids and plans were made to smuggle arms to the island.

By this time all the relative departments of the British Government, Colonial, Foreign and Ministry of Defence, were agreed on the need to retain Cyprus. In 1951 the Greek Prime Minister Sophocles Venizelos had made a 'bases for Enosis offer'. However, he was willing to concede that maybe in view of the 'international situation' the time was not right, but in the future steps should be taken 'to ascertain the wishes of the inhabitants of Cyprus'.[12]

Meanwhile the next year, Field Marshal Alexander Papagos, the nationalist victor of the Greek Civil War, was elected prime minister. He too raised the question of Cyprus with Anthony Eden who brushed aside the Greek claims stating: '... Cyprus had never belonged to Greece.' Papagos felt the only recourse now was to approach the UN.[13]

In London many felt there was no possibility of an insurgency on the island. In the House of Commons it was stated: 'It was all paper agitation. There is no need for us to do anything about it. The Cypriots are ...

civilised people. They will never do anything violent or drastic.'[14] However, others in the security services and Colonial Office were concerned about Greek Cypriot intentions. In 1954 the Security Intelligence Services on the island were reorganised. A.M. MacDonald of MI5, who had done much to organise the Intelligence Services of Kenya during the Mau Mau state of emergency, did the same for Cyprus. He was seconded to the Colonial Office to serve as full-time security intelligence adviser.[15]

Field Marshal Sir Gerald Templer, a former Director of Military Intelligence, wrote a report on the state of the Colonial Security Service; he visited the trouble spots from Cyprus to Uganda and concluded:

> It is possible that, had our intelligence system been better, we might have
> been spared the emergency in Kenya, and perhaps that in Malaya. It must
> be our objective so to improve the present system that we are, so far as is
> humanly possible, insured against similar catastrophes in future.[16]

However, the intelligence was: 'The most serious imperial intelligence challenge after the Malayan Emergency came in Cyprus.' This was mainly due to lack of resources within the Cyprus Special Branch which was described by a head of Security Intelligence Middle East as a 'right royal muddle'. It was not until Donald Stephens became head of security on the island in 1955 that many of the faults were addressed and rectified.[17]

Lawrence Durrell, with his 2-year-old daughter Sappho, arrived on Cyprus in January 1953 at the port of Limassol. He cleared customs where the officials answered firmly in English every question he asked in Greek. His first home was a bungalow on the main street of Kyrenia leading to the hospital, from which he began looking for a house to buy. He liked Ouzo and Commandaria, the tipple of the Crusaders. He found Cypriots even more hospitable than the mainland Greeks and he could never resist the call from a cafe table '*Kopiaste*' to sit down and share.

Durrell found the Colonial Office view on Enosis short-sighted for 'officially it doesn't exist, though unofficially it's a bit of a head-ache'. And no one seemed to have the 'faintest grasp of the situation'.[18] However, equally muddled was the Greek Cypriot position for they had a

'… Quixotic irrational love of England which no other nation seems to have and in a fantastic sort of way it flowered in blissful co-existence with the haunting dream of Union'.[19]

Later he would teach English to the students of the Nicosia Gymnasium where he witnessed first-hand the 'national sentiment in its embryonic state'. He would later work for the Government in the post of Director of the Information Service where he found: 'We had no real policy, save that of offering constitutions whose terms made them unsuitable for acceptance, and of stone walling on the central issue of sovereignty.' But he had no doubt who had fanned the flames of Enosis, the 'implacable priests'. For they knew they had an ideal opportunity and opponent in Britain. 'If we had been Russians or Germans the Enosis problem would have been solved in half an hour by a series of mass murders and deportations. But no democracy could think along these lines.'[20]

Charles Foley on his return to Cyprus to start the newspaper *Times of Cyprus* found the Government Secretariat in a state of normal administrative anarchy. 'They came and they went, a hundred or so officials, few knew whence or whither, least of all why.'[21]

These upholders of the Empire held the top jobs of the Government. Few had the slightest interest in Cyprus and failed to grasp that here they dealt with a literate European population unlike any other colony they had come across. Sir Ronald Storrs, Governor 1926–32, had seen this years before, and felt having officials in Cyprus with only African or Indian colony experience was far from ideal.

However, Suha Faiz who had joined the Colonial Service, first serving in the Gold Coast, returned to Cyprus in 1951 as Assistant District Commissioner in Limassol. He found the British administration 'autocratic'. The governor was British, as were the heads of departments, and the five district commissioners and High Court Judges. But all other senior posts were held by people who came from the local population. Presidents of District Courts, District Judges, Magistrates, Superintendents of Police, the professional services medical, agricultural, public works, forestry, customs were Cypriots. To him this administration of the British, Greeks and Turks, worked efficiently and its people were 'concerned with the well-being of all'.[22]

Before taking up his post Suha visited his mother in Nicosia; he was not aware of any contacts between Greeks and Turks in the normal sociability of daily life. 'The residential Greek and Turkish quarters of Nicosia were quite separate, and even the shopping areas were largely apart.'[23] And he found something he had not come across before. 'I began to get a feeling of an unfamiliar unease in the air. There was apprehension, even fear, in the atmosphere.'[24]

Back in Athens, Grivas attended another secret meeting of the Liberation Committee in March 1953. Makarios was still lukewarm as to the use of force other than for acts of sabotage against property. Grivas turned to Marshal Papagos, recently elected prime minister of Greece, for help; he soon got a reply. Papagos 'did not wish to become involved with the movement (EOKA) nor did he wish it to be known he had been informed of its plans'.[25]

According to Grivas the Greek Government now tried to warn him off. In their view the campaign was unlikely to succeed and Britain was an ally of Greece and the route of diplomacy held better prospects. Again in June, Makarios repeated his support for a sabotage campaign only, nor did he want any mainland Greek to get involved in the Enosis movement on Cyprus itself. Grivas felt increasingly isolated and frustrated. 'I began to believe that Makarios did not want to use force at all and that he had merely yielded to pressure in going this far.' However, Grivas persuaded other members of the committee to back his plans regardless of the Archbishop, and later even Makarios gave in.[26]

Even now there was a chance to give diplomacy a try, for the Greek Government had managed to get the question of Cyprus brought before the United Nations in the following year. Grivas says he was even threatened with arrest unless he dropped his plans.

Again it is clear Grivas was the driving force for he argued the British withdrawal from the Suez Canal bases, and the decision to make Cyprus the Middle East Headquarters forced EOKA to start the campaign. True, at this critical time Cyprus began to become far more important to Britain after leaving Suez in October 1954. In the Cold War against Russia, RAF bombers in theory could reach deep into the Soviet Union from bases on Cyprus.

However, the Grivas view does not stand the test of time. For Britain has retained her bases on Cyprus to this day, so in effect the island remains an aircraft carrier for Britain in the region. Also at the time he must have known his campaign was bound to turn Turk against Greek and leave Britain in the middle between warring ethnic and religious factions, and would be detrimental mostly to the very people he was supposed to serve, the people of Cyprus. Here Grivas as a military quasi-political leader shows a lack of adaptability; in fact he boasts about this trait in his character. 'I always take my decisions after careful thought, but once taken they are, for me, irrevocable …'[27]

In 1954 Britain was largely preoccupied with events in Egypt. By the middle of the year it was agreed 65,000 British troops and airmen would leave the Suez Canal bases, under an agreement reached with the Egyptian leader Colonel Gamal Abdel Nasser. British arms and equipment were to be mothballed and the base would be maintained by Egyptian civilians, while Britain retained the right to return in the event of an attack on Turkey or any Arab State. In the UK on 3 July the Government announced the end of all rationing after fourteen years. And Roger Bannister, the runner, broke the four-minute mile barrier with a time of 3.59.4.

In the summer of 1954, twin brothers Richard and Mike Chamberlain came to Cyprus with the Royal Corps of Signals to do their National Service. Richard arrived first in May and after pressure from the family and their MP on the Army, Mike, who had been sent to the Canal Zone, arrived in the summer to serve at the same base of Gazi Magusa near Famagusta. They found Famagusta had a 'great atmosphere'.

The island as a whole was still an idyllic backwater. They saw a lot of the island spending 'some time in the Troodos, hiring a car and going to the south for a week'. They would leave Cyprus shortly after the start of the troubles for which 'we were never told to be careful' for 'no one really took the threat seriously'. They were not conscious of divisions between Turks and Greeks at the time but did notice there were 'quite a lot of Turkish Cypriots working with us in the army …'[28]

Richard was helped out of a 'scrape' by a Turkish Cypriot:

One of the Turkish Cypriots took me on the 'post run' and afterwards we stopped at the market to do a bit of shopping. I was sitting waiting for him, but the truck was in the way of a bus. I couldn't drive, but I started the truck- when I was revving up I suddenly shot forward and hit the back of the bus, denting our wing and breaking a light. The Turkish Cypriot came back and said 'we're in trouble now'. But he drove to another army camp at Dhekelia and his friend there knocked the wing out and put another light on. I was so grateful I gave the Turkish Cypriot a load of cigarette coupons.[29]

In early 1954 George Grivas again tried to visit Cyprus but this time his visitor's visa, like hundreds of others, was refused. The British had at last woken to the heightened tensions on the island.

On a remote stretch of the Attica coast a small arsenal of arms was loaded onto a caique, a small seagoing fishing boat. Among the arms were British Bren and Sten guns, American Thompsons and Italian Beretta sub-machine guns, and various rifles of similar vintage with 32,000 rounds of ammunition, hundreds of hand grenades and a small quantity of explosives.

Days later this cargo reached a small sandy cove near the village of Khlorakas on the west coast of Cyprus a few miles north of Paphos, where under the supervision of Andreas Azinas the arms were hidden in the fields around the village. However, a second shipment was in some doubt. Makarios was again vacillated in his support and it was he who controlled the purse strings. For all Grivas's bluster he needed the Archbishop for finance and the goodwill of the local population.

The Greek Government were still unhappy with Grivas and advised him in April 1954 'that recourse to violence would cause incalculable damage to the Cyprus question'. Indeed according to Grivas, Prime Minister Papagos hinted that he would take steps in Cyprus to spoil the campaign.[30]

By this time Grivas was keen to get to Cyprus. He left Greece from Piraeus in October 1954 for Rhodes where he went into hiding '… in case the Government (Greek) agents tried to stop us reaching Cyprus'.[31] A bad winter storm kept Grivas frustrated on Rhodes for ten days. The weather cleared on 8 November and at midnight Grivas set sail for Cyprus from the little bay of Kalithea. The 30ft boat *Siren* ran into another gale off the Turkish coast, where the captain wanted to seek shelter, but Grivas would not hear of it. 'I told him I would rather we all went to the bottom than fall into the hands of the Turks.' So the boat rode out the storm and sighted the coast of Cyprus about noon on the 10 November. They waited for dusk and then closed on the west coast.[32]

Grivas was rowed ashore in a dinghy to the same cove near the village of Khlorakas where the first shipment of arms was landed: 'When we were a few yards from land a voice called, "Who is there," I replied "Dighenis is here". And the correct response came back, "Akritas is here".'[33]

Colonel George Grivas was 56 years old, when he stepped ashore that night, short and sprightly and balding with a full moustache. Usually smartly turned out, he might appear more like an agreeable grandfather or uncle rather than a retired Greek colonel and guerrilla leader. On reaching dry land and his welcoming committee Grivas wrote in his theatrical style, 'The storm had ceased and everything was calm.'[34]

Throughout this period of Cyprus history a story of rising tensions, power politics, and terrorist plots, a vital contribution to the well-being of the people of the island, goes virtually unrecognised. Tabitha Morgan wrote:

> There is no plaque, no monument, no grandiose public building to mark the achievement, which came about when the Colonial Government was about to enter its final bitter phase, and which has subsequently been over-shadowed by the story of the armed struggle for independence.[35]

Mehmet Aziz, the island's chief health inspector in 1946, led a campaign, paid for by the Colonial Development Fund, to drive the malaria mosquito, one of the plagues the island had endured for centuries, from the shores of Cyprus. He had suffered from the disease since childhood.

Ronald Ross, the Indian-born Scottish malariologist, had established the connection between the disease and the anopheles mosquito which carried the malarial parasite in 1899. He worked hard to prevent the disease in various parts of the Empire. In 1913 he visited Cyprus where he inspired Aziz to take up the battle. However, with the coming of the First World War funds were limited for preventative work. By the mid-twentieth century Cyprus was reporting 10,000 cases a year.

In 1946, with funds in place Aziz, planned his campaign dividing the island into a grid of 556 blocks, his regiment of Turkish and Greek Cypriot workers being sent out. Each block was covered by one man in twelve days covering every square foot spraying every likely mosquito breeding place with insecticide. The watery places were vital pools, streams, and marshy ground; 'wherever water and breeding places could be found' got the insecticide treatment. Wells and caves were covered. Then the area was checked for evidence of mosquito larvae; if found the area was sprayed again. The operation started on the Karpas Peninsula and moved westward. Vehicles travelling between treated and untreated areas were also sprayed.[36]

Early in 1950 Cyprus was officially declared malaria free. At that time Aziz was acclaimed with his team as the liberators of the island. They went to London where the Secretary of State for the Colonies, Arthur Creech Jones, congratulated them for gaining 'fame among the doctors and scientists all over the world'. Aziz was awarded the MBE.

However, Mehmet Aziz, rather like Doctor Alan Fowdrey, true heroes within the history of Cyprus, on the island today remain virtually unknown. In 1902 Ronald Ross was awarded the Nobel Prize for Medicine and his discovery of the life cycle of the malarial parasite.[37]

Notes

1. FO-(PRO) 371/58891, and Dimitrakis Panagiotis, Military Intelligence in Cyprus p. 61, 'The civil war brought Greece …'
2. ITA 4/12/2007
3. Major J.C. Beadle, *The Light Blue Lanyard*, pp. 174–6, 'Arnold Hadwin OBE …'
4. LTA Thomas Crosbie 14/1/2014
5. BECM Oral Tape 044 Mrs Lloyd-Phillips
6. Charles Foley (ed.), *The Memoirs of General Grivas*, pp. 3–4, 'When the Allied victory …'
7. Ibid., p. 5, 'The occupation was a terrible …'
8. Ibid., p. 13, 'At the same time …'
9. Ibid., p. 1, 'On the first visit …'
10. Ibid., p. 17, 'Soon after my arrival …'
11. Ibid., p. 18, 'When I began declaring …'
12. FO-(PRO) 371/95133 and Dimitrakis, pp. 71–2, 'In Britain the …'
13. Dimitrakis, p. 72, 'Meanwhile, the nationalist …'
14. Ibid., p. 74, 'Officialdom in London …'
15. Christopher Andrew, *Defence of the Realm*, p. 456, 'Shortly after the declaration …'

16. Ibid., pp. 458–9, 'Sir John Shaw …'
17. Ibid., p. 462, 'The most serious …'
18. Lawrence Durrell, *Bitter Lemons of Cyprus*, p. 119, 'He was an interesting …'
19. Ibid., p. 127, 'This indeed was …'
20. Ibid., pp. 152–3, 'Apart from these …'
21. Charles Foley, *Island in Revolt*, p. 17, 'Much had changed …'
22. Suha Faiz, *Recollections and Reflections of an Unknown Cyprus Turk*, pp. 120–1, 'That this administration …'
23. Ibid., p. 117, 'While in Nicosia …'
24. Ibid., p. 118, 'It was now …'
25. Foley, *Memoirs of General Grivas*, p. 20, 'Marshal Papagos had now been …'
26. Ibid., p. 20, 'While blocking this sort …'
27. Ibid., p. 13, 'I always …'
28. LTA Richard Chamberlain 20/11/2000 and his article in *Cyprus Today* 12/8/2000
29. Ibid.
30. Foley (*Grivas*), p. 22, 'I began at once …'
31. Ibid., p. 24, 'I sailed to Piraeus …'
32. Ibid., p. 24, 'At last, on the afternoon …'
33. Ibid., p. 24, 'We approached …'
34. Ibid., p. 35, 'We stepped ashore …'
35. Tabitha Morgan, *Sweet and Bitter Island*, p. 197, 'The single unequivocally …'
36. *Cyprus Review*, June 1948, and Morgan, p. 198, 'In 1946 Aziz …'
37. *Cyprus Review*, February 1950, and Morgan, p. 198, 'Aziz, acclaimed …'

6

A Corporal's
War 1955

The Middle East in 1955 was the centre of a complex political power game. America, Britain, Egypt, France, Iraq, Israel and Syria were the main nations involved.

The USA, with a growing commercial interest in the region, wished to cultivate a defence treaty in the Middle East. America was already providing economic and military aid to the central treaty organisation (Baghdad Pact) comprising Turkey, Iraq, Iran, Britain and Pakistan. Relations between Egypt and the USA deteriorated when Turkey officially recognised the state of Israel. An offer of American military aid to Egypt was rejected by Nasser. On the Cyprus question the USA was initially in favour of self-determination for the Cypriots, but was soon to retreat from this position when Turkish sensibilities became apparent. France had a strong interest in Syria and was suspicious of Britain's support for an Iraqi-Syrian Union. The Algerian conflict had led to increasing enmity between France and the Arab Nations. Britain was mainly concerned with the activities of EOKA in Cyprus and the withdrawal of its forces from Egypt.

The island over which the Cyprus Emergency – as it came to be known by the British, and might be better called the fight against EOKA – took place, is the third largest in the Mediterranean, after Sicily and Sardinia, and has an area of 3,584 sq. miles. It is 140 miles long by 60 miles wide. A narrow Karpas Peninsula, 10 miles wide and 45 miles long, juts out from the top eastern corner and runs east-north-east from Trikomo to Cape Andreas. The British called it the 'Pan Handle' and the whole island resembles a battered frying pan. There are two separate and different mountain ranges. The saw-tooth Kyrenia range runs along the north coast for 100 miles, rising to 3,343ft. In the south-west is the more extensive pine-covered wave-like Troodos range rising to 6,406ft at Mount Olympus. Between the two ranges lies the central arid plain of the Mesaoria which means 'between the mountains'. Six main towns, Nicosia, Famagusta, Larnaca, Limassol, Paphos, and Kyrenia, were connected by a good road network. Nicosia is the only inland town, the others being coastal.

Cyprus in the December 1960 census had a population of 577,615, divided into 442,521 Greeks and 104,350 Turks. The other 30,000-odd were made up largely by the British and the smaller Armenian and Maronite communities. Much of the population were employed in agriculture as they had been for centuries and had, even with the benefits of British rule, remained stubbornly poor; tourism, which would later revolutionise the economy, although a growing factor, was still in its infancy. The middle classes, from which EOKA gained much of their support, ran their own businesses or worked directly for the Government.

On the eve of the campaign most advantages of terrain and population lay with EOKA. A good network of roads built by the British after the Second World War aided movement, and there were the mountain ranges to hide in. A large population was pro-Enosis, although this was more confined to the towns; the rural population had more concern just surviving and at least at the start were largely pro-British. The British administration was riddled with EOKA supporters or people that could be easily intimidated by EOKA.

In December 1954 the United Nations announced the shelving of a demand by the Greek Government that Cyprus be given the right of self-determination. The result was widespread rioting on the island by the Greek Cypriots. Britain had blocked the Greek request declaring that Cyprus was no concern of any other country. In the summer, when Sir Anthony Eden announced Britain's withdrawal from Suez, a Tory backbench revolt was only quelled by repeated assurances that there would be no withdrawal from Cyprus.

Seven times in the debate the Minister for Colonial Affairs, Mr Henry Hopkinson, repeated there could be no question of any change in British rule over Cyprus. He even added he saw no 'reason to expect any difficulties in Cyprus as a result of this statement'. How things had changed in six months.[1]

However, it was the Greek Government who agreed to the American resolution to postpone the question. The USA was the prime mover in this, having woken up to the importance of Turkey on the eastern flank of NATO. Britain had to hang on to Cyprus for the sake of the Western Alliance; to allow the island to fall into the hands of an unstable Greek Government could be disastrous.

On 26 January 1955 the plans of EOKA were dealt a heavy blow. Archbishop Makarios had paid for another arms shipment. The caique *St George* left Greece in mid-January but this time the British had been warned.

The Royal Navy conducted standing patrols with destroyers from the 1st Destroyer Squadron Mediterranean Fleet off the west coast of Cyprus: the operation was code-named Purse Net.

On the morning of 25 January HMS *Comet* relieved HMS *Charity*. Visibility was good. Comet stayed 45 miles off the coast for most of the day and then as darkness approached closed the coast just off Paphos.

The *St George (Agios Georgios)* was spotted by aircraft off Cape Arnauti shortly before *Comet* closed on the coast. The Coral Bay Battery spotted the small craft heading south at 6 knots. *Comet* picked it up on radar at 2000 hours. *Charity* had already observed green lights at a small sandy bay not far from Khlorakas Village during her patrol. The caique was allowed to close on the coast and prepare to unload. The *Comet* kept in touch with the police on the shore. *St George* was stopped while trying to leave by the Navy using one round of .303 which had the 'desired result'. The three-man crew were arrested and the boat was taken into Paphos harbour. Commander Burton, captain of the *Comet*, felt the communications between all concerned made this appear a 'simple operation and each phase of the plan materialised with clockwork regularity'.[2]

Police Commissioner Wren's Special Branch deserve much of the credit, capturing the eight-man reception party at Khlorakas, including Socrates Loizides, who had been expelled from Cyprus in 1950 for his seditious activities. Found on him were documents relating to a secret organisation devoted to the overthrow of the Cyprus Government, and a proclamation declaring the struggle for self-determination.[3] Archbishop Makarios had warned Grivas that they had been betrayed and the British knew of the *St George*. This Grivas called a 'staggering blow'. He fled Nicosia for the Troodos Mountains village of Kakopetria and stopped all training.[4]

However, the British were unable to follow up their advantage. Wren's tiny force was unsure what they faced. The police force and even the Army garrison on Cyprus were small, the latter with two infantry battalions and support units from the Royal Artillery and Royal Engineers. There was no alternative but to wait for EOKA to show its hand.

After a few days Grivas returned to Nicosia to reorganise his people for he still hoped to open the campaign with a wave of sabotage. The explosives lost on the *St George* were replaced by dynamite smuggled from the asbestos mines at Amiandos, and by salvaging shells the British had dumped in the sea off the coast of Famagusta.[5]

The wave of sabotage began on the night of 31 March/1 April. The Government radio station in Nicosia was badly damaged but otherwise little damage was done. Leaflets were thickly spread in the towns demanding Enosis and signed 'Dighenis'. However, the first death in the campaign came from a misguided act of vandalism. Michael Chamberlain heard of this death shortly before he left Cyprus after National Service with the Royal Signals. 'The first thing we knew was when we heard on the radio that a Greek Cypriot had got a wet rope and put it over the electricity wires to cut them, but had held onto the rope and electrocuted himself.'[6]

In Britain, in April, Sir Winston Churchill, now 80 and frail, resigned from the premiership. He was succeeded by Sir Anthony Eden, who had been groomed for the post. Later in the month Eden called a general election, which the Tories won with an overall majority of fifty-eight. The new Government was soon under pressure, declaring a state of emergency to deal with the national dock strike, for 60,000 men had heeded their Union's call to stop work.

Meanwhile on Cyprus, riots broke out when 700 schoolchildren overwhelmed the police in Nicosia and the Army was called in. This was just what EOKA wanted. Pictures of British soldiers with pick helves chasing children were good publicity for the cause and made headlines world-wide. Radio Athens was encouraging the Greek Cypriots to rebel and 'drink deep of the wine of 1821!', when Greece had rebelled against the Ottoman Empire, and that, 'Freedom is acquired only by blood'.[7]

A bomb attack on Empire Day against the Governor Sir Robert Armitage just missed the target. He had watched a film at the Pallas Cinema in Nicosia with the bomb contained in a Coca Cola bottle only a few feet away. However, he and his party had left before it went off, wrecking the gallery.

In February 1954 Robert Armitage had taken up the reins of governor. He was not the best choice, regarded as tentative; he even wrote to his parents: 'the problem of *enosis* is like the velvety blackness of a nightmare, it clutches one everywhere and one strains to see a glimmer of light to guide one to safety and nowhere is there light.'[8] Lawrence Durrell thought Armitage was immersed too fully in the colonial world and that the Cyprus 'problem was not being regarded as a European political problem but as a purely colonial one'.[9]

By June the campaign had turned on the police. A police station in Nicosia was bombed, EOKA taking their first victim, a Greek bystander, while another dozen, mostly Turks, were injured. This was followed by intercommunal rioting in most of the towns. Later the remote village police station of Aminados near the asbestos mines was attacked by masked raiders with Sten guns who killed the sergeant in charge and looted the armoury.

It was into this turmoil that Jay Lennard, an Assistant District Commissioner, and his wife Mary-Pat with two small children, arrived: 'There were so many incidents,' says Mary-Pat, 'and demonstrations, we wondered what we had let ourselves in for. I remember going to Metaxas Square in my little car, a Fiat I think, when I got caught up in a riot, but they only banged on the roof, but I was pretty frightened.' Mary-Pat may have been lucky she was driving an Italian car as rioters often burnt British cars:

> It was a super climate to live in but the emergency was difficult. And I lived in hope every day that Jay would return safe from the office. He was eventually issued with a revolver and told to take at random seven different routes to the office. [10]

Michael Zavros, a 21-year-old Special Constable, was gunned down in the Nicosia streets by two youths. His brother had a defiant letter printed by the *Times Cyprus* in which he attacked EOKA for being 'the real traitors who betrayed the cause of self-determination by forcing their opinions on others by violence'.[11]

This was rapidly followed by the murder of PC Herodotus Poullis on duty in plain clothes at a left-wing meeting. Hundreds saw him gunned down, the gunmen escaping through the crowd, but nobody came forward to help the police.

Soon Greek Cypriots were leaving the police in large numbers. Police Commissioner G.H. Robins was nearly powerless to keep order and said: 'If my men can't rely on the public, I can't rely on them.' Turks came forward to fill the gaps but were largely inexperienced.[12]

In July, Grivas left Nicosia for the Troodos Mountains to get his mountain groups into action. He stayed at the house of a school teacher in the Marathassa Valley village of Kakopetria.

At the end of August Sir Robert Armitage flew to London for a Tripartite Conference called by British Prime Minister Anthony Eden. It was two weeks after the killing of the first British soldier from the Royal Scots.

Harold Macmillan, the Foreign Secretary, chaired the conference. Present were representatives of the Turkish and Greek Governments. It was the first time Turkey was present in talks. Macmillan offered a new constitution with internal self-government and the participation of both Turkey and Greece as interested parties. But without Enosis the Greek Cypriots were not interested and the conference collapsed. However, the Turkish Premier, Adnan Menderes, demonstrated he could be counted on to oppose the union of Cyprus with Greece. Also, half a million Turkish troops stood on Russia's doorstep. Menderes, in return, expected America to finance Turkey. Britain was relieved of the long-standing task of supporting the sick man of Europe; surprisingly US Secretary of State John Foster Dulles called the country a 'bastion of democracy'.

After the conference rioting broke out in Nicosia and Istanbul; in the latter the Turkish Army was deployed on the streets to restore order. Armenians, Greeks and Jews seem to have been the main target in the Turkish capital, where shops were looted and churches set on fire. Greece retaliated by refusing to join any NATO exercises in which Turkey took part.

In September on Cyprus, the British Institute, a two-storey building on Metaxas Square, was set on fire by schoolchildren. The police and army took three hours to restore order, by which time the finest English Library in the Middle East had gone up in smoke. The last person to lecture there was the Cretan and Greek wartime resistance leader Patrick Leigh Fermor.[13] The Army blamed the police, for when the soldiers did arrive it took only five minutes to clear the area, but they could not intervene until called on by the civil authority. The police had been unable to cope, a 'stand-to' had been called but all that meant was the reserves were called out, a total of twelve men, to join the two constables on duty.

Lawrence Durrell found the situation was changing. He 'borrowed a pistol from a kindly Scots major in the police' which he felt 'symbolised the trend of events perfectly, for Cyprus was now no longer a political problem so much as an operational one …'[14]

In the same week sixteen EOKA men had escaped from detention in Kyrenia Castle by simply knotting their sheets together and climbing down a wall to the exclusive country club beach below. However, seven of the prisoners were recaptured within a day. On 25 September it was announced that Sir Robert Armitage had been relieved as governor. In his place was appointed Field Marshal Sir John Harding, KCB, DSO, MC. Lawrence Durrell welcomed the appointment, for here was a man who had been 'trained to decisions based in a trained power of the will'.[15]

However, the military build-up was in gear days before this. On 6 September, 3 Commando Brigade Royal Marines on Malta were ordered to move to Cyprus. The Brigade consisted of 40 and 45 Commandos and Brigade HQ. The Commandos moved by various ships of the Amphibious Warfare Squadron. Four days later a troop of 45 Commando was on patrol in the Kyrenia Mountains and captured four of the escapees from Kyrenia Castle.

Colonel Tim Wilson, who spent thirty-three years in the Royal Marines, recalls the deployment of 40 Commando to Cyprus when he was a lieutenant of 24:

40 Commando went to Limassol and was immediately greeted by rioting. One rioter was shot dead on the second or third day. We were still trying to set up camp and our arrival after dark on the first day was quite a performance. We drove on and on into the 'ulu' to be greeted by one hurricane lamp on a carob tree under which were piled all the Commando stores. We were in Limassol until early 1956 when we moved to Paphos. Our routine in both areas was much the same. Vehicle and foot patrolling, dealing with riots, guarding police stations, and frequent cordon and search operations.[16]

Major Halliday, OC Baker Troop, 45 Commando recalls:

For three months B Troop was on location at Boghaz near Famagusta where the Inniskilling Fusiliers were stationed. How those Irish laid into the rioters.

We introduced a new tempo in patrolling, reconnoitering, and ambush activities to the island, marching and climbing many miles in the Kyrenia range by day and night.

For assisting the civil authorities, although vital in restoring law and order, was a passive role, it did not carry the fight to EOKA or dominate the ground. Often these fighting patrols of perhaps only a section, six to ten men, led by corporals or senior Marines put tremendous responsibilities on often young shoulders making this a real corporal's war.[17]

On the night of 14 September, 45 Commando carried out its first cordon and search of the village of Mandres: Operation Stormsail. The search revealed nothing of importance. However, the unit was willing to try to win 'hearts and minds'. The unit MO, Surgeon Lieutenant Guy Bradford RN, went into the village to give free medical attention, 'feeling rather like a uniformed hawker of patent medicines'. Although reluctant at first, the villagers were still attending surgery two hours after the first call.[18]

Brian (Bomber) Clark, a Marine of Baker Troop, 45 Commando did several of the village cordon and search operations:

When we first went out there doing village searches, the locals always wanted you to stay and talk they would get out little glasses of ouzo or brandy and sweet meats.

At the time the Greek Cypriots certainly were not anti-British. I served on Cyprus for just under a year and in that time the situation changed, but even then the individual Greek Cypriots could be super.

Brian was a National Service Marine and tells us how NS men faired in the Royal Marines.

Most NS men who entered the Royal Marines had chosen to serve in a unit which offered a physical challenge, a disciplined existence and at that time the strong possibility of Foreign Service.

Entry was by no means easy and conscripts entering the Corps were to a certain extent 'volunteers' and already by the nature of the selection process ideal raw material to produce Marines worthy of comparison with their regular counterparts. Few NS men were found above the rank of Marine for those in charge were veterans of campaigns from the Second World War, the Canal Zone, the Jungles of Malaya and the Korean War. Also every one in the Corps was treated the same, regular or National Service.[19]

Some other Army Infantry Units had similar standards and it was these who bore the brunt of the fight against EOKA.

The new Governor Field Marshal Sir John Harding was markedly different to Armitage the Colonial Service man. Harding had left school at the age of 15 when he went to work for the Post Office and joined the Territorial Army. He was commissioned in the First World War. At 57 he had just finished his term as Chief of the Imperial Staff. He had been about to retire to his farm in Dorset when he took on the job as governor and commander in chief in Cyprus. This followed his successful role in the Malayan Emergency 1948–52 when he had combined the two roles. He was small in stature, often compared to T.E. Lawrence in appearance, with a sparkling personality.[20]

With the field marshal came Brigadier George Baker, who became Director of Operations, and also the Chief Constable of Warwickshire, Colonel Geoffrey White, who became Commissioner of Police. The police were expanded with Turks filling the ranks and 300 British 'bobbies' brought their experience to the force, which was now backed by 12,000 soldiers and commandos.

Grivas took Harding's appointment as a compliment to him and EOKA, for why else would the British send a man with such 'a reputation and so brilliant a career'.[21] But Harding was not the man to rest on his reputation; he brought direction to the administration, the law would be upheld and force would be met by force, but there was room for negotiations. Even Makarios is said to have commented: 'Why did they not send us such a man a long time ago?' The soldier and Archbishop were soon in talks.[22]

Early in October the talks broke down, which was inevitable given neither side were willing to shift on the question of Enosis. EOKA were quick to renew the campaign; another police station was blown up and an RAF officer shot. It was about this time that Sergeant Jack Taylor from the Yorkshire Constabulary came onto the streets of Nicosia:

> In the latter part of the introductory course, we were called out to assist the Town Officers and the Army in the search of a Greek Orthodox Church. This was situated quite close to Ledra Street, better known at the time to the security forces as 'The Murder Mile'.
>
> The Army had placed a cordon around the church, and we were ordered to enter the building and give them a thorough, good search. It was strongly suspected that members of a 'killer group' were hiding their arms here after use.[23]

No arms were found but a priest was detained being under suspicion of working with EOKA. An Army padre accompanied the search parties to ensure nothing was broken, damaged, or stolen, for the Church was quick to accuse the police or Army of all sorts of violations. The press too could be economical with the truth as Jack says: 'Of course following the search, *The Times of Cyprus* printed quite a number of unkind remarks about the searching of churches.' Quite remarkable, given this paper at one point employed Nicos Sampson, one of the worst EOKA gangster terrorists, although the news editor soon became aware of him and he moved to a Greek paper.[24]

In October the Greek Prime Minister Field Marshal Papagos died – he was said to have clandestinely supported Grivas and EOKA – and was replaced by the more liberal Constantine Karamanlis. In Washington, talks were about to open with Egypt and the USA on the financing of the planned dam on the River Nile at Aswan.

By November the situation in Cyprus had deteriorated further; curfews were now in force in many towns and villages. A state of emergency was declared and several new regulations came into force: the death penalty for anyone carrying arms, and a life sentence for those caught in the act of sabotage or the possession of explosives.

Early in the month 45 Commando moved from the Kyrenia area, where the 1st Royal Leicesters took control, to the Troodos Mountains, which had become the main base area of the EOKA guerrillas and the HQ of Grivas. There were few Turkish Cypriots in the area which was a stronghold going back to medieval times of the Orthodox Church.

Lieutenant Colonel Tailyour OC of 45 Commando set up his HQ at the Hotel Splendid at Platres high in the mountains. He had under his command some 800 troops which included two companies from 1st Gordon Highlanders, A Squadron the Life Guards and members of the Cyprus police force. Major Halliday, OC Baker Troop, 45 Commando spent seven months in the Troodos Mountains:

> Baker Troop went to Troodos Camp near the top of Mount Olympus 6000 ft high. I was camp commandant two other troops being there, though one were usually on police station duties.
>
> EOKA were quick to start ambushes on mountain roads with some initial success, some troops in vehicles being killed or wounded. My Troop was involved in anti-ambush drill for vehicles and we did intensive patrolling in vehicles and spent several weeks lying out in the mountain forests. We spent one night in a snow blizzard lying in ambush in the mountain pass between Khondria and Polystipos.
>
> EOKA carried out several successful raids on police stations before they were guarded by troops, the Greek Cypriot Police being frightened to resist and, in some cases, being EOKA members themselves.
>
> Baker Troop raided Omodos one night with A Troop under command. We captured half the local EOKA village group. Their leader we missed, but he was captured later. I found his pistol in the rafters of his home through a small concealed trapdoor. A small Cypriot boy kindly told us which his home was.[25]

As a result of this operation, from documents captured the security forces learned that EOKA was trying to obtain all the shotguns on the island. The Government immediately ordered shotguns to be handed in. Many guns were handed in, although no doubt others found their way to EOKA, while others were buried, the owners not wanting EOKA or the British to have them.

On Sunday 11 December, 45 Commando and companies of the Gordon Highlanders were on Operation Foxhunter searching the villages of Spilia and Khandria: unknown to them Grivas had his headquarters dug-out on a ridge above Spilia.

That winter's morning broke cold, damp, and misty. The Gordon's started searching the village just after sunrise, finding EOKA plans and papers. One man tried to escape and when challenged, would not stop; he was shot and wounded and taken to Nicosia. However, Grivas was now alerted to what was happening below.

Part of the cordon, Z Troop, was searching the higher slopes around the village and arrested one man, Georghiou Zavlis, carrying a rifle and forty cordex fuses. Under interrogation in the village he gave away the Grivas hideout. Soon a forty-man patrol with police dogs set out for the hideout. The route to the caves was rough and the mist was thick, visibility reduced to 10 yards in places. A burst of fire from above sent the patrol to ground who returned fire while 2in mortar fire was used to cover the final assault. One mortar bomb exploded on tree branches, slightly wounding two Marines.[26]

The firing had given Grivas enough warning to escape, although he seems to have been tardy in doing so. The caves were taken, which contained abandoned stocks of food, ammunition and clothing. The pursuit was kept up until darkness and for twenty-four hours Grivas and his comrades were forced westward. Major Halliday says: 'At Spilia the terrorist leader, Grivas, was shot in the foot by our pursuing troops and in the fog was helped away by Afxentiou and Lenas.'[27] Grivas says the pursuit was a disaster for the British who: 'began to fire wildly in the mist and kill each other. The shooting went on for nearly half an hour. I lay flat behind a pine tree with a soldier who had been leading me on a rope. I heard later they had suffered at least fifty casualties.'[28] He goes on to say

Lieutenant Colonel Tailyour was killed; this is strange as he went on to become Commandant General of the Royal Marines and retired in 1968. As to the other casualties, only the two slightly wounded by the mortar bomb are in the Commando Battle Diary.[29]

Grivas also says Costas Zavros betrayed his position and a member of the Fontis family both were later executed by EOKA.[30] This seems unlikely to say the least, as not until Z Troop grabbed Zavlis, an EOKA member, did the troops have any idea about the hideout. It was Zavlis who betrayed the hideout.[31]

In mid-December another ambush against British troops affected Archbishop Makarios's own family. An EOKA guerrilla group, under Markos Drakos from the Kykko Monastery area, laid an ambush on the remote north coast road, near the ancient Persian Palace of Vouni, which means 'a mountain peak'. The road here snakes through low hills and old copper workings.

Captain Brian Coombe of the Royal Engineers and his driver Lance Corporal Morum had been working with 45 Commando in the Troodos Mountains. On the return they ran into Drakos's ambush. The first burst of fire killed Morum and the vehicle ran into a ditch. Coombe crawled away from the Champ to a ridge, where he opened fire on the terrorist group below but soon exhausted his ammunition. Returning to the vehicle he took Morum's weapon and returned to the ridge renewing the fight. The EOKA men tried to trick Coombe with a faked surrender, but Coombe spotted a concealed gunman just in time. He shot down the three in the open and then concentrated his fire on the remaining man before his ammunition ran out. At this point the last terrorist ran for it. Coombe had killed one man and wounded two others. Drakos had escaped also wounded. The dead terrorist was Charalambous Mouskos, the Archbishop's cousin.

The Greek Cypriots made a hero out of Mouskos. Thousands turned out for his funeral which turned into a riot when they would not disperse. Coombe talked to the press who had besieged him for his story. He told them at Lance Corporal Morum's quiet burial at the British Military Cemetery outside Nicosia he had read the lesson in which he had talked of 'no more death' for there had been too much on Cyprus. And he asked the press for 'no exulting over this affair'. Which may not have been what they wanted to hear.[32]

The arrival of Harding began a marked improvement in the security and intelligence services on the island. For example, he was shocked to learn that ciphers used for decoding and encoding official dispatches were kept in a safe in the lavatory of Government House.[33]

On 26 November 1955, Governor Harding declared a state of emergency after the increase of EOKA bombings and shootings. Severe punishments were introduced, including capital punishment for the possession of explosives and ammunition. The Director of Military Intelligence about this time reported on the deplorable state of security on the island, finding that 'virtually no Colonial Service official nor staff spoke Greek or Turkish' and that:

> The ordinary police are powerless and the fear of EOKA means that almost all the Greek villages in the island are now 100 per cent against the administration and pro-Enosis. The hard core of EOKA is small and efficient. The Enosis movement is much wider and chiefly supported by the teenagers.[34]

One intelligence report reached Eden, which caused great consternation in London, saying that Greek submarines had been delivering agents and explosives to Cyprus. An arrested man had revealed submarine operations would take place on 28 December 1955 and 2 January 1956. Harding asked for the use of anti-submarine weapons if a submarine was detected.

As the Government grappled with this thorny problem, Greece being a relatively new member of NATO, Naval Intelligence was able to inform them that all four Greek Navy submarines were in their Salamis base and none were at sea in late December. Equally there was no incident involving a submarine on 2 January. In this case the Special Branch intelligence had been wrong.

In December 1955 MacDonald criticised the Special Branch and submitted his report to the governor: 'It would be futile to deny that the EOKA tactics of making Special Branch a primary target have in large measure succeeded, but I do not believe that given resolute leadership in the field the organisation is incapable of rallying.' He went on to advise that operational intelligence would be better handled by Military Intelligence officers.[35]

Notes

1. Charles Foley, *Island in Revolt*, p. 11, 'Enosis had been banished …'
2. ADM-(PRO) 1/26847 HMS *Comet* at sea 26/1/1955
3. Dimitrakis Panagiotis, *Military Intelligence in Cyprus*, p. 76, 'However British spies …'
4. Charles Foley, *The Memoirs of General Grivas*, pp. 29–30, 'The caique St George left …'
5. Ibid., p. 30, 'To help me with this problem …'
6. LTA Richard Chamberlain 24/11/2000 and *Cyprus Today* article 12/8/2000
7. Durrell Lawrence, *Bitter Lemons of Cyprus*, p. 185, 'The nights became stretched …'
8. Tabitha Morgan, *Sweet and Bitter Island*, p. 208, 'In February 1954 …'
9. Durrell, pp. 145–6, 'I had found Sir Robert …'
10. BECM Oral Tape 806A J. Lennard
11. Foley, *Island in Revolt*, pp. 35–6, 'The dead man …'
12. Ibid., p. 37
13. Morgan, p. 216, 'Just over a week …'
14. Durrell, p. 20, 'The next day …'
15. Ibid., p. 209, 'By now, terrorism …'
16. LTA Colonel Tim Wilson RM 6/9/2000
17. LTA Brian F. Clark (Bomber) 5/9/2000 and the supply of unpublished journal Baker Troop 45 Commando, p. 3, compiled by H.J. Cooper
18. David Young, *Four Five*, pp. 220–1, 'Although nothing of …'
19. INA Brian F. Clark 14/9/2000
20. Durrell, p. 209, 'Small of person …'
21. Foley, *Memoirs of General Grivas*, p. 45, 'This was the last …'
22. Durrell, pp. 209–10, 'Up at the Abbey …'
23. Jack Taylor, *A Copper in Kypriou*, p. 11, 'This happened to be …'
24. Ibid., p. 12, 'Accompanying us …'
25. H.J. Cooper, *Journal of Baker Troop 45 Commando*, pp. 5–6
26. Young, pp. 232–3, 'By now the mist …'
27. Cooper, p. 4
28. Foley, p. 56, 'The British …'
29. Young, p. 57, 'The Commando battle diary …'
30. Foley, p. 57, 'We discovered …'
31. Young, p. 232, 'Grivas and his aides …'
32. Foley, *Island in Revolt*, p. 52, 'His quiet voice ran on …'
33. Morgan, p. 218, 'Harding's greatest …'
34. WO-(PRO) 216/889 p. 2 and Dimitrakis, p. 82, 'Meanwhile, the intelligence …'
35. Dimitrakis, pp. 84–5, 'On 30 December London …'

7

1956 CLEARING THE FORESTS

1956 would be a momentous year for Britain, with the Government, under Sir Anthony Eden, trying to reassert the country's crumbling position in the Middle East. The prime minister was under pressure from his supporters to get tougher. The USA was now trying to smooth the way for the new moderate Greek Premier Karamanlis who was supported by massive American aid, but beset at home by fierce opposition to any betrayal over Cyprus, so President Dwight D. Eisenhower personally appealed to Eden to ease the way to peace. At home, in the UK, Hugh Gaitskell became Labour Leader; the party's official line was to champion the cause of self-determination for Cyprus.

At the turn of the year the 16th Independent Parachute Brigade under Brigadier Mervyn 'Tubby' Butler arrived on Cyprus, consisting of 1 and 3 Parachute battalions:

> We were one of the first units to operate against EOKA, operating right across Cyprus. We had a number of successful operations in which people were arrested and weapons confiscated. At different periods, depending on how talks to settle it were going on, our rules of engagement could vary between 'shoot to kill', 'challenge and shoot' and 'challenge and not shoot'.
>
> It was different almost every time we went out. It was tremendous training for the Brigade. It was also very frustrating, EOKA were well versed and

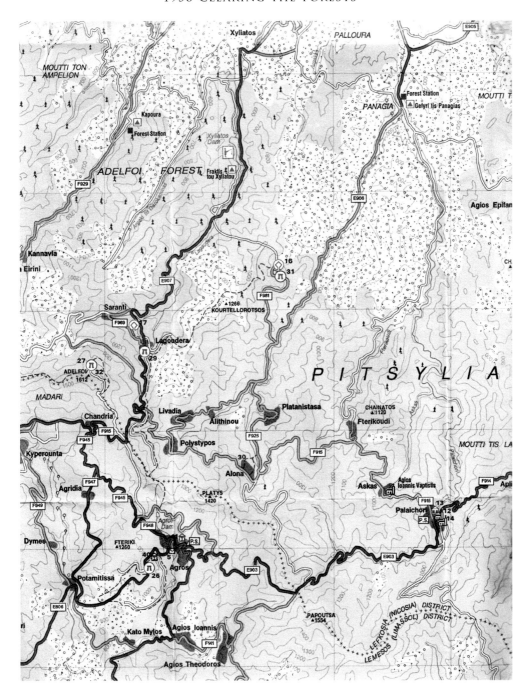

Troodos Mountains Eastern Area

knew the area much better than we did and were able to flit in and out very quickly. We would arrive minutes after a group had moved out of their hill-top location but generally we were not capturing large numbers.[1]

Dr Themistocles Dervis, the Mayor of Nicosia, might declare 'We are all EOKA', but in fact it was a small organisation.[2] By Grivas's own admission the 'hard core' guerrilla's never numbered much more than 300 men. Even the second-line EOKA, who were poorly armed and acted more in the role of sabotage and couriers, numbered about 750, so it is not surprising only small numbers were captured.[3]

It was 3 Para that got the job of arresting Makarios. The Archbishop had been due to leave the island on 9 March for Athens, where he would make contact with the new Government, and then travel on to London. His Beatitudes Palace was quickly surrounded. The amber-tiled roofs and grounds were soon swarming with red berets. 'Black Mak', as the troops called him, was soon in custody. Also the Bishop of Kyrenia was taken from his residence with his secretary. The exiles were flown by the RAF to Mombasa and there taken aboard a Royal Navy frigate for the Seychelles in the Indian Ocean.[4]

Harding and Makarios had talked on and off for months before the arrest, which was the direct result of evidence having been obtained of direct links between the priests and EOKA, but the feeling comes down the years that the soldier and Archbishop had a sneaking admiration for one another. It was never friendship, but respect, which bred a hope which in itself was notable, given the area for negotiation was so small. Francis Noel-Baker, a Labour MP, had come out to act as mediator with the blessing of the Conservative Government. He was equally at home with Greek or English, had interests in Greece and knew Cyprus well. Then Secretary of State Alan Lennox-Boyd arrived; agreement seemed close but then the talks broke down over the make-up of a future Cyprus Parliament. Riots quickly broke out in Nicosia.[5]

The Government then went down the road they had in 1931 when Governor Sir Ronald Storrs had deported the troublesome priests. Then it had been the 'sudden and unexpected deportation of the leaders known only when they disappeared, that cracked the insurrection'.[6] The trouble was,

Troodos Mountains Western Area

in 1931 there had been no EOKA. Lawrence Durrell saw 'the deportation of the archbishop which was operationally just, was politically nonsensical' for 'his absence left the field to the extremists'.[7] In the House of Commons in London Hugh Gaitskell said the deportation was an 'act of folly'.[8]

The Government's official reason for deporting Archbishop Makarios was that he was not 'a responsible political leader, and still less as the head of a Christian church, but in that character which he has himself chosen to prefer, the leader of a political campaign which relies on the use of ruthless violence and terrorism'.[9]

Harding had a dim hope that moderate elements within the Greek Cypriot community might come forward to fill the gap, but John Clerides, the last Greek Cypriot member of the Executive Council, resigned over the deportations. Harding and his soldiers were on their own and the governor would not shrink from using them, which he would have to, now that Grivas no longer had a political brake on his ambitions.

It was now the governor who became the target. Within forty-eight hours of the deportations Government House was infiltrated. A trusted Greek Cypriot valet, Neofytos Sophokleus, smuggled in a time-bomb strapped to his waist which passed a careless search. He placed the bomb under the mattress of the governor's bed. The bomb was discovered by a batman making Sir John's bed the next morning, having failed to go off. Changes in temperature due to an open window may have affected the fuse, although many EOKA bombs were badly made. Whatever, it had been a close call. Harding was upbeat, declaring that he had 'never slept better', but the Greek Cypriot staff of Government House were all dismissed.[10]

Major W.C. 'Harry' Harrison, RAOC, more commonly known as 'Bomber', was the first Army officer to be seconded to the hard-pressed Cyprus police force and given the title of 'Cyprus Government Explosives Expert'. His six-man team was so highly successful in destroying EOKA bombs that he soon went to the top of the EOKA target list.

EOKA were using time pencils of British origin that had been dropped by air to Greek guerrilla forces during the Second World War. By the time EOKA were using the pencils they were some 15 years old and highly unstable. These unsafe pencils saved the passengers and crew of a DC3 of Cyprus Airways destroyed on the ground at Nicosia Airport.

After investigation by Harrison and his men, they found the fuel tank had been sabotaged. However, the time pencil, in this case a No. 9, had exploded prematurely.

Harrison also solved the mystery of two RAF Canberra Bombers that had disappeared en route from Cyprus to Khartoum, Sudan, by finding evidence, in the wheel of a Canberra recovered in some fishermen's nets, of sabotage to the undercarriage of these aircraft.

Harrison's own team did not escape loss; two staff sergeants were killed by a mine booby trap. In August 1959 Major Harrison was awarded the George Medal in 'recognition of gallant and distinguished service during the Cyprus emergency'.[11]

The attack on Government House was followed by the first execution, of Michael Karaolis, the murderer of PC Poullis, who had been tracked down because he left his bicycle behind after shooting Poullis. Karaolis was a mild-mannered youth who had worked for the Government in the Income Tax Department, by no means a hard core EOKA yet a murderer all the same. Shortly after Karaolis, Andreas Demetriou was to hang; he had shot and wounded a British civilian.

Lawrence Durrell's Greek Cypriot friend Panos, the school master, who would later be shot dead in the narrow streets of Kyrenia Harbour, one can only assume for being friendly with an Englishman, summed up the ordinary people's feelings: 'of course Karaolis must hang. The Governor is right. I would do the same thing. But it is not Karaolis only who will be hanged, the deep bond between us will have been broken finally.'[12]

On the morning of the execution Durrell returned to the Village of Bellapais in the foothills of the Kyrenia Mountains overlooking the north coast. He walked slowly through the village to his house, Bitter Lemons, on a steep and stony incline. His 'footsteps echoed harshly on the gravel'; he passed the cafe near the 'Tree of Idleness', which was crowded with people but utterly silent. Everybody looked away or at the ground 'awkwardly and with a shy clumsy disfavour'. His 'good morning' to friends and neighbours who had treated him with utmost kindness, who had called him with affection Mr Darling, was barely acknowledged.[13] It was as if Durrell was the hangman. Within a few hours he had left Cyprus forever, unable to be a Greek-speaking Englishman living among Greek Cypriots.

Adrian Seligman, Master Mariner and writer, spent several years on Cyprus; he became friendly with the Turkish Cypriot Rauf Denktash. However, the rising tensions between the two communities were too much for him and he decided to bring his family home, soon after a lemon with a razor blade sticking out was thrown at him. And he found his 4-year-old son Simon with 'Enosis' written on one arm and 'Onion', thought to be a misspelling of 'Union', on the other arm.[14]

Many British residents did the same as Durrell and Seligman and left the island that was home. For they could not trust the most innocent-looking locals and any local friends could easily be put in peril of their lives for associating with the British.

Two British soldiers who had fallen into EOKA hands were executed on Grivas's order in reprisal for the execution of Karaolis. Private Gordon Hill and Corporal Ronnie Shilton were shot and buried. The bodies were later discovered when captured terrorists gave the positions of the graves.

Owen Parfitt served with 1st Battalion Parachute Regiment at this time; even off duty they went armed:

> In Nicosia one day, I wasn't on duty; I was just out with a group of friends. When we went out we had to carry weapons. I carried a Browning pistol and somebody else a sub-machine gun. We went in groups of four, and each carried a personal weapon.
>
> We used to cover one another, and somebody was actually shot near the old city, near the wall. I remember helping to get this body that had been shot in the head; he was a Cypriot.
>
> I can remember we took potshots at someone who was moving during curfew, and one fellow was shot, and it turned out the poor devil was deaf, and he hadn't heard the 'Halt! *Stomata!* (Greek) *Dur!* (Turkish).'[15]

Sandy Cavenagh, a medical officer with the 3rd Battalion Parachute Regiment, arrived on Cyprus in June 1956 aboard an aircraft carrier:

> A mere five days after leaving Portsmouth, HMS *Theseus* had anchored off Famagusta on the east coast of Cyprus. The laborious transfer of vehicles,

baggage and ammunition into lighters began. It seemed surprising that in eighty-odd years of colonial rule Britain had not managed to construct a deep-water harbour.

Had she done so the island's economy would have benefited enormously. But again and again we were to see the harvest which these lost opportunities had reaped. Much good had been done on the island, but parsimony or laissez-faire caused much to be neglected or postponed. More money and more energy expended peacefully a few years ago might have forestalled the enormous expense and tragedy of EOKA.

As darkness fell a smart explosion under the ship reminded us that EOKA existed. The captain appeared at once on the quarterdeck and asked what was going on. It transpired that the commander, suspecting a frogman below, had dropped a grenade over the side.

He had won the VC in a midget submarine attacking a German pocket battleship, and could be expected to know the potentialities of frogmen. Our subsequent alarms were not always so false.[16]

In the spring of 1956 with the winter snows gone, in the mountains the Army, now with fifteen battalions on hand, moved against the 'hard core' terrorists. In May starting with Operation Pepper Pot and Operation Mustard Pot; during the latter the Kykko Monastery was searched. Tim Wilson of 40 Commando takes up the story:

Operation Pepper Pot was the first saturation operation in the forest, (conducted in the Troodos Mountains, around the Kykko Monastery.) It was based on a pattern of placing stops out on the hill tops to create a cordon and sending patrols and ambush groups into the area surrounded in the hope of finding terrorist groups who were known to be based there. The units involved were 40 and 45 Commandos, 3 Para, and the Royal Norfolks.

Once a cordoned area had been searched the net would be moved to a different section and the process would be repeated. I remember covering many miles on foot and frequently going up and down several thousand feet at the same time. We were seldom in one place for more than two days and the operation lasted two to three weeks.[17]

Spike Hughes of Support Troop 45 Commando was also on Pepper Pot:

> When the weather broke we did a lot of village searches. This usually started
> in the middle of the night, with us being transported to some remote place,
> crossing the mountains in the dark in single file and quietly surrounding a
> village. The 'searchers' would go in at dawn, always greeted by the church
> bell ringing the alarm, only to find nothing but blue and white 'EOKA' flags
> flying from the village hall and church. (These flags were often just Greek
> National Flags, although sometimes they had the word EOKA in black on
> them.) We all wanted one for a souvenir but 'looting' was strictly forbidden.
>
> Not that the 'Cyps' had anything of value anyway. I was personally
> amazed at the poor living conditions that prevailed. We had long iron rods
> for poking into wine vats and odd corners. One Marine was about to poke
> an upturned wicker basket when the lady of the house screamed at him.
> She then picked up the basket and three chickens ran out.[18]

The operation did scatter five groups in the area, one containing Grivas,
who admitted 'Harding had improved his tactics'. Two groups were captured and Grivas was forced south-west, deep into the Paphos Forest,
where he went into a new hideout on a 4,000ft peak in the area of Dipli.[19]

Sandy Cavenagh of 3 Para saw these large operations as having basic
disadvantages for the Army:

> The pursuit of EOKA by the security forces resembled a display of shadow-
> boxing. Most of the British hammer-blows landed on air, as their targets
> vanished into the forests, the farms, or the dark, twisting alleyways of the
> towns … Great cordon and search operations, involving thousands of troops
> and great movements of trucks, inevitably sent out vibrations which were
> picked up by the sensitive antennae of EOKA, and messages of warnings could
> often be sent off ahead of the darkened convoys twisting through the night.
>
> It was the extreme efficiency with which EOKA had permeated every
> organisation on the island which made this possible. Postmen, telephone
> operators, contractors, foresters, policemen, all passed on what was required
> of them in the way of information. Each of them knew that it was literally
> as much as his life was worth to fail to do so.[20]

However, Brigadier Baker kept the pressure up with the even bigger cordon and search operation, in the Paphos Forest, Lucky Alphonse, which spanned 8–23 June. Tim Wilson of 40 Commando:

> The Gordon Highlanders, King's Own Yorkshire Light Infantry and 1 Para were added to the forces that had been deployed on Pepper Pot. (Also the South Staffordshire Regiment, the Royal Horse Guards parts of the RAF Regiment and a small landing party from HMS *Diamond*.)
>
> During Lucky Alphonse there were two or three confirmed contacts by the patrols, including a patrol from 3 Para sighting a group which included Grivas and several known hard men who, sadly, managed to escape. I was personally lucky enough to capture a group of nine hiding, literally, in the bushes just outside the forest. One of my observation posts saw a farmer with a donkey go to the bushes and pass some loaves of bread to someone in the bushes.
>
> The farmer was probably able to tell them a lot about where we were deployed and they probably felt safe just outside the cordon. From our point of view it was a lucky break as the OP was about half a mile away. I took a patrol down to the area, surrounded the hide, and called for whoever was in there to come out. They did, with their hands up. Two of the gang had £5,000 rewards on their heads and were on the most wanted list.[21]

Sandy Cavenagh described the dense forests of Paphos and Troodos in which these operations took place:

> The steep, wooded slopes tower monotonously, wave on wave for about two hundred square miles. It is a bewildering country to the stranger. The secret valleys and nullahs wind indeterminately beneath a blanket of pine trees, and slopes soar up evenly, at an angle of forty-five degrees to undulating crests between three and five thousand feet high. The few motorable roads and narrow one-way tracks are hidden in this sea of trees and you come across them with surprise. It was the perfect place for a mountain redoubt, and Grivas, the professional soldier, had not wasted his opportunity. The Monastery at Kykko in the centre of the area, acted as a nerve-centre for EOKA.[22]

It was a patrol from C Company, 3 Para, led by Sergeant Scott, which just missed Grivas. But they did capture his camp intact complete with diary, radio and bedding. Just after this C Company 1 Para's Sergeant Major Jimmy Foster took out another patrol; unfortunately they walked into a 3 Para ambush on the edge of the battalion area. Foster was shot in the chest with a single bullet which passed through him into the next man and the next. The sergeant major was killed and the other two men seriously wounded. The patrol took cover, the ambush party gave a radio contact report but it soon became apparent from grid references what had happened.

Again a patrol from 3 Para were ill fated on 14 June when they opened fire on suspected terrorists only to find they had engaged a stop-group from the Norfolk Regiment. Lance Corporal Elliot of the Norfolk's Support Company died of his wounds in this incident.[23] Lance Corporal Colin Ireland of Baker Troop 45 Commando believes they also just missed Grivas:

During Lucky Alphonse the Paphos Forest had been a hive of activity. We had marched all day and finally found a resting place, a good ambush position at a likely watering spot and we settled down as dusk fell to watch this space.

Seven section had been split into rifle and Bren group astride the watering hole. Watches were set and those not on watches settled down to a couple of hours rest. I drew the first watch as Bren group commander.

An hour or two passed and I was dreaming of home. A movement caught my eye something white amongst the trees leading down to the waters edge.

I debated whether or not to wake my two colleagues. It could be a deer or some other creature coming for a drink. But, no, it was standing on two legs, and looked like a man answering the description of Colonel Grivas.

I nudged my companions and indicated the target. We had no way of communicating with our colleagues in the rifle group across the stream so we opened fire. The night was shattered by twenty-eight rounds from my sten shots from a rifle and a prolonged burst from the Bren.

The rifle group must have wondered what on earth was going on. Sergeant Gordon had us stay in position. I told him I was sure it was Grivas. 'Alright, we'll get the tracker dogs in he said'.

At dawn the army dogs duly arrived and located a scent in the area of the water hole. We trailed off to the top of a by now sun-soaked ridge where the scent gave out due to the sun's heat.

In hindsight, I am certain that I had Grivas in my sights, and, I should not have missed plus my two comrades were good shots and we all fired at a target some 100 yards away. We may or may not have hit our man but he got away.[24]

Spike Hughes of 45 Commando Support Troop remembers Lucky Alphonse for being anything but lucky:

The plan was to surround a large area of the Paphos Forest in sub-areas like the petals of a flower. The central area was called the 'Magic Circle' and Grivas and his merry men were supposed to be there.

To make it more dramatic Vickers Medium Machine Guns and Mortars would fire on selected targets that were difficult to search on foot. Good fun for us, a chance to fire our three inch mortars. A Troop would also be firing two inch mortars at the same time; suddenly we got the order to 'cease firing'.[25]

It appears support mortars had dropped a bomb on Able Troop, four or five of which were wounded. It seems they were using out-of-date mortar bombs. Whether a bomb had exploded prematurely or hit a branch was not found out, but Spike is pretty sure of something else:

We also noted that the opposite hillside was alight. 'It will burn itself out' someone said. I was not so sure. The following day the fire spread and the operation began to collapse.[26]

Brian (Bomber) Clark of Baker Troop 45 Commando was caught in the fire:

The fire during Lucky Alphonse was horrible. A forest fire is really terrifying it moves faster than you can run. In Cyprus there's a lot of Pine and Cedars of Lebanon, conifer trees. The heat was so intense it would start burning up the trunk then suddenly it would explode, this was the resin inside. I think there were nineteen or twenty people killed in it. (Mostly Gordon Highlanders.)

In one instance we were out and virtually surrounded by this fire. Lucky for us we had a guy with us who used to work for the forestry commission. His view was that as the fire burns and moves it uses up combustible material rapidly. So the fire front is never very deep, ten or fifteen feet. He said the way out was through the flames.

Now that was all very fine but God it took some doing. But it was true, although just the other side there was smoke and everything so you could not breathe again. I and my section owe our lives to that guy.

A lot of the Gordon's were caught in a situation where the wind changed so quickly. There was a truck went off the road and I think they stayed with the truck instead of moving out. The Gordon's were a good bunch of lads and we enjoyed working with them.[27]

Elenitsa Seraphim, a female EOKA member, insists:

The fire was started deliberately by the British who were hoping to capture Dighenis and his men. The fire grew stronger as it advanced threateningly in the direction of Kykko and it went on raging all day. Gales hampered the attempts of the men from the Forestry Department and supporting areas to extinguish the blaze …[28]

Captain A.W.C. Wallace, a Royal Marine on duty with Commando Brigade HQ in Limassol, was detailed to form a troop of men from HQ staff to take the field during Lucky Alphonse. His 'odds and sods' served with the Norfolk Regiment. Captain Wallace observed mortar fire from his position during the night of 15/16 June: 'I could see quite clearly the semi circle of flames spreading from the points of the explosions.' He felt definitely this was the cause of the fire and it was 'not deliberately started by EOKA as stories circulating later suggested'.

Wallace and his men were soon ordered to join a force with men from the Gordons and the Norfolks to help assist Turkish Cypriot foresters fight the fire. At an RV he took his men with a group of foresters 'up a hill away from the fire and began to create a fire break near the crest, taking my directions from the foresters'.

He had been promised more troops by a major from the Gordons. When these became 'long overdue' he returned to the original RV at a road to find the major, but he had gone. He continued along the road and came across another group of troops from the Norfolks and Gordons with Foresters. 'They were standing by their 3-ton trucks. The young officer in charge told me he had been given another task and was not our relief.'

Now events began to overtake Wallace:

By now the fire was closing on us and the Foresters were concerned for our safety. I remember clearly thinking that I had time to walk back toward the RV, but was soon prevented by a wall of fire crossing the road in front of me. I was forced to return to the group I had just left. The foresters advised us that the situation had become critical and we should follow them up the hill. Someone, I don't know who, decided it was better to escape the inferno by using the trucks and he gave the troops orders to embark and move off. With my driver I chose to follow the foresters and headed up the hill. It is very hard to describe the heat. It was almost impossible to breathe and difficult to climb the hill. Near collapse and exhausted, an elder Turkish Cypriot forester saw my plight and helped me toward a burnt out patch of ground. I was left alone sitting there as the fire swept past me on both sides. Strangely, at no time did I actually consider myself in danger.

It was not long before Wallace heard explosions coming from the road. And later two near-naked men emerged from the smoke, their clothes all but burnt off. Wallace moved gingerly back to the road where he 'saw the trucks had been caught in the blaze. It appeared as if they had driven straight into a tunnel of flames. The troops had tried to escape by running up an incline, but failed and their dead bodies were spread everywhere.'

It now became apparent what the explosions were: the troops' ammunition bandoliers worn on their waists. Soon a group of Norfolks with a senior NCO turned up and began to recover the bodies to the road.

Captain Wallace again:

Later we discovered the reason why these soldiers were unable to escape was because their Bedford trucks could not continue down the single track road as they had been blocked by a Scout car travelling in the opposite direction …

More troops arrived with another officer now in charge. I went off to find my own platoon and driver. I had left them in the care of the foresters. Half a mile up the road, I found them sitting 'having a smoke' one of them casually remarked 'We thought you were a goner sir.'[29]

Sandy Cavenagh recalls the Lucky Alphonse operation. 1 Para searched the Kykko Monastery, Horace McClelland, the padre, accompanied the search party to ensure all was done properly with due reverence. However the search was fruitless. 'The news that Grivas was somewhere in the cordon area had led to large reinforcements being drafted into the area.' This included the Norfolks, Gordon Highlanders, Royal Engineer units and the RAF Regiment. The hunt went on for several days, only being brought to an end by the forest fires.

Eventually it seemed that the terrorists might have escaped southwards towards the positions of 40 Commando, and their 3in mortars pounded the area where Grivas and his party might be hiding. It seems likely that the explosions of these mortar bombs in that tinder dry country set fire to the forest. Grivas later claimed to have lit the fire himself … Whatever the cause, the fire rapidly increased its hold, despite all efforts to contain it. The professional Cypriot Foresters were called to help, for the technique of fighting fire in the resinous, dry trees is a specialist business.[30]

The accidents and fire undoubtedly distracted the troops and Grivas escaped. For thirty hours he played cat and mouse in the forest covering several miles – A remarkable feat of endurance across rough terrain for a man in his late 50s. Grivas and his group headed north, back into the area already searched, slipping through the net. Eventually they got food and shelter at the Trooditissa Monastery back in the Troodos and 5 miles from Mount Olympus. Grivas then moved south-east to a camp near Saittas Village. On 19 June a car took him the last 10 miles into Limassol where he went into hiding at the house of Dafnes Panayides.

In his memoirs Grivas goes into a long tirade against the British Army's poor performance and how he had outwitted them. However, this rather masks the fact he had been forced to abandon the ground he had chosen, for a cellar. Indeed, the Greek prime minister would point out Grivas had become famous by hiding.

The EOKA member Elenitsa Seraphim maintains that 'Greek Cypriots tried to put out the fire, rushing to help the soldiers …'[31] And Grivas says in his own colourful style, 'When a British Officer in tears begged the (Greek) Cypriot fire fighters to help, they choked down their hatred of the tyrant and, heedless of the danger, ran into the flames to carry out the dead and the dying.'[32]

However, Frank Delamere, a Gordon Highlander, felt the Greeks tried to keep the fire going. 'Just as we put out one blaze the Greeks came up behind us and started another.'[33]

Later, at the Court of Inquiry, Captain Wallace was called to give evidence:

At one point, I was asked if the Turkish Foresters had run away – deserted the British troops. I replied that on the contrary the Turks had given sound advice and repeatedly it had been ignored. I suggested that had their advice been followed and the urgency of the situation been appreciated, the tragedy may have been avoided.[34]

The Inquiry's report came to no conclusion, and there was no definitive evidence to prove whether the fire was started by EOKA, to mask the escape of Grivas, or had been caused by the British troops. Whatever, it was the largest loss to the British Army in a single day during the EOKA conflict.

Grivas says the 'dead numbered more than sixty'.[35] The number quoted by the Royal Norfolks historian is twenty-one, which was also the same figure as the official announcement, at the time; of course several soldiers were severely burnt during the fire. Some reports say seven terrorists died in the flames, we have no real way of knowing that, but seventeen were captured during Lucky Alphonse.

Penelope Tremayne, a fluent Greek speaker who worked for the Red Cross, was in the high Troodos ten days after the tragic events of Lucky Alphonse driving to a remote settlement for a visit. She soon noticed '… away ahead of me, rising over the mountain line, an enormous pillar of smoke, stretching for several miles as dense as feathers. Unmistakably a very big forest fire.' In Lucky Alphonse she felt the fire had been 'Started deliberately by the EOKA …'[36] With all the medical supplies on board her Land Rover, she felt she should go toward the fire. Eventually, taking a narrow track, she got close to the fire but could find nowhere to turn around:

> The track made several bends, and then brought me abruptly into sight of the head of the valley. Both sides were steep now; fairly close together, and burning splendidly. Hot sticks and fragments were beginning to fall on the Land Rover, and I thanked my stars that it had a tin top instead of a canvas one. But straight ahead, apparently completely closing the head of the cleft rose a huge precipitous mountain shoulder, thickly forested, and aflame from foot to crest.[37]

She felt herself mad to go on but had little choice. Then into view came two men 'with sticks plodding in a tired way towards' her.[38] They were both exhausted and she gave them some water, and learnt they had been fighting the fire for twelve hours. Further up the track were 100 men still fighting the fire. She decided to go on. Finally she found the men; in command was a Greek Cypriot Forestry Department official.

The fire had first been reported by the Army but by the time the foresters arrived it was out of control and there was no sign of the soldiers, and now they were exhausted. She had never come across 'Such concentrated bitterness against the English …' and they felt the '… British were not taking any action because they wanted the Cypriots to burn' after they had lost so many men ten days ago.[39]

However, they welcomed her because they had no medical supplies for cuts, burns, and bruises. She made her way to the Stavros forest station that they were using as a HQ, where she did what she could for the firefighters. A lot of the villagers working for the Forestry Department, she learnt, were only there for the 'special pay' and did not care about the forest.[40]

As things were clearly getting worse she offered to try to find the Army to assist. The foresters felt she was wasting her time. Twenty miles away at the Kykko Monastery was an Army post. There she learnt the Army knew nothing about the fire; they thought the billowing smoke was fog. Soon aircraft and helicopters were dropping supplies to the firefighters, and ferrying out the injured. Once the Army was there in force it took them twenty-four hours to get the fire under control. The foresters felt the discipline of the Army was key – what they asked for was done – whereas the labourers would tell them, 'You … off, or we'll bash your head in.'[41]

The Commandos were far more use than anyone else, because they could run uphill so much faster. 'Pretty well as fast as we can, actually, and we're born to it.' He beamed in admiration of them, 'In fact,' he said, 'all we need have had, really, was a hundred Commandos. I don't know why they bothered to send the rest.'[42]

In spite of EOKA's disruption and losses in the mountains and forests, killings in the towns went on as before and the Government hit back with collective punishment. When a Greek Cypriot police officer was shot dead in a Nicosia hospital waiting to see his wife and newborn baby, the authorities closed all cafes, bars, dance halls, clubs, restaurants, cinemas, anything that entertained. Sports meetings were curtailed and a night curfew introduced.

At the end of May posters went up all over the island offering a £10,000 reward for the capture of Colonel Grivas. Informants were offered protective custody and a passage to 'anywhere in the world'. Greek Independence Day celebrations, always popular with Greek Cypriots, were banned. Collective fines were also introduced. By June 1956 the fines had risen to more than £100,000. The fines were levied on the basis of individual income, but hit the poor the hardest and did nothing to endear the British to the very people who, if they had their way, were probably pro-British.

Then bad inter-communal rioting broke out which had not occurred much before in the emergency. In Nicosia, shops were looted and burnt. The capital was roughly divided between Greeks and Turks with rolls of barbed wire, which became known as 'The Mason–Dixon Line'.

Many of the EOKA town killer groups made so many mistakes against, in general, soft targets, that it clearly shows they had a lack of direct control from Grivas, who was well aware of the value of good publicity and bad. One example of this is the bombing in Nicosia of the 'Little Soho' restaurant, a popular watering hole of the American community. Two homemade pipe bombs were thrown through the door. They exploded close to the table of four Americans; three were injured and the fourth, William Boteler, the American Vice Consul, was killed. All of the Archbishop's hard work in the USA to gain support was dealt a severe blow. Grivas called it a 'tragic mistake'. [43]

In July George Karberry, a customs official new to the island, and his pregnant wife were driving through the Mersinki Pass in the Kyrenia Mountains. It was a Sunday, they were going for a day out on the coast and were ambushed by EOKA terrorists. The wife died in the first burst of fire, while her husband was beaten up before being killed.

Three more executions were due to be carried out: the two men who had been captured during the Coombe ambush and another man who had killed a policeman. EOKA then kidnapped a 'British Intelligence Agent' who was to be shot in reprisal. The hostage was a 78-year-old retired civil servant who lived near Kyrenia. However, as soon as Andreas Zakos, the senior condemned man, found out, he asked EOKA publicly to release the old man at once and unconditionally, which they did. [44]

There is no doubt EOKA were as cruel with their own community. Major Halliday of 45 Commando:

EOKA members ruthlessly slaughtered their own people, including women and their own priests. They would line up a crowd in a coffee shop at night; make them all face the wall, and drill one through the head with a bullet because he was suspected of being an informer, as a lesson to the others. These methods Grivas brought from his Greek Guerrilla warfare days.

Perhaps one of the worst EOKA murders was carried out in the Church of St George in the village of Kythraea, this church being in Makarios's own diocese. Four EOKA men entered the church, ordered the congregation to face the walls, and then calmly shot dead the man, a member of the choir, in the presence of his children, his crime being an 'informer'. Was it Herodotus who said 'Unhappy Greeks barbarians to each other?' [45]

About this time, the British Government in Whitehall managed to bungle one of the best chances of catching Grivas. Harding had written to the

Times of Cyprus a lengthy defence of Government policy in which he said to end violence: 'Let the murderers make the first move.' The next day, 16 August, Grivas ordered a ceasefire from his bunker. In his memoirs he indicates this was in response to the Greek Government trying to find a diplomatic solution and not in response to the governor. However, neither explanation seems all that likely. Rather it was a tactic of his that would become familiar whenever EOKA had been subjected to a battering; Grivas would reorganise behind a ceasefire.[46]

Grivas, a compulsive diarist, had had several diaries and documents found by the Army. When EOKA abandoned the ceasefire, Lennox-Boyd had selected extracts published implicating Makarios and the Greek Premier, Marshal Papagos. Thus the Government and governor could show the 'duplicity' that had gone on.[47]

On 20 August more diaries came into Harding's possession but these were different for they detailed EOKA's organisation. If kept secret it was only a matter of time before Grivas fell into a trap. The EOKA leader, who was now constantly changing his hideout, would, at some time, stay with Andreas Lazarou, the main informer on the security force's payroll.

However Whitehall again published against the advice of people on the ground to make a political point, and information that could have only come from the diaries was let slip while interrogating EOKA suspects, instead of keeping the diaries secret. Days later Lazarou, a watchmaker and father of six, was gunned down in his shop in the Nicosia suburb of Kaimakli.[48]

At home, in the UK, many in the press still supported the Cypriot right of self-determination. However the Archbishop of Canterbury, Doctor Fisher, after criticising the Government over the exile of Makarios in the House of Lords, was called to order to denounce terrorism. A measured censure of EOKA was unacceptable in Britain while her soldiers risked their lives. However, for Makarios to denounce EOKA, an organisation he helped start, meant to repudiate the men who had become heroes to the Greek Cypriots, and this was a British requirement to political progress.

Against this background Lord Radcliffe arrived in Cyprus as Constitutional Commissioner. He was to undertake a survey on the island and then draw up a detailed constitution, which Eden said, would be introduced when law and order was restored. No Greek Cypriots would call on him at Government House which was understandable given the climate of terror within the Greek Community. So Radcliffe toured the island and was well received in general. After two weeks he returned home hopeful, if both sides could be conciliatory the Constitution might stand a chance.

However, Britain would soon be swept away by Suez fever after Nasser seized the Canal at the end of July. Eden told the public that Suez was 'a matter of life and death'. And a man with Colonel Nasser's record could not be allowed 'to have his thumb on our windpipe'. This sudden Egyptian move came in the wake of the refusal by the USA and UK to finance the building of the Aswan High Dam. The reason given was that the Egyptian economy was too weak to sustain such a project, even with Western help, although the purchase of large quantities of arms from the Communist Eastern Bloc by Egypt may well have swayed the decision.[49]

In August, 3 Commando Brigade was withdrawn from Cyprus to Malta to prepare for the Suez Operation. Unfortunately they were replaced by green troops from the UK. However, this was partly offset by the arrival of 2 Para battalion, although each Para battalion in rotation returned to Britain for parachute training in preparation for Suez.

In September, Grivas launched a fresh terrorist wave of attacks, but he was marshalling his forces for a bigger effort for when 'as seemed likely, the British attacked Egypt and provided us with a chance for a major onslaught in Cyprus'.[50]

Lord Radcliffe, the man who had drawn up the partition plans for India and Pakistan, was drawing up a provisional Constitution for Cyprus. None of which interested Grivas for it did not include Enosis.

In early October another large cordon and search, Operation Sparrowhawk, took place in the Kyrenia Mountains. All three Para Battalions, along with the No. 1 (Guards) Independent Parachute Company, took part. Some twenty terrorists were captured along with stocks of arms.

3 Para was given the area around Kalogrea Village to cordon and search. Kalogrea lay at the eastern end of the northern Kyrenia range of saw-tooth mountains. The village was surrounded before dawn. B Company sent a patrol into the village. They were greeted by a single shot which

missed. The company was to search the village and now: 'If the search was carried out with more than the usual thoroughness, that would be no more than the village deserved.'[51]

In mid-morning Governor Harding visited the unit, arriving by helicopter. In the afternoon Sandy Cavenagh went into the village. He found a Danent wire enclosure set up on the school playground ready to contain suspects for interrogation. B Company was in the middle of their search:

> Below the school was a row of little houses, their backyards open to the sky. From my eyrie on the playground I could see it all. A few hens scratched around disconsolately in the heat of the day. One of the Toms was methodically going over the nearest backyard. With his bayonet he prodded through a pile of rubbish.[52]

All around him the Paras were 'ransacking' the village. As the doctor and his batman walked along what went for the main street he was approached by a sergeant, who told him he thought there was a child in one house the doc should look at. They followed him into a house where 'on the stone floor, covered in flies, lay a pale, emaciated child of about eighteen months'. In the house the eyes of the malevolent women watched him suspiciously. However, as soon as they realised he was a doctor he was 'plunged into a hectic round of visits. The village teemed with disease, both real and imaginary …'

He knew his first concern was 3 Para but at that time he found:

> The medical plight of the villagers was more pressing. They were such real, unaffected and sincere people.
> Like country people everywhere their inherent good manners kept showing through the film of dislike and distrust between us, but their menfolk were being rounded up for questioning and hatred was never very far beneath the surface.[53]

No EOKA men were found in the village. Even the village priest became a patient for Cavenagh, as he had been stung by bees when the soldiers had searched his beehives.

2 Para had some success while searching the ground between Kyrenia and Bellapais. They found two EOKA men hiding inside the walls of a farmhouse. The Paras searched several villages over the period of a week, mostly in 'vain'. Cavenagh found that 'luckily medicine was always in demand. "*Iatros! Iatros!*" And off we went again, eking out our dwindling supplies of "*Hapia*" (pills) with the odd "*Inesin*" (injection), in which the villagers had a complete and childish trust.'[54]

However, late in October while on another operation in the Paphos Forest the 16th Parachute Brigade was withdrawn for deployment to Egypt. About this time one of the worst bomb attacks against British troops took place at the football field of Lefkonico High School which members of the Highland Light Infantry had been using. After a game the troops had gathered around a tap for a drink and wash. A bomb had been placed under the tap and was detonated by remote control after a prearranged signal from some schoolchildren. Two soldiers were killed and several badly injured.

Grivas seems to have had no qualms that this attack was carried out by children. However, when the villagers of Lefkonico received some rough treatment by the Highlanders, although no villager was killed or badly injured, he cries: 'There was a great outcry in the island at this vandalism …'[55] In view of the circumstances, in this case, the Highlanders showed great restraint.[56] Worldwide events were overshadowing Cyprus at this point, as hard as EOKA might try to grab the headlines.

While the Marine Commandos and Paratroops trained for the Suez Operation code-named Musketeer and ships were assembled, the politicians tried to find a diplomatic solution. However, the Soviets were now hard at work supporting their new arms customer and ally Egypt, and trying to gain more friends in the Arab world. It was also a heaven-sent opportunity, even if Communists did not believe in such a place, to divert attention away from Hungary where a revolt in Budapest by its citizens and students was crushed by tanks of the Red Army.

Israel was encouraged by France to lend a hand against Egypt, which they were more than willing to do before Nasser got too many modern Soviet weapons. Meanwhile, the USA, beset by presidential elections in November, prevaricated. John Foster Dulles, the American Secretary of

State, pressed the British and French to negotiate but put no pressure on Egypt.

Even at home the British Government was becoming increasingly isolated with opinion leaning toward the United Nations. But here Dulles advised Eden and Selwyn Lloyd, Secretary of State for Foreign Affairs, that the Security Council route would be blocked by Soviet Russia's veto. All this resulted in frustration for Eden, who compared the United Nations to the League of Nations. France believed Britain would cave in to American pressure and therefore roped Israel further into the plan.

Although Britain tried to deny this later it now appears clear they went along with the French plan. The military operation was put in motion after the UN Security Council debated the Suez Crisis and refused to condemn Egypt or permit any Anglo-French attack under the UN banner.

On 24 October Nasser announced a military pact with Syria. Israel responded by calling up her reserves. Three days later Israeli tanks entered Sinai and the day after the British fleet sailed from Malta joining the French at sea. On 31 October, Canberra bombers took off from Cyprus to attack targets around Cairo, Alexandria and Port Said.

In the UK public opinion was split by the Suez Operation. Thousands demonstrated in Trafalgar Square demanding 'Law not War'. However, it was the American pressure that was most telling. President Eisenhower and Secretary of State Dulles were infuriated while the Russians not only condemned the Suez attack but threatened the UK and France with military action. When the British troops went ashore on the morning of 6 November Eisenhower telephoned Eden with an ultimatum: an immediate ceasefire and withdrawal, or face economic isolation. Eden, surrounded on all sides by enemies abroad in the Commonwealth, in the UN, by the unlikely alliance of the USA and the USSR, at home by Labour and the Liberals and on the streets by demonstrators, had to climb down to humiliation, a blow he would politically never recover from.

Charles Butt served as a security sergeant with 253 Field Security Section based on Famagusta during the Suez Crisis:

The day we declared war on Egypt, I had gone down to Vorosha to collect my new car and had just driven it back to my headquarters when the Sergeant Major put his head over the balcony and told me he had just received notification of the declaration. Instead of driving the new car I had to get into an old Bedford 1 ton 'Nellie' and drive it between the beach just beyond Caraolis Camp and the HQ carrying loads of sandbags.

The whole unit, less those actually engaged on dock duties, spent the rest of that day filling sandbags and stacking them across doors, windows and any other place in need of protection in case of air attack. It was feared Famagusta would suffer air raids as it was the only port in the island and was just 240 miles from Egypt in easy range of their aircraft.[57]

EOKA took advantage of this period; Charles Butt goes on to describe another bomb incident:

A bomb exploded behind a couch in the rest room where an Arabic Course was being held in the Waynes Keep Camp, which was the main transit camp in Cyprus for the whole of the Middle East, the squaddies used to call it the 'black hole of Calcutta'. Several people had been injured when we got there.

All the Cypriot employees were assembled on the square which was just in front of the NAAFI. They were sitting on the ground with their hands on their heads while the commanding officer was screaming at them in a high old state.

It had always been my opinion that up to that time the security at Waynes Keep was poor.

One reason I was told for this was that the CO believed that none of his employees would dare to do anything nor wish to upset him. The main reason for his view was that he had a Greek Wife.

The man who planted the bomb was never found. I think it must have been a local employee of the NAAFI because it was placed in the room for the course and exploded just after they had resumed after the mid morning break. The course attacked had been for doctors and medical orderlies learning Arabic. Several were badly injured in the explosion.[58]

November 1956 soon became known as 'Black November' on Cyprus, with 416 EOKA attacks as Grivas had planned. Over forty people were killed, half of them British soldiers.

At the end of 1956 Anthony Eden, suffering from the strain of Suez, was advised by his doctors to take 'immediate rest'. R.A.B. Butler, the Leader of the House of Commons, took over the temporary leadership of the Cabinet.[59]

Notes

1. Max Arthur, *Men of the Red Beret*, p. 313, 'Anyway, in big spirits …'
2. Charles Foley, *Island in Revolt*, p. 46, 'Nicosia's mayor …'
3. Charles Foley (ed.), *The Memoirs of General Grivas*, pp. 66–6, 'The exile of the Archbishop …'
4. Peter Harclerode, *Para*, p. 217, 'After its arrival …'
5. Foley, *Island in Revolt*, p. 63, 'In spite of street troubles …'
6. Ibid., p. 66, 'Five minutes later …'
7. Lawrence Durrell, *Bitter Lemons of Cyprus*, p. 243, 'But what could I tell him …'
8. Harold Macmillan, *Riding the Storm*, p. 223, 'By the beginning …'
9. John Reddaway, *Burdened with Cyprus*, p. 67, 'So long as there were …'
10. Foley, p. 68, 'The way was now clear …'
11. IWM, The papers of Major W.C. Harrison RAOC
12. Durrell, p. 242, 'This is a Greek island …'
13. Ibid., pp. 247–8, 'It was a beautiful …'
14. David Matthews, *The Cyprus Tapes*, p. 99, 'At the same time …'
15. Adrian Walker, *Six Campaigns*, pp. 109–10, 'In Nicosia …'
16. Sandy Cavenagh, *Airborne to Suez*, pp. 23–4, 'Hands on hips Tubby …'
17. LTA Colonel Tim Wilson 6/9/2000
18. LTA Spike A. Hughes 10/9/2000. Also see Robin Neillands, *A Fighting Retreat*, pp. 282–4
19. Foley, *Memoirs of General Grivas*, p. 76, 'We did not have long to wait …'
20. LTA Colonel Tim Wilson 6/9/2000
21. Cavenagh, p. 72, 'Malicious mockery …'
22. Ibid., p. 72, 'The forest of Paphos …'
23. Harclerode, p. 218, 'At the beginning of June …'
24. LTA Brian F. Clark 5/9/2000 and H.J. Cooper, *Journal of Baker Troop 45 Commando*, pp. 7–8
25. LTA Spike A. Hughes 10/9/2000
26. Ibid.
27. ITA Brian F. Clark 1/10/2000
28. David Carter article, 'The Tragedy of Lucky Alphonse', britains-smallwars.com, and 'The Cyprus Liberation struggle 1955–1959 through the eyes of a woman EOKA area commander'
29. Ibid.
30. Cavenagh, pp. 76–7, 'At the same time …'
31. Carter, article
32. Foley, p. 84, 'I cannot close …'

33. Carter, article
34. Ibid.
35. Foley, p. 84, 'I learned later ...'
36. Penelope Tremayne, *Below the Tide*, p. 35, 'As I neared the cross-roads ...'
37. Ibid., p. 36, 'The track made ...'
38. Ibid., p. 36, 'It was a mistake ...'
39. Ibid., p. 38, 'Such concentrated ...'
40. Ibid., p. 39, 'Gathered from the ...'
41. Ibid., p. 56, 'It's discipline ...'
42. Ibid., p. 57, 'These accounts made ...'
43. Foley, p. 72, 'The attack continued ...'
44. Foley, *Island in Revolt*, p. 86, 'Passions were heightened ...'
45. LTA Brian F. Clark 5/9/2000 and H.J. Cooper, *Journal of Baker Troop 45 Commando*
46. Foley, p. 95, and *Times of Cyprus* 16/8/1955
47. Ibid., p. 98, 'Lennox-Boyd lost no time ...'
48. Ibid., pp. 99–100, 'The informer ...'
49. Harold Macmillan, *Riding the Storm*, p. 103, 'But if Eden had been ...'
50. Foley, *The Memoirs of General Grivas*, p. 92, 'Our first activities ...'
51. Cavenagh, p. 8, 'In the half-light ...'
52. Ibid., pp. 83–4, 'B Company was ...'
53. Ibid., pp. 84–5, 'There's a kid ...'
54. Ibid., pp. 86–7, 'For a further week ...'
55. Foley, pp. 96–7, 'The explosion blew ...'
56. Robin Neillands, *A Fighting Retreat*, pp. 286–7, 'There were a great ...'
57. LTA Charles R. Butt 8/1/2001
58. Ibid.
59. Macmillan, pp. 173–4, 'It was therefore ...'

Hoisting the British flag in Nicosia, 12 July 1878. (*Illustrated London News*)

Sir John Tenniel's cartoon in *Punch* on conclusion of the Cyprus Convention 1878.

HMS *Himalaya*
off Limassol 1878.

The British land on the west coast
near Baffo. (*Illustrated London News*,
28 September 1878)

Garnet Wolseley courting Cyprus.
(*Punch*, 3 August 1878)

Garnet Wolseley courting Cyprus.

GRAVE OF
SERGT.
M^CGAW
V.C

No. 141 SERGEANT SAMUEL McGAW
- V.C. -
42ND ROYAL HIGHLANDERS:
THE BLACK WATCH:
DIED ON THE LINE OF MARCH TO
CAMP CHIFLIK PASHA OF HEAT
APOPLEXY (sic) 22ND JULY 1878
AGED 40 YEARS.

Early grave of Sergeant
Samuel McGow VC.
(*Illustrated London News*,
17 August 1878)

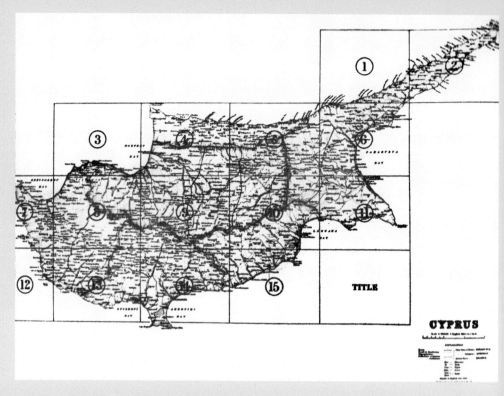

Subaltern H.H. Kitchener's index map of Cyprus.

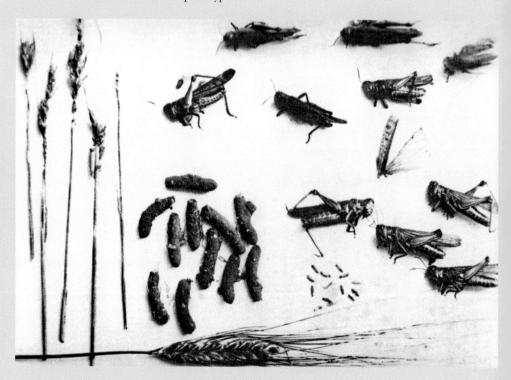

The plague of Cyprus locusts, around 1890.

Old Government House, Nicosia, burnt down by rioters in 1931. Sir Hamilton Goold-Adams is in the foreground. (Harry Luke)

The 7th Australian Division Cavalry Regiment, Cyprus, spring 1941. A 2-pounder anti-tank gun is mounted on a Morris truck.

7th Australian Division Cavalry Regiment, Cyprus, Spring 1941. Vickers light tanks are on patrol.

Ships unloading at Famagusta, 1943.

Cordon and search operation in the Troodos Mountains.

HMS *Chivalrous* operated from Cyprus during the Palestine Emergency 1947–48, seen here leaving Venice. (AFT Simmons collection)

EOKA hide found in the Troodos Mountains by Royal Marine Commandos. (40 Commando Association)

Burnt-out 3-ton Bedford after Greek Cypriot rioting.

British troops search a Cypriot bus during the Emergency.

Foot inspection for troops of 3 Para during cordon and search operations.

No. 1 Maritime Headquarters Unit examines a Lightning fighter on a visit in 1971 to RAF Episkopi. (RAF Command Public Relations)

No. 1 Maritime Headquarters Unit examines a Vulcan bomber on a visit in 1971 to RAF Episkopi. Cyprus acts like a permanent aircraft carrier in the eastern Mediterranean. (RAF Command Public Relations)

HMS *Hermes* flight deck evacuation of civilians from the war zone during the Turkish Invasion of 1974. (Royal Navy)

Royal Marines of 41 Commando observe Turkish operations in 1974. (Royal Navy)

Tristar caught on the ground during the Turkish Invasion of 1974, remaining in the Green Line at the old Nicosia airfield. (Author's Collection)

The Green Line in Nicosia dividing the city. The Line divides Turkish Northern Cyprus from the Greek Cypriot South. (Author's Collection)

British position near Kolossi Castle, Western SBA, 1974. (Author's Collection)

42 Commando on exercise near Pissouri, Southern Cyprus, mid-1970s. (Royal Navy)

'Bitter Lemons': the house in Bellapais where Lawrence Durrell lived in the 1950s. (Author's Collection)

British legacy: Royal Engineers supplied mains water to most Cypriot villages in the 1950s. Due to neglect some villages now have to truck water in. (Author's Collection)

British legacy: Bellapais Abbey. Note the marks on the wall – the result of British troops using it as a rifle range. (Author's Collection)

British legacy: post boxes still in use. (Author's Collection)

British legacy: Bedford buses in Limassol. (Author's Collection)

The oldest British Sovereign Base: radar station in the Troodos Mountains. (Author's Collection)

Waynes Keep British Military Cemetery within the Green Line. (Author's Collection)

8

1957
STALEMATE

Early in 1957 Suha Faiz came to the regretful decision he was going to leave Cyprus, the land of his birth:

> Such was the dreadful climate of animosity, mistrust, fear and hatred which had engulfed the island. And in that atmosphere Lalage [his English wife] and I now had anxiously to consider what future there was for us and our child in this new Cyprus. We were both coming to the conclusion that whatever the future held for us, it was scarcely likely to be in Cyprus where the two communities were being violently driven into themselves, in seemingly inescapable violence and counter violence.[1]

It had become apparent that once the British left, as seemed likely, there could be only one result, for against the Greek call for Enosis and only Enosis the Turkish response had become 'either partition or death'; it could only end one way, with civil war.[2]

The *Times of Cyprus*, which had become sympathetic to the Greek Cypriot view, was bombed on Christmas Day 1956 by Volkan, the Turkish counter-terrorist organisation. Volkan had been formed to protect the Turkish community from EOKA attacks. Increasing numbers of Turkish Cypriots had joined the police, to fill the gap left by their intimidated

Greek Cypriot colleagues. Many Turks believed the Government was incapable of protecting them.[3]

The security services on the island had much improved and in November–December 1956 forty-four important EOKA suspects were arrested in the Limassol and Larnaca districts. While captured EOKA documents confirmed '… that EOKA was modelled very much on Communist lines'. In most cases there was a group leader and a political commissar both holding the same rank, but it was only the latter who was likely to have access to Grivas.[4]

Early in January Anthony Eden, having returned from his Caribbean rest, called his Cabinet together and announced his decision to resign because of ill health. Macmillan found it 'dreadful that he waited so long for the Premiership, and held it for such a short time'.[5] On 3 February the Queen sent for Lord Salisbury and Sir Winston Churchill; many thought Butler would take over but it was Macmillan who was sent for to 'kiss hands' and take over as prime minister.[6] As far as Cyprus was concerned the change of leadership was probably for the good. Macmillan had, during his time as Foreign Secretary, devoted much 'fruitless endeavour' to the 'Cyprus Tangle', and was well aware of the 'painful' journey that lay ahead.[7]

Sir Winston Churchill had done much to repair the relationship between the UK and USA in a direct appeal to President Eisenhower after the Suez Crisis. And he pointed out the Middle East was a vacuum in which 'our friends are beset by bewilderment and uncertainty for the future'.[8]

By January many troops had returned to Cyprus from the Suez Operation to bring the garrison strength up to eighteen infantry battalions and the security forces came down hard on EOKA. In the early weeks of the New Year the Army accounted for some thirty hardcore EOKA terrorists and was now under the command of Major General Joe Kendrew.

The Pitsilla Mountains form the eastern end of the Troodos range. The ground is not so wooded here as in the west, given over to acres of vineyards, although pines flourish on the northern slopes. It was in this region Markos Drakos, once leader of EOKA's youth movement and the only terrorist survivor of the Coombe ambush, was killed in a gun battle with troops during Operation Black Mak.

In the same month Nicos Sampson, the leader of the Nicosia Killer Group, was arrested. Sampson had been what Charles Foley called '*The Times of Cyprus* enthusiastic correspondent from Famagusta'. The man that often arrived at murder scenes, before the security forces or ambulance had arrived, clutching his press card, who had in all probability often committed some of them himself.[9]

Sergeant Jack Taylor of the Cyprus police tells the story of Sampson's arrest in January in which he was directly involved himself by arresting Lazarou Ioannides, who had been the courier between Andreas Chartas, the Nicosia EOKA town commander, and Sampson the execution group leader. Ioannides was questioned by two Turkish Cypriot officers 'who had never heard of such things as "The Judges Rules" and was roughed up'.[10] After Ioannides' visit with the Turks:

> he told the Special Branch Officers that Sampson was hiding in the village of Dhalli, a company of the Guards Regiment had gone out to hold a cordon around the village, while three sergeants of Special Branch got into the house.
>
> On entering Sampson had apparently rolled off the bed trying to grab a sten gun, one of the sergeants had thrown a loaf of bread at him and stamped on his fingers while another had hit him with a chair.[11]

Jack Taylor was disappointed he had not been on the raid to arrest Sampson, who required medical treatment afterward, for the Cyprus police had lost two sergeants killed by the Sampson group.

EOKA terrorists could expect rough treatment if they were captured. Alan Staff of C Company 2 Para witnessed some after capturing some terrorists in the Kyrenia Mountains. 'Well, we just guarded these blokes and were getting quite matey when the police arrived, Special Branch, and they were bastards. They really knocked these blokes about, I could hear them crying.'[12] However, the treatment in this case bore quick results by finding out the location of arms and explosives.

Two Army captains were court-martialled for beating up a suspect with metal chains. Found guilty, they were dismissed from the service. However, in general the security forces showed a high degree of discipline and restraint. Such methods were not necessary as there were many informers willing to betray EOKA. Many of the important successes of the security forces 'was due to some betrayal and EOKA were ruthless in dealing with "traitors"'.[13] Yet informing affected both sides.

Grivas was protected by a mole within Special Branch. Inspector Georgios Lagodontis, who often warned prominent members of EOKA of impending operations against them, although some feel he was a 'double agent' working for the Government: 'Possibly Lagodontis's backing for Grivas was indeed known by the British who kept him in place to follow his warnings to EOKA members and arrest them.'[14]

The Duke of Wellington's Regiment, early in March, killed Grigoris Afxentiou, Grivas's second in command at that time. He was trapped in a cave on the slopes of Mount Kionia in the Pitsilla region near the monastery of Makheras, which today houses a one-room museum to Afxentiou. Half a mile below the monastery is the cave marked by a Greek flag, and maintained as a shrine, where he met his end.

Rain and wind had shielded the Army movements as the cave was surrounded at 3.30 p.m. on 3 March. At dawn the occupants were called upon to surrender; four did, but Afxentiou stayed to fight it out. He shot a corporal dead. Explosives and petrol bombs were used to get him out but Afxentiou died in the flames rather than surrender. He had been betrayed by a local shepherd, for there had been £5,000 on the EOKA man's head. Although losses for EOKA had been heavy there were always new, albeit inexperienced, volunteers to replace them.[15]

Philip Shepheard served in the Royal Navy off Cyprus in 1957 as a midshipman aboard the minesweeper HMS *Sefton*:

After Suez we headed off to Cyprus to do a tour. It was normally six weeks and then back to Malta, and I think we did three tours. The routine was that we worked out of Famagusta as home port, there were five minesweepers. The sea around Cyprus was split into patrol areas. The Army and Army Intelligence thought they had a pretty tight hold on the arms that were available to EOKA within the island; our job was to prevent gun-running.

Though we were never involved in a search of a large ship, we did stop fishing boats, and once apprehended a man who bore a striking resemblance to Grivas in the book of photographs we carried. He protested at first but came along quietly. We found out later that he had been pulled in many times because of his face, but was harmless. Our patrol area would be, typically, that you would start in Famagusta and go up to the Panhandle on the eastern end of the island. That would be one night, and then you would move on, rotate round the island and do however many it was, five or six, and then have twenty-four hours in harbour, and then start again …

We used to carry revolvers when we went ashore in Cyprus. We stopped from time to time to pick up fresh supplies, if we could get them, around the island in a fair number of places. During the day in summer we would anchor and have a good swim. We had very little sense of there being a dangerous situation on shore; it was theoretical. If you went ashore, you took someone else with you to act as an escort and keep a lookout. We had contact with Army units which gave us a good idea of what was going on, such as the Argyll and Sutherland Highlanders on the north of the island, north-east of Kyrenia.[16]

One of the most significant events of early 1957 was the UN debate on Cyprus which began on 18 February; the Greek Foreign Minister Engelo Averoff put the Greek Cypriot case. Averoff was now in touch with Grivas, using the code name 'Isaac' and the Greek consulate in Nicosia to deliver mail; he warned him the USA would support Britain on the basis of the Radcliffe Constitution as the best way forward. If they did not agree to negotiation, division of the island was a real possibility. The debate lasted five days and ended with a resolution calling for negotiations in a peaceful atmosphere.[17]

Again the Greek Government pressed Grivas for a ceasefire, for they believed Governor Harding was advising Macmillan to force through the Radcliffe Constitution. Grivas had no faith in the British but agreed to offer the ceasefire. The battered state of EOKA was undoubtedly a factor but the release of Makarios was a pre-requisite. The EOKA proclamation of 14 March 1957 read:

In accordance with the spirit of the UN resolution, which expressed a desire for the just and peaceful solution of the Cyprus problem on the basis of the UN charter principles, and in order to facilitate the resumption of negotiations between the British Government and the only representative of the Cypriot people, Archbishop Makarios, our organisation declares that it is willing to order the suspension of operations as soon as the Ethnarch Makarios is released.

Signed Dighenis.[18]

About the same time as Grivas was making his offer, Lord Ismay, the Secretary-General of NATO, offered his services as a mediator. Macmillan wrote of this: 'This gives us a more respectable entry into a new position than the EOKA pamphlets. I rang Lord Ismay in Paris, and arranged with him to send his letters to the UK, Greek and Turkish representatives at NATO forthwith.'[19]

However, to persuade the British Cabinet was a different matter, for if they accepted the NATO offer it would almost certainly mean releasing Makarios from the Seychelles. The Cabinet agreed if the Archbishop would make a statement opposing violence by EOKA they would end his detention.

But Makarios was ambiguous. There were statements about a new start and he tried to bargain for the abolition of the emergency regulations. Even so Macmillan was still in favour of his release. 'So long as it was not related to any action concerning the emergency regulations.'[20]

R.A.B. Butler and Alan Lennox-Boyd, Secretary of State for the Colonies, along with Governor Harding, were in favour of releasing Makarios but not permitting his return to Cyprus. Lord Salisbury, Lord President of the Council, one of Macmillan's most trusted advisers who had recommended his take over from Eden only months before, strongly disapproved and threatened to resign, which he did on the 29 March. Macmillan wrote of it: 'Naturally the loss of so old a friend was a personal sorrow to me. Moreover, Lord Salisbury's own distinction in politics, and his high standard of integrity, was impressive and widely recognised. He had resigned with Eden in 1938, as a protest against the policy of appeasement toward Mussolini.'[21] Lord Salisbury looked on Makarios in much the same light as the Italian dictator Benito Mussolini.[22]

Nevertheless, it was a humiliation for Britain internationally, while others loomed on the horizon, although President Eisenhower sent

Macmillan a message of sympathy over Cyprus and it was clear the American's had abandoned their original support for Enosis.

While at home, so Macmillan wrote, the resignation 'caused far less sensation than I expected. Indeed, it seemed to me then that he (Lord Salisbury) had chosen an issue on which no strong public opinion would be aroused'.[23]

The opposition Labour Party was reluctant to take advantage of the Government's discomfort. In public they might still support the Cypriot right of self-determination but in reality it was a hot potato. James Callaghan, who would become Colonial Secretary when Labour came to power, was worried about the troops whose relatives were voters: 'Talk to the man in the street or my Dockers at Cardiff. It's their youngsters who were being shot in the back and they don't like being pushed around by Makarios either.'[24]

Harold Macmillan could shortly get away with telling the British people 'we've never had it so good', as he told a cheering Conservative rally at Bedford on 20 July 1957.[25]

Grivas was not impressed by the offer from the British Government of safe conduct out of Cyprus for EOKA members. And even less so by the message from the Greek Government that they considered the struggle over and they were expecting him to return to Greece. He replied in no way would he 'abandon the struggle' without 'guarantees for a permanent solution'.[26]

Makarios, although released, was still banned from returning to Cyprus and so took up residence in Athens. The Archbishop soon confided to his supporters on the mainland that the struggle for Cyprus would be over soon and that Grivas should return to Greece. But Grivas was not interested in peace or the Radcliffe Constitution and remained a barrier with his own agenda; it would be peace on his terms and he would 'stay where I was until I got the terms I wanted'.[27]

3 Commando Brigade had not returned on block to Cyprus after the Suez Operation but now its two units alternated, 40 Commando doing the first tour in the Troodos. Then in May 1957 they were relieved by 45 Commando. After their success with helicopters in Suez, 45 Commando were quickly used for airborne operations on Cyprus. David Henderson, a Royal Marine with 45 Commando, took part in the early helicopter training on Cyprus with RAF Sycamore helicopters:

We would travel down to Nicosia Airport and act as guinea pigs as the
RAF boys and our officers worked out ways of loading us on and off the
craft and then we would climb aboard and fly off to see if their latest idea
worked … The mountains we operated in were heavily forested and that
was where any self respecting terrorist would run to, so the problem was
how to get us on the ground.[28]

This was solved by roping down while the helicopter hovers, something
that is done to this day but was quite new then; however all did not go
smoothly at first:

At Nicosia Airport the pilots could hold the helicopters as steady as they
wanted as we dropped off down the ropes but at high altitude it was a
different matter. The approach would be fine and the hover would be
achieved but without warning the craft would drop a foot or two like a
stone or swerve off to the side, so any poor sod on the rope at the time was
either dropped with a thump on the deck or dragged through the tree tops.
But the pilots got the better of the sideways waltzing and by reducing the
amount of passengers by one the hover was controlled.[29]

During this training period there was a bad accident when a Sycamore
at the hover failed to lift off and crashed into the ground turning over, its
rotor blades breaking up and turning into lethal weapons flying through
the air in all directions. Sadly Sergeant Major QMS Graham Casey sus-
tained massive injuries and soon died of shock and Marine Miller was
seriously injured.

The first heli-borne operation 'Sherry Spinner' took place on 24 July.
It was part of the cordon and search operation of the villages of Arakapas,
Pharmakas, and Sykopetra in the Pitsilla Mountains. A large deployment, it featured parts of the KOYLI, the RUR, and a company from
the Grenadier Guards plus 45 Commando. 'Sycamore' helicopters were
used allowing the rapid placing of OPs and cordons. No major kills or
arrests took place, for this was a quiet period.[30] R.W.Viant served with a
Transport Company of the Royal Corps of Transport at this time:

Cyprus I found very pleasant but EOKA made a lot of problems. My post-
ing was to a transport company Royal Army Service Corps at Dhekelia.
The camp was fairly open, there was no barbed wire, but it was patrolled by
armed guards round the clock. Generally EOKA did not attack Army installations; they were keener on tackling single officers and mining the roads.

I lived in a tent which was good even in winter. We only had three
weekends when the curfew was lifted, when we could get out and about.
Once, I and several pals decided on a trip to the Troodos Mountains, which
was occupied by a Marine Commando.

A couple of us borrowed cars, I took my own which broke down and
I had to spend the night in the Commando location.

Generally life was good; we had access to the beaches and the NAAFI.
It was in the towns where you had to be wary, we travelled armed there.
We lost no one during our tour to EOKA action although our Sergeant
Major was killed in a road accident. But of course it was the infantry that
took the brunt of the terrorist campaign.[31]

In July Sergeant Jack Taylor of the Cyprus police moved from Nicosia to
the Troodos Mountains village of Pedhoulas, to become the local police
sergeant there. Pedhoulas, 1,100m high at the top of the Marathassa Valley
in the high Troodos, has a clear view of the north coast and the sea from
its lofty position. Even before 1957 it was a popular holiday resort with
red-tiled whitewashed houses and some large hotels, while in the lower
village were the Pan Cyprian Gymnasium and the domed church. In the
village centre was the bungalow that served as the police station with a
Union Jack flying outside.[32]

A Greek Cypriot sergeant had been in charge until Jack's arrival; also
on strength were four constables and a special constable who became
Jack's interpreter and batman. However, basically Jack was the only Brit
in a Greek Cypriot village; his nearest Army unit was Support Company
KOYLI at Pinewood Camp several miles away along difficult mountain roads.[33] As Jack put it: 'I appreciated my life was going to be very
lonely and far different from my days in Nicosia.' However, he soon got
into the swing of things and began to get to know the locals:[34]

One of the duties that always amused me was, I often received application forms from Greek Cypriots in my area to emigrate to England. Having checked them over, I made enquiries, either by phone to Platres or radio to Lefka, then from there to Nicosia checking any records of the applicant. I was soon informed, and it was surprising the number, who, as youths and young men, had convictions for distributing leaflets or being concerned in riots calling for Enosis and now they wanted to emigrate to England, those with a record I recommended that they apply to Greece.[35]

With the new truce in force the curfew was lifted and troops were on the streets unarmed for the first time in months.

Grivas was not idle during the ceasefire. 'I spent much time in filling the gaps in our ranks and in redistributing arms and men among the various groups.' Also he felt acts of sabotage were outside the perimeter of the ceasefire so to keep things boiling he continued with this tactic.[36]

Meanwhile Makarios sat in Athens while the British Government refused to deal with him. Charles Foley visited the Archbishop at this time who told him he would go to America for the next UN appeal; he also asked Foley what the people were saying in Britain. Foley told him the 'people were complaining that instead of helping things he was sitting in Athens as if it were an enemy capital, setting new conditions for peace and cooking up atrocities about the troops'. Makarios was taken aback by this but felt, with his current situation, there was little he could do.[37]

Even Radcliffe, who had penned the self-governing Constitution, saw little hope of a solution: 'The Cypriots may think that if they hang on long enough we may get bored and cut our losses, or that outside pressure may become too strong, or that Britain may discover that Cyprus is not really important and pull out altogether.'[38]

As far as the last comment was concerned there was a growing group in Britain who questioned the wisdom of further involvement in Cyprus. They pointed to the fact that in August Malaya would become an independent country within the Commonwealth after 170 years of British rule. It too had a mixed population of Malays, Chinese, Indians, Eurasians, and Europeans. The British had also fought a highly successful campaign against the Communist rebellion. The British would leave as friends surely something similar were not beyond the realms of possibility for Cyprus.

For the servicemen on Cyprus, as the diplomats talked and the politicians 'stonewalled', life went on with what passed for normality on the island. Raymond Ferguson served with the RAF at this time:

I served as a radar operator in Cyprus from April 1957 until my demob in May 1959. Initially I served at 7 signals unit, RAF Kormakiti until November 1957 when I was posted to 751 signals unit, RAF Cape Greco.

The domestic site at Kormakiti was situated some distance from the technical site and to get to it we passed through the small village of Kormakiti. (Kormakiti lies in the peninsula of the same name that juts out from the north coast westward into the sea to the west of Kyrenia. Today it is the last village of the island's thousand-year-old Maronite Community. During the EOKA troubles they tried to stay neutral as much as possible.)

From memory I think this was mainly populated by Maronites and despite the daily military traffic through the village they were friendly towards us.

Although there didn't seem much to offer servicemen in the way of entertainment some of us occasionally made the effort to visit the village when the emergency situation was relaxed.

Myrtou another village was not far away; this boasted an outside cinema and a cafe. The locals were mainly Turkish Cypriots and were friendly toward us, possibly because quite a lot of money was being spent in the village.[39]

I can't remember there being any trouble between us and the local population. However I remember our CO constantly reminding us of the need for vigilance and good behaviour.

When I was posted to Cape Greco (on the south coast) the situation changed quite dramatically. Again the station was isolated from the main military garrisons at the time and we had to pass through some hostile areas. In particular the village of Paralimni being a strong Greek Cypriot Village its allegiance was firmly with EOKA. During periods of high tension our convoys were stoned by the villagers on many occasions.

Many servicemen and their families were resident in Famagusta with its mixed Greek and Turkish community. I spent many off duty periods with some of these families and always found the next door neighbours friendly, be they Turkish or Greek Cypriots. One bar the 'Trianon Bar' became a regular 'base' for 751 personnel when we were allowed off camp. This bar was owned and operated by two partners a Greek Cypriot Chris, and a Turkish Cypriot Ali. Throughout the troubles they seemed able to survive all that was going on around them.[40]

Following is a typical situation report list for the month of September 1957 which gives a flavour of daily life on Cyprus for the security forces at that time. It was recorded by Major W.C. Harrison RAOC:

September 1957.

2　Government printing works bombed.

4　Greek Cypriot shot dead Nicosia by EOKA.

7　Turkish Cypriot killed. UK Police officer shot in Nicosia by EOKA. Bombs in official's house Nicosia.

8　Four soldiers wounded by beach bombs.

9　GHQ Army Episkopi C-in-C house bombed.

10　Police station set on fire. Greek Cypriot shot dead by EOKA.

13　Four time bombs British Military hospital Dhekelia. Two masked men shot dead (informers against EOKA).

15　Soldier shot dead Nicosia. Greek Cypriot and wife killed in car by EOKA in Paphos.

23　One Airman killed and one wounded. Four beach bombs Kyrenia. Greek Cypriot shot and wife wounded Nicosia by EOKA.

24　Three soldiers wounded by bomb thrown at lorry Famagusta.

25　Army sergeant killed and eleven injured bomb at Paphos.

26　British Officer (RAOC) shot and killed Nicosia.

27　Seven soldiers wounded Army Camp Nicosia by a bomb.

28　Two British Police Officers shot dead Nicosia. One soldier and one woman (Royal Volunteer Service) shot dead in Ambush Kyrenia whilst delivering books to British Regiment. Ban on the use of bicycles proclaimed.

October 1957.

3　3000 troops (mostly Paras) started operation 'Sparrowhawk' in the Kyrenia Mountains. And so it continued.[41]

In early October 1957 Sir John Harding asked to be relieved of the governorship. It had been two busy years which had affected his health. Also, to a degree, he had defeated EOKA as far as it was possible with military means. Even Grivas said of him in his memoirs:

> In Cyprus he was given a task outside his powers but he was the strongest man I faced there. It must also be remembered that while in the military field he was lord and master, politically he was in the hands of the old Colonial Officials.[42]

On 22 October the field marshal left Cyprus. At the airport, to the waiting reporters, he admitted mistakes: 'But if I had my time again I would have to come to the same major decisions and followed the same general policy.' He also pointed out it would be a bad move to allow Archbishop Makarios to return to Cyprus.[43]

In September, 45 Commando and the Support Company KOYLI came to the end of their tours in the Troodos Mountains and were relieved by the Royal Ulster Rifles. Jack Taylor witnessed the arrival of the new battalion at Platres with 'pipes playing and orange kilts swaying'. He soon got to know his new neighbours. The new soldiers were quite amazed that he lived in a Cypriot village alone as the only Brit, one RUR corporal told him:[44] 'I wouldn't live alone in a Greek Village on my own, not if you paid me £100 a week.' But things had been quiet for Jack so far, even on '*Oxi day*' the Pedhoulas villagers had greeted him with *Kala Maras*.[45]

Early in October, Michael Ashiotis surrendered to the RUR after killing two companion terrorists in a hide near Kakopetria Village in the Troodos Mountains. The reason he gave for his surrender was that he had found his name on a death list issued by Grivas for being an untrustworthy member of EOKA.

Alan (Gunner) Riley of the RUR went to recover the bodies; they reached the scene near nightfall:

> We reached the hideout, a large burrow under the ground, and there were two dead terrorists inside. The Sergeant, a Korean War veteran said 'Grab a leg. He won't bite you, as he's dead.' Until that night I had never seen

a dead body let alone touched one. We laid the bodies on the ground …
Someone heard a voice and we adopted defensive positions. I was only
a few feet from the terrorists' bodies, when I thought I saw a movement
and aimed my sterling at it. As it became lighter, around sunrise, I saw the
movement was just a bush moving against a silver birch tree.

The Special Branch arrived and wanted to know where the EOKA radio
receiver and binoculars had gone and they accused us of stealing them.
Later that morning we went down the mountain to a farm to get a donkey
so we could take the bodies down.

Our Turkish interpreter did his best to translate but could not get the
peasant to understand, so we took the donkey anyway. I'm certain the peasant was just acting dumb, as to help the SB meant death.

We were relieved later by a patrol that included one of my National Service
draft, and he told me that he was being shipped back to the UK the following day, a month earlier than expected and that I was going with him …

Before we left the scene Lieutenant Knox arrived with explosives and blew
up the terrorist hideout. Half the mountainside seemed to go up with it.[46]

Ashiotis was given a new identity and sent to live in the UK. But he soon
returned to Cyprus where he was executed by EOKA.

'*Oxi day*', 28 October, celebrated the day Greece denied access to the
Italians to Albania during the Second World War. Greek Cypriots liked to
celebrate this, although during the EOKA troubles in the bigger towns it
usually ended in riots between Greeks and Turks.

During this quiet period there were, as Grivas puts it, 'isolated acts
of sabotage to show the British that they could not do exactly what
they liked'. These attacks culminated with a raid on RAF Akrotiri on
25 November resulting in several aircraft being damaged.[47]

Early in December the new governor, Sir Hugh Foot, aged 50, arrived
on Cyprus. One of the first actions of this liberal diplomat was to delay
the sacking of 5,000 Greek Cypriots who worked in British camps and
bases. The mass dismissal had been requested by the security forces after
the 'Akrotiri incident'. Foot told the Cypriots he was their 'friend and
servant' and would 'deal with you honestly and sincerely'; he asked the
people for time to review the situation and make recommendations to

the UK Government. However, time was short for there was another UN debate on Cyprus due on 9 December.[48]

However, Sir Hugh Foot had the basis of a plan in mind, yet no 'official version has yet been published and what has appeared is only the barest outline'.[49] Foot did write in his autobiography:

> In November on my way to Cyprus I again went over my ideas with Ministers in London. The essentials I thought were four. A period of five or seven years before any final decision. An end to the Emergency and the return of Archbishop Makarios to the island. Negotiations in the Island with the leaders of the two communities to evolve a system of self-Government. And an assurance that no final decision would be taken at the end of the five-or-seven-year period which was not acceptable to Greeks and Turks alike.[50]

The new governor came from a traditional Liberal family, although his brothers Dingle and Michael were ardent socialists and Labour MPs. Indeed he may have been embarrassed by the Labour Party resolution, passed by the party conference at Brighton, committing the party to self-determination for Cyprus 'within the lifetime of the next Labour Government'.[51]

It had been sponsored by Tom Driberg and Barbara Castle and upset the Government, although many in the Labour Party, as soon as the resolution was adopted, began to distance themselves from it.

Many troops on Cyprus mistrusted Sir Hugh Foot from the start. Charles Butt, who served with 253 Field Security Section, felt the appointment of Foot was a bad move:

> Morale did take a blow with the appointment of Foot as Governor, as his pro-Greek sympathies were well known as was his dislike of the military in general. This distrust was reinforced by his habit of entering condemned cells and personally shaking the hands of reprieved killers of British Servicemen. There was consequently a feeling that HMG was preparing a sell-out and a betrayal of lives of the murdered soldiers, policemen and civilians and the efforts of those involved in combating terrorism.[52]

A few days before the appointment of Foot up in the Troodos, Jack Taylor had gone to the village of Spilia where a house had been blown up. Here EOKA men had been making bombs. Searching the wreckage, the police came across parts of three different people and parts of the bombs they had been making.[53]

In Nicosia, after the Greek resolution on Cyprus was defeated in the UN, the usual riots quickly turned inter-communal; 140 people were injured including forty police and soldiers, looting and burning had been widespread.

Up in the mountains on 9 December even Jack Taylor was expecting trouble in so-far peaceful Pedhoulas. A section of the RUR was in close support. A running battle soon developed between the soldiers and demonstrators. Jack had not expected it to reach the severity it did. Bottles and rocks were greeted with tear gas and pick helves.[54] At the end of the day some of the older villagers approached Jack in the hope he could help some of the students arrested. However, he had no time for this as he was dripping blood on the station floor from various cuts and grazes, some that required stitches, and a broken tooth. He angrily chastised them:

> I have lived amongst you for several weeks, thought of you all as being friends, but you all stood by and allowed a mob of students to take over the village, and then you ask me to help them. When I find out the ringleaders, I will see that they are prosecuted.

After this Jack decided to go and live in Pinewood Camp with the RUR.[55]

Notes

1. Suha Faiz, *Recollections and Reflections of an Unknown Cyprus Turk*, p. 177, 'Such was …'
2. Ibid., p. 176, 'In the event …'
3. Tabitha Morgan, *Sweet and Bitter Island*, p. 323.
4. Panagiotis Dimitrakis, *Military Intelligence in Cyprus*, p. 88, 'The arrests …'
5. Harold Macmillan, *Riding the Storm*, p. 170, 'On the morning of …'
6. Ibid., p. 185, 'After the resignation …'
7. Ibid., p. 657, 'The problems of Cyprus …'
8. Ibid., pp. 175–6, 'There is not much …'
9. Charles Foley, *Island in Revolt*, p. 139, 'A new wanted poster …'
10. Jack Taylor, *A Copper in Kypriou*, p. 42, 'When we returned …'

11. Ibid., p. 43, 'There Jock told us …'
12. Peter Harclerode, *Para*, p. 219, '2 Para was deployed …'
13. Foley, p. 186, 'Informers were the last …'
14. Dimitrakis, p. 88, 'General Kenneth Darling …'
15. Foley, p. 140, 'The security forces …'
16. Adrian Walker, *Six Campaigns*, pp. 144–6, 'After Suez …'
17. Charles Foley (ed.), *The Memoirs of General Grivas*, pp. 91–2, 'The British Government …'
18. Ibid., p. 115, 'Although, then I had …'
19. Macmillan, p. 226, 'In spite of the obvious …'
20. Ibid., p. 227, 'It was difficult …'
21. Ibid., p. 229, 'Naturally the loss …'
22. Ibid., p. 229, 'He had resigned …'
23. Ibid., p. 229, 'The resignation …'
24. Foley, *Island in Revolt*, p. 151, 'James Callaghan, who would …'
25. Harold Macmillan, Conservative Rally Bedford 20/7/1957
26. Foley, *The Memoirs of General Grivas*, p. 116, 'I replied at once …'
27. Ibid., p. 116, 'My personal safety …'
28. Cyprus, britains-smallwars.com
29. Ibid.
30. David Young, *Four Five*, pp. 238–9, 'The helicopter …'
31. BECM Oral Tape 356 R.W.Viant
32. Taylor, p. 81, 'Ironically the day of my transfer …'
33. Ibid., p. 83, 'John was able …'
34. Ibid., p. 80, 'So my days …'
35. Ibid., pp. 105–6, 'Sunday, I intended …'
36. Foley, p. 120, 'If the British …'
37. Foley, *Island in Revolt*, pp. 152–3, 'I told him …'
38. Ibid., p. 152, 'Radcliffe, in Sunday sweater …'
39. LTA Raymond Ferguson 4/10/2000
40. Ibid.
41. IWM Papers of Major N.C. Harrison RAOC
42. Foley, *The Memoirs of General Grivas*, p. 126, 'Nevertheless, I continue …'
43. Foley, *Island in Revolt*, pp. 161–2, 'A thin white line …'
44. Taylor, p. 116, 'On the morning the Royal …'
45. Ibid., p. 125, 'Back at the police station …'
46. Cyprus, britains-smallwars.com
47. Foley, *The Memoirs of General Grivas*, p. 126, 'The Army left …'
48. Foley, *Island in Revolt*, pp. 168–9, 'Foot began on his first day …'
49. John Reddaway, *Burdened with Cyprus*, p. 105, 'The Foot Plan …'
50. Ibid., p. 159, 'A start in freedom …'
51. Foley, pp. 211–12, 'Mr Gaitskell disowned Mrs Castle …'
52. LTA Charles R. Butt 8/1/2001
53. Taylor, p. 143, 'As I continued to drive …'
54. Ibid., p. 145, 'As the head of the procession …'
55. Ibid., pp. 148–9, 'We had been in the police station …'

9

1958 BLOODY
CIVIL WAR

As the year turned so had the British position, in that the military bases were increasingly seen as her only requirement on Cyprus, and the British role on the wider island was to keep the peace between the two communities. The Turks, fearing abandonment by the British, had dangerously set up their own counter-terrorist organisation, TMT, the Turkish Defence Organisation.

At the end of 1957 Sir Hugh Foot returned to London to lay a new plan for Cyprus before the Cabinet. Basically it was based on a breathing space of five to seven years of Colonial self-government, a cooling off period, after which the Cypriot people would decide their own future, with one proviso, that if the majority still wanted Enosis they could only have it with the approval of Turkey.[1]

After winning over the Cabinet, Foot, who had come into the Cyprus crisis like a whirlwind, was optimistic of success, and would stop in Athens to try to win over Makarios. However, the Turkish Premier, Adnan Menderes, as soon as he heard, was against any attempt to pacify the 'blood stained priest in Athens'.[2]

Turkish Cypriots took to the streets in Limassol and Nicosia where rioting broke out leaving seven dead and hundreds injured. Despite the curfew the hitherto largely peaceful Turks took to burning garages and cars, and stoning the security forces. The rioters were heard to shout 'Down with Foot' and 'Long live Harding'.[3]

In March the Government in Athens collapsed when Constantine Karamanlis resigned as prime minister over an internal crisis. At the same time Grivas launched a new EOKA campaign warning the new governor: 'The credit of time you asked for has run out and so has my patience. The fight must go on, because there is no other way to deal with Britain's uncompromising attitude.'[4]

Grivas had been deeply shocked by the loss of Afxentiou, learning with 'pain' of his death.[5] Even more so that the British had known of his mountain hideout, and Afxentiou had stayed in place because he believed the police would never find his hiding place. Several of EOKA's mountain groups had been broken up. Many of the arrested had cover stories that deliberately led the security forces to real hideouts and arms dumps but away from the real target, the head of the insurgency, Grivas.[6]

In Athens Greek counter-intelligence found out that Prime Minister Constantine Karamanlis's private telephone lines had been tapped by the British. Eventually, three spies working at the British Embassy were deported.

EOKA's new campaign also introduced fresh tactics with the use of 'passive resistance', which relied on minor sabotage and a boycott of everything British. Charles Foley found the passive resistance exasperating:

> English lettering was forbidden by Grivas, every paint brush on the island seemed to be at work as English street names vanished in a blur. Next the Turkish names were painted out and then the Turks retaliated by obliterating the Greek names, soon there were no street names at all.[7]

British goods were boycotted but even the threats of Grivas could not overcome the Cypriot passion for gambling and in particular the pools. 'The same little crowd gathered round the office radio every Saturday night to hear the announcers': 'Chelsea-ena … Tottenham Hotspur-dio …'[8]

For Britain in the early months of 1958 there seemed to be trouble everywhere. On Malta anxiety over the scaling down or even closure of the dockyard due to envisaged defence cuts and the scale of Britain's aid limit to the island of £5 million brought about the resignation of Dom Mintoff and his Labour Cabinet on 24 April. This was followed by widespread strikes as a national protest, which degenerated into rioting, and pitched battles between the rioters and police. The Governor Sir Robert Laycock dissolved the Legislative Assembly and assumed powers to maintain law and order.[9] Aden was also sliding toward trouble being fostered by Egypt; in May Governor William Luce declared a state of emergency.

Geoffrey Saunders, who served with the Oxford and Buck's (which later formed part of the Royal Green Jacket's) during his National Service, arrived on Cyprus early in 1958:

> It was quite an interesting trip, with three days to get to Gib, three days to get to Malta and then, finally, three days to get to Limassol Cyprus. As soon as we got to Limassol, we were taken up to the tented barracks just outside the town, just away from Berengaria Village.'

Geoffrey was soon in action armed with the new FN, the Belgian *Fusil Automatique Leger*, produced under licence by the British as the L1A1 Self-Loading Rifle, the SLR. He continues:

> There was a village called, I believe, Mutiarka, which is a little north of Limassol, into the bottom of the south Troodos Mountains. Our Intelligence Corps people had been told Uncle George was in the village with his men, so they immediately threw out about 2,000 troops. The whole of our battalion was set out around the village, in a circle completely enclosing it.
>
> There was another village a little way away, and another battalion, which may well have been the 3rd Parachute, because they were operating a little north of us into the Troodos encircling that village, and the Gunners were entrenched in a complete circle around these circles. So basically, the first night out, we were sat in pairs twenty yards apart, right around the village. I have never been so scared in my life, waiting for a terrorist with a knife to come and stick me in the back. The greatest protection I had was my rifle with twenty rounds of ammunition; we had the FN. We were the first to have the FN; we had this magnificent little rifle with twenty rounds automatic to keep you going. We sat there for about seven or eight days. We learnt later that Uncle George got out on the first night.

There was a little gully, and there were people sitting either side,: he flicked some stones toward them. 'Who's there?' No response. So he knew exactly where they were, and went up the gully and out. A little later Engineers came and, any hole they could find, they stuck dynamite in it and blew it.[10]

It was at this time the young Auberon Waugh came to Cyprus during his National Service as a cornet with the Royal Horse Guards. Waugh flew to Malta and then to Cyprus in RAF transport planes; he soon got into the swing of things. 'Outside the camp, the activities of the EOKA terrorists made us behave rather like an army of occupation, carrying pistols the whole time and being a little nervous of any sudden movement.'[11]

Waugh felt the troops were very much caught in the middle. 'EOKA shot the British, Turks massacred the Greeks and in any lull in the fighting between EOKA and the Security Forces, EOKA would turn and attack the LWGCS [Left Wing Greek Cypriots].'[12]

The 19-year-old Waugh found the life exciting and busy. In letters home he wrote:

> Nearly every day we are out on some raid, road block, search or patrol'. But at 'the moment they (EOKA) are not shooting much … Bombs, however, are exploding at the rate of three every 24 hours, and we sometimes go rushing to the scene, quite often the Cypriots blow themselves up, as they are not very expert in handling them.[13]

However, this was all about to change. Grivas relaunched his terror campaign on 4 May when two military policemen were shot dead as they patrolled the streets of Famagusta. They were the first British Servicemen to die in thirteen months. EOKA said it was a reprisal for the 'ill-treatment at Camp K'.[14] The detention camps were always a focus of dispute. EOKA claiming they were a hot bed of torture, punishment and revenge. The same evening the two MPs were gunned down; the death penalty for carrying arms, which had been lifted by Harding soon after the truce started, was restored by Foot, who flew to London for talks with the Government.

Toward the end of May Major General Joe Kendrew, the new GOC, launched his troops on Operation Kingfisher, an attempt to find Grivas, who was said to be hiding in or around the village of Mathy Koloni in the southern foothills of the Troodos Mountains, an area which lay among hills honeycombed with ancient caves.

Auberon Waugh took part in this operation. 'I was under canvas in the Troodos Hills with the rest of my squadron, a regiment of the Ox and Bucks and a regiment of Marine Commandos who were horribly fit and keen, rushing everywhere at the double.'[15] He took part with his men acting as infantry in a large cordon and search operation, after which they switched to searching the caves and terraces; some of the latter were pulled down with picks and crowbars after they had probably stood there for thousands of years. 'After a time, the troops grew bored with this and started letting off explosives charges in the side of a mountain. One explosion was much louder than the rest, and I noticed rocks falling all around me. "Look up, look up" they shouted.' Unluckily, Waugh did not move in time and one rock struck him on the head knocking him out. He suffered concussion and double vision but no more than that.[16]

In the early months of 1958 Macmillan and his Cabinet tried to get to grips with a new plan for Cyprus, based on the Sir Hugh Foot attempted solution. But as Macmillan wrote, 'informed negotiations through the Ambassadors revealed that neither the Greeks nor the Turks were likely to be attracted by our new scheme'.[17] The Greeks would not abandon Enosis and the Turks were equally attracted to partition.

Macmillan likened the 'Cyprus Tangle' to the child's game of getting three balls into cups at the same time. Two are relatively easy but the third verges on impossible. It was necessary here to get agreement between Greeks, Turks and Cypriots.[18] Macmillan explained:

After much thought we agreed to regard our plan as an interim proposal, to be accepted for a seven-year period during which no change in the international status of the island should be made. We hoped by altering our scheme from a final to a provisional solution, to meet some of the rooted objections of the rival parties.[19]

The USA supported the British position with diplomatic pressure and argument, but really seemed doubtful about the merits of the 'Tri-Dominium Plan'.[20] On 16 June the plan was put before the NATO council who welcomed Britain's efforts, although as to be expected the Greek and Turkish representatives were reserved.

Three days later Macmillan put his proposals before the British Parliament, after a meeting with Gaitskell and some of the shadow cabinet. On 26 June the full debate took place. As Macmillan points out, the House of Commons Members were largely distracted by other matters, 'the long bus strike had just ended, the railway strike was in the balance, and the Middle East crisis was in full swing'.[21]

It is well to look at the plan in some detail, for although not the settlement that would end British rule, it did demonstrate the Government's resolve to find a solution. The new Constitution allowed for:

1   A separate House of Representatives for the two communities with legislative authority in communal affairs.
2   Internal administrations would be handled by a council of the Governor, Representatives from the Greek and Turkish Governments and six councillors from the House of Representatives, four Greek Cypriots and two Turkish Cypriots.
3   External affairs were the reserve of the Governor after consultations with the Greek and Turkish Governments.
4   The Greek and Turkish Governments could block any legislation they considered discriminating which would need then to be considered by an impartial tribunal.[22]

For all the British Government's efforts it seemed to make little difference on Cyprus, for in June occurred one of the worst atrocities during the troubles. A party of fifty or so Greeks had gone to the village of Skylloura, about 15 miles north-west of Nicosia, where they had heard the Greeks were being attacked, but on the way they were stopped by a patrol and taken to Skylloura Police Station. From there they were brought to Nicosia in trucks escorted by an armoured car, but as the police had no charge to bring against them they were driven out into the countryside to Guenyeli. They were then released and told to walk home across the fields to their own village, 8 miles away. To drive people some distance from their destination and release them was a security practice known as 'cooling them off'.[23] This incident, perhaps more than any other, reinforced Greek Cypriot suspicions that the British were collaborating with Turkish Cypriots in order to oppress them and is still remembered with bitterness today.[24]

Guenyeli was a Turkish village. Its inhabitants set upon the Greeks, whom they may have thought were going to attack them, chasing the Greeks on motorbikes across the fields wielding axes and knives. Auberon Waugh was early upon the scene:

> The Turks poured out of the village and quite literally hacked them to pieces. It was a very messy business. Nine Greeks were killed and many others mutilated. Hands and fingers were all over the place and one officer wandered around, rather green in the face, holding a head and asking if anyone had seen a body which might fit it.[25]

Something akin to a blood lust broke out after the massacre, as Charles Foley put it:

> After Guenyeli any semblance of a civilised society vanished. The killings and fire-raising continued through June, yet it was not their frequency but their savagery which most appalled. Men and women and boys were stabbed and shot and beaten, their throats were cut while they slept, they were hacked to death with axes as they worked in the fields, they were burnt alive in their homes.[26]

Auberon Waugh also became a casualty, about this time, as the result of a freak accident. 'On patrol, we always travelled with a belt in the machine guns of the armoured cars, but without a bullet in the breech.' Waugh had trained in Britain on the Besa machine gun, which to put a bullet in the breech needed two cocking actions. However in Cyprus the armoured cars were equipped with the Browning .300, which needed only one action to cock. Waugh continues:

It is most probable that I cocked the gun in a moment of absent minded-
ness, but that did not explain the subsequent events which were the result
of excessive heat and a faulty mechanism.

I had noticed an impediment in the elevation of the machine gun on
my armoured car, and used the opportunity of our taking up positions to
dismount, seize the barrel from in front and give it a good wiggle. A split
second later I realised that it had started firing.[27]

Waugh was hit six times: four bullets went through the shoulder and
chest, one through the arm and one through the left hand. The gun
fired off nearly the entire belt of 250 rounds before a corporal got in
the turret and stopped the gun.[28] Few thought the young Waugh would
survive but the medical team in the British Military Hospital Nicosia
'performed brilliantly'. He lost a lung and spleen, and his National
Service was over. In February 1959 he was discharged from the Army
and became a war pensioner.[29]

About this time, July 1958, Makarios began to be more critical of Grivas
and his handling of the campaign. Despite the 'success', wrote Makarios,
'of passive resistance, the economic effects regarding the consumption of
British products are probably more unpleasant for the Greek Cypriots
than for the British economy. The organisation must not, of course, give
the impression of admitting to a mistake on this issue, but should quietly
relax the boycott both in intensity and extent.'[30]

Grivas wrote to the Bishop of Kitium in July complaining about
Makarios: 'I begin to doubt whether the Archbishop is capable of handling the Cyprus question and I am no longer disposed to give him carte
blanche to express the opinion of, or to represent the organisation.'[31]

Later that month an Army patrol tried to remove Greek slogans hung
in the village of Avgorou near Famagusta; a riot soon broke out, when
200 people attacked the five armoured cars with anything they could.
The troops opened fire, killing two people, an old man and young mother,
while fifty other villagers were injured and twenty-three soldiers.[32]

Three days later in the shopping centre of Famagusta two National
Servicemen were shot dead and so it continued in a barbaric but familiar style. Inter-communal violence had not slackened either. On 13 July

fires blazed all along the Mason–Dixon Line, five Turks and three Greeks being killed in the fighting. Governor Foot reluctantly ordered a month-long night curfew which started with a forty-eight-hour blanket curfew.[33]

However, for all the murderous violence going on in Cyprus, it was not making the worldwide headlines, for in July, the Middle East was con-vulsed by a chain of events that started with a coup in Iraq. Army officers, inspired by Colonel Nasser of Egypt, deposed the pro-Western regime of King Faisal. The king was murdered along with his uncle Prince Abdulillah and his Prime Minister General Nauri al-said. The coup put pressure on Jordan, Iraq's partner in the Arab Union, and in Lebanon where the Government was fighting rebels funded by Egypt. President Chanoun of Lebanon demanded Western aid.

The aid was quick in coming. On 15 July, 1,700 Marines from the US Sixth Fleet landed at Beirut. While two days later, RAF Beverly trans-port aircraft landed some 2,000 British paratroops, mainly from Cyprus, at Amman Airport in answer to a request for help from King Hussein, after Syrian troops had been massing on Jordan's border.[34] These moves by the NATO Allies left Nasser and the Soviet Union demanding the UN order the withdrawal of the British and US forces. However, the American rep-resentative to the UN, Mr Cabot Lodge, argued that 'if the UN cannot deal with indirect aggression the United Nations will break up'.[35]

In Britain, Labour Leader Hugh Gaitskell talked of 'serious doubts' but Macmillan won the vote on the issue. Meanwhile British forces were bolstered by reinforcements sent to Bahrain, Malta and Cyprus to act as a fire brigade force if needed.[36]

Back on Cyprus, on 25 July Mrs J. Somerville, wife of a serving Royal Artillery Officer, wrote in her diary:

> As expected there is a strike today in protest against the round-up of EOKA men. It happened yesterday in Nicosia (Mrs Somerville lived in Famagusta) when the curfew was lifted I was summoned to the NAAFI where we had a record day. Opened 8a.m and by 1.20 the last customer was served and doors closed. We had simply never stopped.

On 28 July she wrote:

NAAFI staff on strike because union leader taken in sweep as EOKA member.

And of the week ending 5 August:

> Strike goes on for over a week. Shop functions very well to surprise of Greek staff … At the end of the week organised two teams but strike finished next day. Still, all ready for next time.[37]

On 26 July parts of 45 Commando returned to the unhappy island. They arrived in Limassol aboard HMS *Bermuda* and the transport LST *Striker* for their third and final tour during the troubles. Within days the Commando took over responsibility for the by-now familiar Troodos area. Soon they were involved in Operation Swan Vesta, part of an island-wide search for terrorists.[38]

45 had also set up 'Heliforce' which had been in Cyprus for weeks before the main body arrived. This operated from RAF Nicosia and consisted of a tactical headquarters and two rifle troops, and 728 Flight Royal Navy with four Westland Whirlwind helicopters. The use of helicopter-borne troops was still in its infancy but many lessons were learnt on Cyprus, in particular with regard to night operations.[39]

Early in August appeals for peace on Cyprus were issued by the Greek, British and Turkish prime ministers and endorsed by Makarios. Within days EOKA called a ceasefire which was followed two days later by the TMT.

Harold Macmillan now appealed to fellow NATO Allies Greece and Turkey, with personal visits blessed by the USA, to back his plan for Cyprus. This was, five to seven years of colonial self-government, a cooling-down period, during which the Greeks and Turks would have separate councils, with elected members, and two Viceroys from Greece and Turkey who would sit in the Governors Council, after which the Cypriots would decide their own future – with the proviso that, if the majority still wanted Enosis, they could have it only with Turkish approval.

Macmillan visited Cyprus before returning to London – more in this case to visit the troops, including his old regiment the Grenadier Guards, rather than to gain favour for his plan. He arrived at the village of Lyssa near Limassol by helicopter and wrote in his diary:

Here we landed in the square outside the church. An operation was going on. A cordon of troops (3rd Battalion Grenadier Guards and A Company Royal Scots Fusiliers.) had been put round the village some days ago and was still maintained. A search of every house and of the church had revealed a lot of arms, including twenty–thirty bombs.[40]

The battalion was commanded by Colonel P.C. Britten, son of Charles Britten, who had served with Macmillan in the 4th Battalion at Loos in 1915. He inspected one company in the schoolroom who looked in 'splendid shape'; he spoke a few words to them. He found it 'very moving' as for him it 'recalled so many memories'.[41]

Thus as far as the political agenda was concerned what could be called the Macmillan plan MK2 would be imposed on the island without further discussion. Greece rejected the plan, Makarios denounced it while on Cyprus the moderate John Clerides called it 'a monstrous plan for divide and rule'.[42] However, Makarios did tell Governor Foot in Athens during talks that it might be reasonable to propose an independent Cyprus within the Commonwealth and to leave Greece and Turkey out of the decision on Cyprus. Had Makarios begun to realise Enosis would never work, what he outlined in fact had been on the table since 1955 when the emergency had begun.[43]

45 Commando's Heli Force, known as the 'Sky Cavalry', was in action on 10 July. Operation Springtime was mounted in the area of Akanthou 35 north-east of Nicosia in the Kyrenian mountain range. Seven villages were cordoned and screened in seven days.

At dawn on the fourth day Akanthou was the target. Ten helicopters were used bringing in troops to look for terrorist hides. The 1st Battalion Royal West Kents were in support. One of the first casualties was the commanding officer of 45, Lieutenant Colonel John Richards, who made a bad landing while roping down and broke his heel. Two men of X Troop were both accidentally killed in a 'friendly fire' incident. Three other Marines were wounded in this incident, and evacuated by air to the British Military Hospital. One Marine, Harry Bostock, later died of his wounds.[44]

The truce of August lapsed and the island returned to the familiar round of ambushes and sabotage and Army operations. Even the neutral

American community were not unaffected for they were stunned when US Vice Consul, John Wentworth, was shot and wounded in his own garden; EOKA alleged an Anglo-Turkish plot intended to show the Greeks in a bad light.[45]

There was a gun battle in Lyssi where three Cypriots and a soldier died. On the murder mile in Nicosia a British police inspector was shot dead. The next day an RAF Warrant Officer was gunned down from a passing taxi. In Liopetri Village a few miles south of Famagusta, four of EOKA's senior guerrillas were trapped in a barn by the Army. The barn was set on fire and the terrorists shot as they came out; one soldier also died. The group leader Christos Samaras had a price of £5,000 on his head: he had been turned in by his brother Elias.[46]

In September focus shifted to the village of Kathikas north of Paphos. The Argyll and Sutherland Highlanders searched the village following the ambush and killing of one of their men. Dozens of villagers were injured in the search and one man was shot dead after attacking the soldiers.[47]

British politicians during the annual summer parliamentary recess visited Cyprus and were shocked by the vicious, violent atmosphere. However, in reality most did little to help, for the island had suffered quite enough from opinionated politicians. Barbara Castle, Vice Chairman of the Labour Party, was a prime example, unlike John Hatch, Labour's Commonwealth Officer, who spent ten days on Cyprus in a quiet manner making a point of seeing as many people as possible. Then, on his return to Britain, talking to Zorlu in Ankara and Averoff in Athens before finally talking to Makarios who, as we have seen, was now talking, albeit tentatively, about an independent Cyprus. Thus Hatch returned to London with the seeds of a solution.

Mrs Castle saw Makarios first, who again outlined his plan. Thus she arrived on the island full of the plan Governor Foot was well aware of, before she had even spoken to the people on the ground. In her tour of Cyprus Mrs Castle was welcomed by both communities but here rather naively put her foot in it about matters she was inexperienced with. In Kathikas she saw people allegedly injured by the Argylls and commented that the troops were 'permitted and even encouraged' to use rough measures after a shooting, on the grounds that they were engaged in 'hot pursuit'.

Foot came to the defence of the Argylls, one of Britain's most famous regiments, and he was 'not surprised' that the soldiers were rough when their comrades were killed.[48] Mrs Castle tried to withdraw the word 'encouraged' but it was too late; it was already on its way to London. Back in the UK it was not the Conservatives that turned on her but Labour.

James Matthews of Labour's National Executive felt Mrs Castle's 'unjustified' remarks had 'not portrayed the party in a good light especially on the eve of the Labour Party Conference'. Hugh Gaitskell disowned Mrs Castle's statement, and the party was finding Cyprus, in view of their earlier support for self-determination, an embarrassment, with a general election on the horizon and public opinion to consider.[49] The press joined in the condemnation. The *Daily Telegraph* felt her statement 'deplorable', which would only further 'inflame the passions' on the island. The *Daily Mail* felt she belonged to the 'always-blame-the-British group'. The *Daily Express* went further, stating she had sided with 'Britain's enemies'.

Mrs Castle saw Makarios again in Athens on her return to the UK and he authorised her to tell the world's press of his position on an independent Cyprus. However, the Government were unwilling to listen to what they saw as the meddling Mrs Castle and largely ignored the Archbishop's new line. They also ignored the less public Labour Party's suggestion for new talks with the Cypriots and the suspension of the Macmillan Plan. Thus much of John Hatch's work came to nothing.[50]

However, it was Grivas who was perhaps the most shocked and upset by the news of Makarios's new position and wrote in his memoirs: 'It was a compete surprise to me … The Archbishop had no mandate to depart from our basic claim for self determination the right to choose our own future and join our Greek Motherland.'[51]

Grivas now made plans for a major new offensive to greet the implementation of the Macmillan Plan, which would consist of sabotage strikes and mass demonstrations and attacks against the British. In the autumn of 1958, EOKA sank to a new level of barbarity in a forlorn last attempt to bounce the British out of Cyprus.[52] General Kendrew escaped unhurt from a spectacular attempt on his life, when one of the largest mines so far blew up a culvert seconds after his car had passed over it. However, an escort in the truck behind was killed.

In October there was a general strike, and in the same month the first British civilian to be killed by EOKA gunmen since January 1957 was shot down, and the next day Mrs Catherine Cutliffe was murdered on the streets of Famagusta. Mrs Cutliffe was the wife of a Royal Artillery sergeant, a mother of five children, the youngest a year old. With her eldest daughter Margaret, aged 18, and Mrs Elfreda Robinson, German wife of another sergeant, she had gone shopping in the town. They were leaving a shop at which they had bought a dress for Margaret's engagement party when they were fired on from behind. Mrs Cutliffe was killed and Mrs Robinson badly wounded.

Hundreds of troops were quickly on the streets. Virtually every male in Famagusta was rounded up, most being knocked about if they did not move quickly. During the night there were four further deaths. A soldier was accidentally shot.

On the Greek Cypriot side a 13-year-old girl suffered a heart attack, and two men were shot, while hundreds were treated in hospital.[53]

Mrs Somerville wrote in her diary on 3 October about the shooting:

Mrs Cutliffe dead and Mrs Robinson seriously injured and flown to Dhekelia. All are deeply shocked … All Greek males being rounded up and taken to cages for questioning. Troops not wearing kid gloves and many broken heads … Furious when we hear the bloody mayor of Famagusta protest about action of troops and not a word of sympathy let alone mention of cowardly shooting.[54]

Hugh Grant, a National Serviceman, was on the streets that day. He served with 1st Battalion the Parachute Regiment on Cyprus from July 1958 to March 1959.

C Company 1 Para moved to Famagusta on 1 October after increased terrorist activities to carry out VCPs and foot patrols. On Friday 3rd they had been playing football in the afternoon when the game was stopped and the company rapidly deployed onto the streets of Famagusta. Hugh Grant takes up the story from his diary: 'As we neared Famagusta the high walls surrounding the old city were black with people crowded up there shouting and waving us on.' They were Turks cheering on the

British troops, which the soldiers thought quite odd. The Paras were dropped off in groups at various points to conduct VCPs. It soon came down the grapevine that service wives had been shot-up while shopping. Pretty 'harsh treatment was meted out to all' Greeks 'who came into our orbit that night'.[55] In Hugh's view the rough treatment of the locals 'brought little credit on the various troop units that cracked down on Famagusta that night'.[56]

Yet on the whole the Army maintained its discipline, which was not, perhaps, what Grivas had gambled on. For if there is one murder that marks the decline and ostracism of Grivas from his own community in Cyprus and on the Greek Mainland it is that of Mrs Cutliffe.

Grivas claims in his memoirs the attack on the service wives 'was as much a surprise to me as to anyone else …'. He goes on to say 'there was no evidence whatever that EOKA was involved'.[57] Not happy to leave it at that he suggests Mrs Cutliffe 'might have been the victim of some crime of spite or passion'. But if that was the case why shoot indiscriminately at both women? No, there seems little doubt that this EOKA killer group had lost control of its executioners. Indeed, groups before had shown a total disregard for their victims and whoever might get in the way. And it might just have been a new tactic of Grivas, ever the gambler.[58]

On the 4th Mrs Somerville went with another service wife to visit the Cutliffes:

Drive in Land Rover with heavy escort through completely deserted streets, not a soul about, all shutters shut and not a flag flying. Few troops in sight … Cutliffes a sad house but everyone bearing up well. Did what we could and came away.

Curfew lifted for two hours for women only. British families who went to shop in the old city were given food free. In Ronnies Village [village under curfew by troops commanded by friend of her husband] strongly left wing, Greeks have said how shocked they were to hear of shooting.

EOKA Times [*Times of Cyprus*] carries headlines 'In searches three more die' and in small print 'two servicemen's wives shot in Hermes Street'. Press denying it is the work of EOKA and suggest it might be Turks or British, laughable. No Turk would be seen dead in Hermes Street.[59]

One Old Turk told Mrs Somerville not to trust the Greeks and to avoid Hermes Street and felt 'the British too gentle, too democratic. If Germans or Turks one woman shot, they shot ten, twenty and set fire to Varosha.'[60]

At the funeral on 6 October the coffin was carried by six sergeants of the 29 Field Artillery R.A. Wreaths came from all the Famagusta units and the Turks of the city. Harold Macmillan wrote: 'The general feeling in Britain was one of relief. Splendidly as our troops had behaved, nothing is more poignant than the suffering of families bereaved through operations of this kind.'[61]

Even the Orthodox Church had to distance itself from the murder. Makarios's deputy, Bishop Anthimos, in a press conference where he had hoped to lampoon the British forces for wanton revenge on the Greek Cypriots, was forced into a corner, and had to admit the murder of Mrs Cutliffe was 'a monstrous crime' and it was 'inconceivable' that Greeks should shoot English women.[62]

The furore grew. CBS broadcast that no 'evidence had come to light suggesting that the murder was not committed by EOKA', and pointed out Athens radio on the night of the murder, probably before they realised the full implications, said that 'Cypriot Patriots' were responsible. The mayor of Famagusta put up a £5,000 reward for information on the killers: none was forthcoming.[63]

The murder of Mrs Cutliffe seems to have grabbed the imagination of all sides, in a strange way, given all the other horrific murders during the troubles: it was a turning point. Although not publicly, for they still wished to appear united, there was a marked shift by many Greek Cypriot groups away from EOKA, a distancing by the Greek Government, the Church and Makarios. The Greek Prime Minister Averoff wrote to Grivas indicating that EOKA stood in the dock with world opinion and not the British and it was time violence came to an end. The Bishop of Kitium reminded Grivas it was a grave mistake not having warned the British about the end of the ceasefire.[64]

A few days later, Grivas, as if rebelling against the censorship of the Greek world, ordered his men to step up their action.

In the first three weeks of October twenty-three people were killed and dozens wounded. A transport plane in Nicosia Airport was blown up shortly before it was to have been boarded by service people returning to the UK. However, the British were well prepared to take up the challenge.

A week after Mrs Cutliffe's murder Major General Kenneth Darling took over as GOC. Speaking to 1 Para, standing on the back of a jeep, the former airborne soldier declared: 'I'm not interested in live terrorists, only dead ones.' The unit was soon to embark on Operation Filter Tip, which was planned to clear EOKA from the Kyrenia range of mountains.[65] Hugh Grant takes up the story:

> The operation was designed to tackle EOKA on their own terms. Two rifle companies of 1 Para were to infiltrate the Kyrenia range in small groups of five to six men. These groups were to lie up in different selected areas throughout the range and monitor all movement. This information would be fed back by radio to a control command post and then relayed to intelligence in Nicosia. This way a complete picture of all movement in the range would be obtained.[66]

However, to get this number of troops into the mountains without alerting EOKA and sending the terrorists to ground created a problem; this was solved by using the company rest camp on the Kyrenia Coast as a Trojan horse. A company would set off for the coast as if for rest and recreation, but at night the majority would slip away in their small groups for the hills. On the following day the balance of the company in the same amount of vehicles returned to Camp Whittington and the process was repeated with another company.

'On the night we headed for the hills,' continues Hugh:

> we were loaded with all the necessary equipment and rations in bergens and set off about midnight. It was no easy task scaling the steep hillside in total darkness heading by compass for our selected area. After two hours we reached and prepared our hide. When dawn finally broke over the Kyrenian range we saw that we were on a high point overlooking the village of Trimithi and the roads leading from it.
>
> A routine was quickly sorted out and we took stages observing the village and roads with binoculars and logging all movements no matter how unimportant it seemed. Life became understandably a bit tedious, but we realised that it was an important part of the overall operation.[67]

After several days the OPs had gathered sufficient intelligence to mount direct operations against EOKA. The village of Karmi was high on the list for a search.

Just before dawn:

> the village was surrounded and then we moved in giving a nasty early morning call to all males over sixteen. They were rounded up and taken down to an open area in the grounds of the village school. We then mounted a guard on the 200 or so males who sat on the ground in detention. In the early afternoon a police vehicle drew up close to our assembled prisoners.
>
> Inside the jeep was an EOKA informer who had been persuaded to reveal the members of the Karmi cell that he knew. The villagers were paraded one by one in front of the vehicle for the informer to identify them, although at no time was he visible to them.[68]

In this way eight men were identified and taken away. The rest were released but the village was put under curfew. This tactic was used in several of the mountain villages dispersing several EOKA cells.

Lieutenant Colonel F.C. Barton, new CO of 45 Commando, faced intense activity in his first few weeks in command. There were five major incidents in the Troodos Mountains in October.

The police station at Kambos and the forestry station at Platania were burnt down. Also there were three road ambushes. 45 lost one Marine killed, while the Royal Welch Fusiliers, who were under command, lost one killed and five wounded; one terrorist was killed. On 6 October a two-vehicle patrol was fired on; however, the ambush was badly set, one vehicle not being in the 'zone'. That vehicle stopped on hearing the firing and the Marines went forward on foot clearing the ambush position. One Marine was killed by a grenade and two wounded. The terrorist was killed.

On 22 October one Marine was killed when his patrol was ambushed. Lieutenant David Spurling died of wounds on 3 November attacking a hide with his section near Pedhoulas:[69]

> Four Five adopted several new measures: where possible patrols moved out on foot to minimize the chance of vehicle ambush; observation posts

were set up and manned for long periods so that careful checks could be made on the likely enemy routes and hides; and intensive training starting at six-thirty every morning, was carried out concurrently with operations to improve alertness and tactics.[70]

On 15 November an important EOKA member Andreas Georghiou Sofokleous was wounded and captured by a 1 Para patrol while hiding in a well in the village of Ayios Yorgios, although a Para was badly wounded when his section was caught in an ambush between Dhavlos and Kantara.

On 19 November a patrol from D Company recorded the main success of the operation when the leader of EOKA in the Kyrenian Region was killed. Kyriakos Christoforou Matsis was cornered in the cellar of a house in Drikomo along with two other terrorists. They surrendered, but Matsis elected to shoot it out. In a brave but futile last stand he was shot and finished off with a grenade.[71]

Hugh Grant continues with his story:

We based our Company HQ in the coffee house of Trimithi Village. From this base we continued to maintain curfews on nearby villages and mount night time ambushes on the tracks leading from the villages to the high tops so as to cut off any support that the villagers might try to send to any terrorists still at large.

Night ambushes could be boring in the extreme and after the warmth of the day it was surprising how cold it could become. We had one luxury to help pass the long silent hours as we lay chilled to the bone in our ambush positions.

This took the form of a tin of self heating soup. The tin had a central core of some slow burning substance. Once two holes had been pierced in the lid, a match applied to a small wick caused the central core to smoulder slowly, heating the soup in the process. We could shelter under the cover of our ground sheet as we struck the match and then the soup tin could be put to one side to allow the heating process to take part. A further bonus was that you could warm your chilled hands on the slowly heating soup tin. In ten minutes you had a piping hot tin of soup under the stars.

An ambush usually comprised four soldiers and, in addition to our own weapons, we carried a Greener Shotgun into the bargain. In the darkness when an accurate shot might be difficult, the shotgun would hit a wider target area.[72]

A week after the killing of Matsis, Hugh Grant witnessed the Bomb Disposal squad in action in a bungalow outside Ayios Georgios where a bomb had been found in a secret cellar:

> We were called out to guard the premises while Bomb Disposal experts from Nicosia were summoned. The bomb expert had a good long look at it before emerging with his findings.
>
> The bomb had indeed been completed, but was too big to be removed from the cellar. 'Bloody EOKA must be employing an Irish bomb-maker now' was his comment. An observation Paddy Tomkins took strong exception to.
>
> As the house owner had been taken away for questioning, and his family dispersed, the decision was taken to blow the bomb up in situ and the bungalow with it.
>
> We withdrew to a safe distance and the bomb detonated. It was quite a spectacle as the bungalow flew skywards under the force of the explosion …
>
> 'Better here than in some street in Nicosia' was the final comment passed by the mild looking bespectacled Bomb Disposal expert.[73]

Even in the British bases life could be deadly. When a bomb in a NAAFI killed two airmen Governor Foot reversed the policy decision he had made on arriving in Cyprus. He announced the dismissal of more than 5,000 Greeks from MOD establishments and NAAFI facilities. Some were replaced by servicemen's wives. A further 500 volunteers were flown out from the UK, while 18,000 people applied for the jobs in the UK. Thus the British people made sure the troops would not go without their sticky buns and tea.[74]

In his memoirs Grivas complains about the 'dismissal of some thousands of Cypriot workers without notice or compensation', yet without doubt the bombers, or help for the bombers, came from these same people. He was even ready to admit the economy of the island was collapsing with little direct effect on the British.

While EOKA was riddled with informers willing to act against it, Grivas was quick to blame others: 'We must blame the Greek Government, the Archbishop and the Cypriot Intelligentsia. For the last year or more I have been warning the Archbishop that if this treatment is allowed to continue all our secrets will be gradually betrayed.' Grivas was insisting the increase in informers was due to British interrogation techniques, rather than an increasing lack of support for EOKA and a yearning for peace.[75]

In November, Anthony Benson, manager of a Nicosia bank, was shot dead as he left at lunchtime. The authorities, unable to guard everyone, decided to issue side arms to civilians.

Benson's mother had a letter published in the *Cyprus Times*:

'You have taken our only son, a young husband and a very recent father, a man of liberal views and sympathies. Is this a proud record? I beg you to stop this senseless bloodshed.' Benson was the last British Civilian killed in Cyprus during the troubles.[76]

At the end of November the Cyprus question again came before the UN in New York, raised by Greece but this time calling for an independent Cyprus. Averoff made the opening speech, talking of the Cypriots as a people in slavery. Zorlu spoke for Turkey accusing Greece of merely wishing to take over the property of another state. Britain answered that the Macmillan Plan must be accepted or the result might well be partition. In the face of Anglo-Turkish opposition backed by the USA the Greek resolution collapsed. The final UN resolution called for continued efforts to reach a peaceful, just and democratic solution.

Such events usually resulted in orchestrated riots and murder on Cyprus, but this time only a few British cars were burnt, for conciliation was in the air. The governor reprieved several prisoners sentenced to death.

While Greece and Turkey were talking in Paris, at a NATO meeting about Cyprus, on Christmas Eve EOKA declared a truce.[77]

President Eisenhower wrote to Macmillan about this time:

I admire your refusal to be disheartened by recent Cyprus developments and your determination to continue to work toward a settlement of this vastly difficult problem. For our part, we always shall be ready to help whenever and however we appropriately can.[78]

Notes

1. John Reddaway, *Burdened with Cyprus*, p. 105, 'The Foot Plan …'
2. Charles Foley, *Island in Revolt*, p. 174, 'Menderes refused to talk …' and James Pettifer, *The Turkish Labyrinth*, p. 189, 'At a popular level …'
3. Ibid., p. 174, 'The Governors arrival in Ankara …'
4. Foley, *The Memoirs of General Grivas*, pp. 132–3, 'EOKA had meanwhile …'
5. Ibid., p. 112, 'I heard the news …'
6. Panagiotis Dimitrakis, *Military Intelligence in Cyprus*, p. 93, 'Grivas was shocked …'
7. Foley, *Island in Revolt*, p. 178, 'Occasional EOKA reprisals …'
8. Ibid., p. 179, 'EOKA's new tactics …'
9. Joseph Attard, *Britain and Malta*, p. 180, 'More than a deadlock …'
10. Adrian Walker, *Six Campaigns*, p.135–6, 'In March, 1958 …'
11. Auberon Waugh, *Will This Do?*, p. 98, 'We flew to Cyprus …'
12. Ibid., p. 99, 'The nationalist movement …'
13. Ibid., p. 99, 'Life is immensely exciting …'
14. Foley, *The Memoirs of General Grivas*, p. 140, 'But appeasing messages …'
15. Waugh, p. 102, 'When Evelyn Waugh …'
16. Ibid., pp. 102–3, 'Meanwhile the search …'
17. Harold Macmillan, *Riding the Storm*, p. 666, 'During the early months …'
18. Ibid., p. 657, 'The Cyprus tangle …'
19. Ibid., p. 666, 'After much thought …'
20. Ibid., p. 666, 'If we are to …'
21. Ibid., p. 670, 'On 26 June …'
22. Ibid., pp. 669–70, 'To allow time …' and Foley, *Island in Revolt*, pp. 187–8, 'The proposals, henceforth …' and Morgan, *Sweet and Bitter Island*, p. 240, 'Yet despite Foot's liberalism …'
23. Foley, *Island in Revolt*, p. 194, 'Two days …'
24. Morgan, p. 244, 'The spring and summer …'
25. Waugh, pp. 103–4, 'It was a relief …'
26. Foley, p. 194, 'After Guenyeli …'
27. Waugh, p. 104, 'My troop was sent …'
28. Ibid., p. 104, 'The machine gun …'
29. Ibid., p. 108, 'My own memories …'
30. Foley, *The Memoirs of General Grivas*, p. 146, 'Despite the success …'
31. Ibid., pp. 146–7, 'At the same time …'
32. Foley, *Island in Revolt*, p. 202, 'On the road to Famagusta …'
33. Ibid., p. 202, 'Three days later …'
34. Peter Harclerode, *Para*, p. 234, 'Based at the airfield …'
35. Mercier Derrick, *Chronicle of the 20th Century*, p. 816, 'These swift moves …'
36. Ibid., p. 816, 'In the House of Commons …'

37. IWM. The diary of Mrs J. Somerville
38. David Young, *Four Five*, p. 243, 'Fresh outbreaks of violence …'
39. Julian Thompson, *Royal Marines*, p. 442, 'In July 1956 …'
40. Macmillan, p. 681, 'We went off again …'
41. Ibid., p. 682, 'The battalion was commanded …'
42. Foley, p. 206, 'The announcement was …'
43. Ibid., p. 209, 'Here a great step …'
44. Richard G.M.L. Stiles, *Mayhem in the Med*, p. 235.
45. Foley, p. 209, 'Even the American community …'
46. Ibid., p. 207, 'When at last …'
47. Ibid., p. 210, 'The place was …'
48. Ibid., pp. 210–11, 'The last of the summer visitors …'
49. Ibid., pp. 211–12, 'Mr Gaitskell disowned …'
50. Reddaway, pp. 115–16, 'The Archbishop used the Labour Party politician …'
51. Foley, *The Memoirs of General Grivas*, pp. 169–70, 'On the evening the radio bulletin …'
52. Ibid., p. 164, 'I now began preparations …'
53. Dave Cranston, britains-smallwars.com, The murder of Mrs Catherine Cutliffe
54. IWM. The diary of Mrs J. Somerville
55. Hugh Grant, *A Game of Soldiers*, p. 81, 'On Wednesday 1st October …'
56. Ibid., p. 83, 'It had been a rough …'
57. Foley, pp. 169–70, 'On the evening of the radio bulletin …'
58. Ibid., pp. 169–70
59. IWM, Somerville
60. Ibid.
61. Macmillan, p. 693, 'The general feeling …'
62. Foley, *Island in Revolt*, p. 215, 'I asked the bishop …'
63. Ibid., pp. 215–16, 'Instead they broadcast …'
64. Foley, *The Memoirs of General Grivas*, p. 170, 'Here, if ever …'
65. Grant, p. 88, 'He stated that …'
66. Ibid., p. 91, 'This was the background …'
67. Ibid., p. 91, 'On the night …'
68. Ibid., p. 93, 'By this time …'
69. Stiles, *Mayhem in the Med*, pp. 254–7
70. Young, *Four Five*, pp. 244–5
71. Foley, pp. 177–8, 'Now, at the start …'
72. Grant, pp. 93–4, 'We based our company …'
73. Ibid., pp. 95–6, 'A week or so after …'
74. Robin Neillands, *A Fighting Retreat*, pp. 289–90, 'The EOKA campaign …' and Macmillan, p. 688, 'On 10th November …'
75. Foley, pp. 176–7, 'The last pretence …'
76. Foley, *Island in Revolt*, pp. 223–4, 'The authorities decided …'
77. Macmillan, p. 689, 'But just before Christmas …'
78. Ibid., p. 689, 'In the course of a long…'

10

1959 Agreement in Room 325

On 15 December 1958, 45 Commando Royal Marines left Cyprus for Malta after its final tour of duty. The unit spent a total of nearly twenty-one months on active service on Cyprus, mainly in the mountains. During this period the Commando made some 800 arrests, 70 of whom were found to be hard-core terrorists. Five terrorists were also killed while the unit lost eight killed and some twenty wounded, most of whom returned to the colours. 45 Commando took part in eighty major operations.[1]

Right up to the end, 45 Commando had been actively dominating the ground. On the evening of 25 November a patrol from X Troop operating in the area of Dhymes to the east of Pano Amiandos challenged two men who tried to run away; one managed to get away in the gathering darkness but the other was shot dead. He was Savvas Rotsides, a man Grivas called a 'veteran guerrilla'.[2] 40 Commando did one further tour of Cyprus during the spring of 1959 before returning to Malta and 3 Commando Brigade.

On 14 December it was 1 Para that relieved 45 Commando. Hugh Grant recalls that winter in the Troodos Mountains:

January saw winter break over the Troodos with a vengeance and it was reckoned to be one of the coldest on record with heavy snow falls. As Operation Mares Nest got under way we were to provide a tactical HQ for an infantry brigade. The weather worsened turning really cold and windy.

During this spell of bad weather, we constantly patrolled and manned observation hides and once again gave due thanks for tins of self heating soup.

One slight diversion was ski patrol training carried out on the heights of Mount Olympus. D Company was based in the valleys of Agros and Alona an area with a reputation for being openly hostile and giving ongoing support to the hard bitten and active mountain terrorist groups. 1 Platoon survived an all-out attack on the police station at Agros. Some weeks later 3 Platoon seized a quantity of explosives in Agros and a full riot developed as they closed in on the terrorist hide. A large and angry stone-throwing crowd assembled and tried to run down fourteen members of the platoon. The tense situation developed further until 3 Platoon fixed bayonets and finally convinced them that it would be in their best interests to disperse.[3]

In the guerrilla war that took place on Cyprus there was no victory or defeat, even if there is such a notion in this type of conflict. There is a clear indication that if the British had arrested or killed Grivas, and thus cut off the head of EOKA, the likely result would have been EOKA sprouting several smaller heads, leading to civil war within EOKA within a civil war. Special Branch under Sir John Prendergast had been getting close to Grivas, via his links to the Orthodox Church. Grivas needed to be in contact with 'Makarios and others in the church circles to make known his views on the resolution of the Cyprus question'.[4] From the early days of the insurgency the elimination of Grivas had been code-named Operation Sunshine.

In February 1959 the Black Watch had been searching for him in his old hideouts in the Troodos Mountains during Operation Mare's Nest with no luck. That month the Greek Foreign Minister Averoff was in London discussing the Cyprus situation. Special Branch had located the house Grivas was hiding in at Limassol.

Peter Wright of MI5 arrived on Cyprus on 17 January 1959, after studying Bill Magan's (Director of E Branch Colonial Affairs) report on the conflict. His first step was 'to place a secure telephone tap on Makarios's palace. We were certain that Makarios, and probably EOKA at certain times, used the line secure in the knowledge that their post office spies would automatically alert them to the presence of a tap.'

However, there were ways around this by tapping the overhead cables that led into the Archbishop's palace 'using a radio transmitter which took power from the telephone circuit to radiate the signal out to our waiting receiver a mile or two away'. John Wyke, one of the best MI6 technical men, was brought in to do this. 'The whole operation was fraught with danger. Wyke had to climb a telephone pole in total darkness, in full view of the road, which was constantly patrolled by the armed bodyguards of Makarios and EOKA guerrillas.' Yet he pulled it off making a connection into the telephone cable. Wright was at the bottom of the pole passing tools up to him via lines it took them two hours freezing at the slightest noise but the line 'gave us the essential base coverage of Makarios'.[5] The first part of Operation Sunshine had gone well; Wright estimated it would take 'six months to complete'.[6]

However, on 16 February Prendergast had to fly to London to get authority to move against Grivas. This was while Anglo-Greek–Turkish negotiations were going on at Lancaster House. Macmillan wrote in his diary: '17 February Cyprus in the balance. The Governments seem pretty firm. The Archbishop is "making reservations". Meetings all the morning and afternoon. I expect the Greek and Turkish Prime Ministers today.'[7]

It's said Macmillan asked Averoff what would happen if Grivas was killed. His reply was a collapse of negotiations and renewal of violence on the island. Whatever did take place, Prime Minister Macmillan cancelled Operation Sunshine.[8] Peter Wright said: 'The carpet was roughly pulled from under our feet, and the entire Sunshine plan was aborted overnight. Magan was furious; particularly when Grivas emerged from the precise area we had foreseen and was flown to Greece, ready to continue to exert a baleful influence on the island.'[9]

Evangelos Averoff, the Greek Foreign Minister and Fatin Zorlu, his Turkish opposite number, had got on rather well during the November UN debate on Cyprus. Macmillan saw Averoff as a man of honour and reliable, while Zorlu could be rough and tough, 'but with an occasional gleam of humour'. Oh, they had flung the expected insults at one another, but more was salvaged this time and they looked forward to further talks at the NATO meeting in Paris.[10]

In the Paris meeting just before Christmas the British Foreign Secretary, Selwyn Lloyd, was approached by Averoff and Zorlu and asked whether Britain would see advantage in their pursuing an agreement on Cyprus, under which the UK would hold the bases in full sovereignty and the two communities would enjoy a measure of autonomy in an independent Cyprus. The British jumped at the chance to have Greeks and Turks talking in this way and working together, but did not interfere; they were told 'Her Majesty's Government welcomed their new initiative and wished them every success'.[11]

A few weeks later in Zurich on 10 February the Greek and Turkish premiers announced full agreement on Cyprus. Another meeting was convened in London, this time to involve all interested parties, including the Cypriots. Would it be possible, after all, to get all three balls in all three cups at the same time?

From the Eastern Mediterranean delegates arrived in London to look at what Governor Foot called 'the Miracle of Zurich'. Archbishop Makarios stayed at Dorchester and even at this late hour he was trying to get further concessions from Averoff and Zorlu, who had now replaced the British as the main negotiators.[12]

The conference was to be staged at Lancaster House on 18 February but was looked on by many as a mere formality about minor details. On the night before the meeting the airliner bringing Prime Minister Karamanlis from Athens was diverted to Gatwick due to fog. Ten minutes later the Viscount carrying Prime Minister Menderes from Turkey crashed on landing at Gatwick. Menderes escaped with shock and bruises from the wreckage where several passengers were killed.[13]

Makarios brought forty-one people in his delegation to Lancaster House. He forced a twenty-four-hour extension of the conference 'after a demonstration of brinkmanship which left delegates guessing over his intentions'.[14] At the conference, the next day, again Makarios tried to object to the plan which amounted to power-sharing between Greek and Turkish Cypriots and powers of veto for a Turkish Cypriot Vice President on some aspects of foreign affairs and defence. At about 5 p.m. the Greek and Turkish delegates were 'fed up' and wanted to go home.[15] However, Selwyn Lloyd got a full meeting called at 7 p.m. Once more, the UK,

Greek and Turkish Governments expressed their agreement with the Cyprus plan. Even the Turkish Cypriots agreed. The Archbishop stated his objections, which were all concentrated on the Zurich agreement – that is, on the Greek–Turkish Constitution and power-sharing for Cyprus.

The meeting was adjourned at 9.15, but Selwyn Lloyd's late calling of it meant it was now too late to go home; everybody stayed in London.[16] A certain amount of arm-twisting went on with Makarios during the night and next morning. Greece warned him, and even the British Labour Party, if his delegation did not support the Zurich deal, then they would wash their hands of Cyprus. What in the end convinced the Archbishop to accept the agreement that night has been the source of much speculation; some suggest that he was 'blackmailed by MI5's allegation about his sexuality'.[17] At last Makarios advised his delegates to accept. At 9 a.m. on 19 February it was announced that agreement had been reached on Cyprus. The agreement was signed that day in Room 325 of the London Clinic where the Turkish Prime Minister, Mr Menderes, was taken to recover after the crash at Gatwick. It was the first time Macmillan had met Makarios:

> I had quite an interesting talk with Archbishop Makarios, whom I saw for the first time. He was not at all as I had pictured him, I had thought of him as a big man like Archbishop Damaskass. Not at all, five foot eight inches or so at the most. Good hands, flexible and artistic. I would have said agreeable, subtle, intelligent, but not strong. This explains, perhaps, his hesitations.[18]

Macmillan says it was a tight squeeze in the room 'into which a mass of people forced themselves, including a Foreign Office Messenger with a fine silver ink pot. We all signed and after some little talk with Prime Minister Menderes withdrew.'[19]

He thought the Greeks delighted, even though the bargain was not the best they could have obtained. 'They could have done better by accepting the Radcliffe Plan or Macmillan Plan. But all our friends like the ambassador and others, are delighted that the long Anglo-Greek dispute is over and that our old friendship can be renewed.'[20]

However, on Cyprus Grivas was far from happy. He had been kept largely in the dark about the agreement and wrote in his memoirs: 'Such, then, was the surrender which I was expected to acclaim as the vindication of our struggle and Averoff tried later to make the Greek Parliament believe EOKA was represented among the Archbishop's advisers who agreed to it.'[21]

EOKA's political and propaganda chief, Tassos Papadopoulos, was present and voted against the agreement; however, those in favour won twenty-seven votes to eight.[22] Now even Grivas realised he had to give up the cause he had struggled so long with, although he did consider 'turning Greek against Greek'. But this would mean 'endlessly prolonged bloodshed, but no final victory for either side. In the end I decided with a heavy heart that I must call a final cease-fire, leaving the Archbishop and his friends to implement the agreement as best they could in the absence of my approval.' Hardly the words of a victor.[23]

Mike Webb, who did his National Service with the Royal Signals from 1958 to 1959, witnessed the transition from near civil war to peace. In 1958 'there were bombs going off everywhere'. And all the staff were changed at the NAAFI after attempts by Greek Cypriot staff to blow it up. He liked Cyprus when he first arrived, even after getting 'burnt to a cinder' after using Brylcreem as suntan lotion: 'But I quite liked it, because we didn't do a hell of a lot for the first few days; just lazed about the beaches.' After the ceasefire Mike appeared to have a fine time:

> After the troubles were over and the barbed wire started coming down things got a bit easier. For instance, you could go out without being armed. The last six months of my service, that would be 1959, after the EOKA campaign was over, we used to go out looking for trouble. To Nicosia and to Famagusta and places like that. Each troop would go out, and come back with a souvenir; it was a sort of competition. What you would do is get tanked a little bit, and grab one of these Greek flags, which was on a massive pole fixed to a wall, and you'd pull it off and all these Greeks would come round, thumping you about, and you'd walk off with the flag.
>
> While the troubles were on, and even afterwards, we never really thought about why we were there in political terms.

As far as I can remember, the Greeks were trying to chuck the British out, and trying to chuck the Turks out as well. Of course, because of this we were friendly with the Turks and not the Greeks, and that's all we thought about the situation really.[24]

After the ceasefire most of 1 Para set off for home in February. However, Hugh Grant was part of the rear party left to tidy up Camp Whittington:

One morning as the day yawned ahead of us, I asked if anybody wanted to go with me for a jaunt over the Kyrenia range to visit Bellapais Village for the last time. I had only one taker John 'Jenny' Wren a fellow C Company member.

Jenny and I set off just after breakfast and crossed the Mesaoria, passing one or two herds of tinkling sheep, watched over by their patient shepherds. They looked at us without any show of emotion as we passed and did not return our greeting.

Grant and his companion wondered if they even knew about the peace talks:

We walked on and once more scaled the crest. Down the steep slopes of the other side we headed for Bellapais. The village still slumbered in the sunshine as we picked our way down the street to a table under the Tree of Idleness where we ordered a welcome couple of Keo beers. The villagers who occupied the other tables studiously ignored us, even when we acknowledged them. After a while, to our surprise, one of the men rose from a table and sat down beside us with his coffee. He turned out to be the local school teacher with an excellent command of English.

Why were we here he asked, as he understood that the Paratroopers had all gone back to Britain. We explained about our presence on rear party and our wish to have a last look at Bellapais.

Talk soon got on to the forthcoming peace settlement and what it would mean for the island. It will be a compromise said the teacher. Cypriots want independence and Britain wants a Middle East Military Base and both will get what they want. In his opinion this could have been thrashed out a decade before and avoided all the bloodshed and bitterness on both sides. We had to admit that we could find no fault in his argument.

I asked him if he had any fears for the future and had the Turkish minority anything to fear from independence. He said the Turkish interests would be protected in any agreement but his personal worry was that Makarios would reward some hard core terrorists with high position in the new administration, who might not share the same agenda with the wily Archbishop.[25]

On the 1 March Hugh Grant and the remainder of 1 Para returned to the UK. On 17 March under amnesty Grivas left Cyprus after a short press conference, which Charles Foley attended, who asked him what he thought of the British now. 'Nowhere in Greece,' he replied, 'was there anyone more pro-British than I. But what could I do? We could not swallow the bitter medicine you forced on us.'[26]

Strange words, in a way, for a man who had spent most of his life away from the island of his birth and was going into exile again. Shortly after this Grivas left Cyprus aboard a Greek Air Force plane.

EOKA gave up a token quantity of arms to indicate their surrender, while terrorists in prison were released under amnesty. The EOKA troubles were over – well, at least for the time being.

As for the British, many wondered why they had bothered. Tim Wilson of 40 Commando wrote: '… it was with mixed feelings that one realised that some of those who had been our "enemies" and whom we had spent dozens of sleepless nights and physically exacting days searching for, were now members of the Government.'[27]

Gordon Burt, who served with the Paras, observed: 'It left a funny taste in one's mouth at that time to see these people who supported terrorists coming to power.'[28]

It may have seemed to these men they had suffered some kind of defeat through no fault of their own. However, time would tell the only real losers were the people of Cyprus.

Transfer of power took place formally on 16 August, when Archbishop Makarios was invested as President of the Republic of Cyprus. In December an election took place in which Makarios was returned as president, although the opposing Democratic Union candidate pooled 33 per cent of the vote.

In his acceptance speech of 14 December 1959 the Archbishop first praised the 'heroes and martyrs' of the liberation struggle, mentioning Colonel Grivas, the EOKA leader. Then he insisted that fanaticism and antagonism must cease. Greeks and Turks must work together, he said, 'in a spirit of great sincerity, with great respect for the natural rights of each other'. Fine words but it remained to be seen whether the people of Cyprus could respect the natural rights of each other.[29]

In Cyprus itself there were many reservations and outspoken criticism within the Greek Cypriot community. Soon it was called a 'rogues deal'.[30] And as time went by 'the idea took root that the Zurich and London agreements were a disgraceful betrayal of the Greek Cypriots by Britain, Greece, and Turkey and this denunciation came to be expressed in increasingly extreme language'.[31]

At home in Britain, in November Harold Macmillan – 'Supermac' – won another general election, the third in a row for the Conservative Party, in which he re-ran the slogan 'You've never had it so good'. One of the new Tory MPs was Margaret Thatcher.

In Macmillan's utopian classless Britain you could buy a new Mini – Austin or Morris version – for around £500 with purchase tax. However, within days of the launch an unofficial strike at the British Motor Corporation (BMC) halted production of the new car.

Notes

1. David Young, *Four Five*, pp. 247–8, 'The bandit in Malaya …'
2. Charles Foley, *The Memoirs of General Grivas*, p. 183, 'The two groups …'
3. Hugh Grant, *A Game of Soldiers*, p. 104, 'January saw winter …'
4. Panagiotis Dimitrakis, *Military Intelligence in Cyprus*, p. 99, 'By late 1958 …'
5. Peter Wright, *Spycatcher*, p. 156, 'The first step …'
6. Ibid., p. 157, 'I began work …'
7. Harold Macmillan, *Riding the Storm*, p. 694 '16 February …'
8. Dimitrakis, p. 99, 'Prendergast was required …'
9. Wright, p. 157, 'The carpet …'
10. Macmillan, p. 699, 'There were, as was only …'
11. Ibid., pp. 689–90, 'Although friendly messages …'
12. Foley, *Island in Revolt*, p. 232, 'Foot with journalistic …'
13. Macmillan, p. 694, 'Just as I was leaving …'
14. Tabitha Morgan, *Sweet and Bitter Island*, p. 252, 'Makarios, who had bought …'
15. Macmillan, p. 695, 'At the same time …'

16. Ibid., p. 695, 'Selwyn Lloyd, seeing the way ...'
17. Morgan, p. 252
18. Macmillan, p. 697, 'After this we went ...'
19. Ibid., p. 698, 'We were taken ...'
20. Ibid., p. 698, 'The Greeks are delighted ...'
21. Foley, *The Memoirs of General Grivas*, p. 192, 'What was I to ...'
22. Ibid., p. 192, 'Such, then, was the surrender ...'
23. Ibid., pp. 198–9, 'The time had come ...'
24. Adrian Walker, *Six Campaigns*, pp. 156–8, 'I must say ...'
25. Grant, pp. 107–8, 'One morning as ...'
26. Foley, *Island in Revolt*, p. 236, 'I asked what he thought ...'
27. LTA Colonel Tim Wilson 6/9/2000
28. LTA Gordon Burt 11/10/2000
29. Derrik Mercer (ed.), *Chronicle of the 20th Century*, p. 837, 'Thousands of people ...'
30. S. Panteli, *A New History of Cyprus*, p. 341; John Reddaway, *Burdened with Cyprus*, p. 125, 'However on Cyprus ...'
31. Ibid., p. 125

11

ANYWHERE'S BETTER THAN HERE 1960–1973

On a blisteringly hot day in August 1960 a small convoy of cars containing the last British Governor of Cyprus and his entourage made its way across the Mesaoria Plain between Nicosia and Famagusta. Off the coast of the ancient sea port waited a British destroyer to take Sir Hugh Foot, later Lord Caradon, away. The British had ruled Cyprus for just eighty-two years, a mere blinking of the eye compared to other foreign rulers.[1]

Yet in a sense the British have never left, only given up power in the majority of the island, for 99 sq. miles remain British in the Sovereign Bases. Negotiations over the size of the SBAs were lengthy. It was the only thing the Archbishop had left to talk about where he had any power. Macmillan appointed his 'son-in-law the staunch imperialist Julian Amery' to take charge for Britain.[2] The result was that independence was delayed several months. So Britain retained the two bases of Akrotiri and Dhekelia and smaller installations like the RAF radar dome on Mount Olympus in the Troodos Mountains, and antenna arrays in Ayios Nikolaos near Famagusta. But there are no boundaries in the SBAs, no barbed wire, people come and go virtually as they please, Cypriot farmers grow their crops on much of the land apart, that is, in the airfields and barracks. Who knows? Perhaps in the future the British will even give this up?

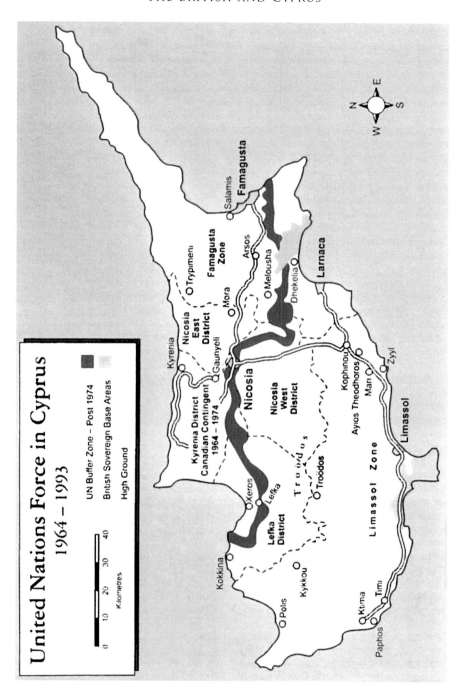

UN Forces Cyprus Map

It appears today the troubles of Cyprus could never be justified. For the agreement out of which came the Republic of Cyprus, a nation state within the Commonwealth, was much the same as that offered by Britain in 1955.

The Cyprus Emergency had cost the lives of some 505 people in four years; 156 British servicemen had died and fifty-one EOKA terrorists, yet by far the largest group of deaths lay with the Greek Cypriots, many of whom were murdered by EOKA in cold blood, and that total with any certainty will never be known.

Even before the British handover of power, the future was full of foreboding. Suha Faiz had returned to Cyprus in the spring of 1958; a year later he served the Interim Council of Ministers. This consisted of Makarios, Dr Kuchuk, leader of the Turkish Cypriots, plus six other Greeks and three other Turks. This body's weekly meetings were intended as an apprenticeship for future Government of the island. Two secretaries served this council, one Greek and one Turkish: Suha Faiz was the latter:

> Week by week I saw regularly all its members. And at close quarters, the chamber where the meetings took place was barely fifteen feet wide and about twenty-five feet long. My desk was only slightly more than an arm's length behind and to the right of Makarios. Governor Foot had him on his right, with Kuchuk on his left. Two of the future Greek Ministers known EOKA terrorists …[3]
>
> At these meetings there was a complete absence of even the slightest evidence from Makarios in word or demeanour, to suggest any intention sincerely to work in true cooperation, much less in partnership with the Turkish side.[4]

To him the Constitution of the new Republic was a sham, and sooner or later the Greeks would have Enosis. Thus early in 1960 Suha left Cyprus again fearing for his home land.[5]

Mary-Pat Lennard recalls one Greek Cypriot friend who was greatly upset when she and her husband left in 1961, confiding to her: 'Why are the British deserting us? We Greeks and Turks in this island will never agree but at least with the British as referee in the ring we'll box ourselves reasonably fairly. But with you gone both sides will use every dirty trick in the book.'[6]

Departing officials were offered generous terms. After suffering years of poor salaries resulting often in uninterested and uninspired British administrators, now they were offered terms 'more generous than those of any other colonial administration in the period of decolonisation'.[7] Even short-term staff and 'ordinary British residents' received compensation. George Meikle, who had been the colony's deputy chief police officer, received £10,000, which was, as his wife Jean remembered, 'a lot of money in those days'.[8]

The years 1960–63 on Cyprus were good for the British. Colin Robinson takes up the story:

> I enlisted into the Army in February 1960 and after training was posted to Cyprus in August of that year. I was part of a draft of fifty-five men all but five of whom were National Servicemen. The call-up for NS had ceased in 1958 and these were National Servicemen who had had their service deferred for a variety of reasons.[9]

On 31 December 1960 the last British National Servicemen received their call-up cards. The last intake was 2,049; 1,999 for the Army and 50 for the RAF, the Royal Navy never having taken large numbers. Since the scheme began in 1939 5,300,000 men went through the rigours of National Service:[10]

> Most of us were destined for HQ Middle East Land Forces. The EOKA campaign was not long ended, both barbwire and security bunkers were still much in evidence but the island was peaceful and the Cypriot people very pro-British and welcoming despite the recent past.[11]

Colin was billeted in Episkopi Barracks with its large Army garrison and some RAF personnel. The summer working routine which lasted most of the year gave plenty of time off for sport and leisure. 'I became interested in horses, learnt to ride and I remained in Episkopi until about July 1962 when I was posted to Dhekelia. I continued to ride and play polo, including taking part in a race for service personnel at Nicosia Racecourse. I was supposed to be in Cyprus for three years but was short-toured and returned to the UK in January 1963, in the middle of a very harsh winter.'

Little did he know, less than a year later he would return to Cyprus in startlingly different circumstances.[12]

Lieutenant Colonel Wilde of the survey battalion Royal Engineers arrived in Cyprus in May 1960:

> I was in Cyprus for seventeen months, it was a pleasant posting. We did mostly staff work and the mapping of the UK Bases which were still being negotiated with the new Cypriot Government. Of course the troubles with the Greeks were finished and we had a great social life and there were all sorts of sports. The British Community was large with married quarters in Limassol and Episkopi, I suppose we were self contained really almost insulated from what was going on, but you could move about the island freely.[13]

As the British basked in this idyllic lifestyle in the twilight of Empire the rest of Cyprus, after independence, descended into anarchy. In the first three years there was a peace of sorts between the two communities although both EOKA and the TMT remained in place; also there were Greek and Turkish mainland troops now on the island allowed under the Zurich Treaty. The 70:30 ratio between Greeks and Turks was supposed to run throughout Government but proved impossible to work in the civil service or the Army. The latter was never set up along such lines; instead Makarios eventually established the all-Greek National Guard.[14]

For much of 1962 Cyprus had no uniform income tax or customs laws. The Turks had obstructed them in retaliation for Greek foot-dragging on the implementation of separate municipalities for the five largest towns which was another concession to the Turkish Cypriots from colonial times and Zurich.

When anybody in the two communities tried to bridge the gaps they put their lives in danger. In April 1962, Ahmet Gurkan and Ayhon Hikmet, two Turkish Cypriot politicians who backed co-operation, were murdered by TMT gunmen. By 1963 the young Republic's Government on the Greek side was full of EOKA men, who increasingly refuted the 1960 Constitution as an agreement forced upon them. The Turks for their part went to the Supreme Court over the number of EOKA men in Government.[15]

The Court ruled in their favour but the Greek Cypriots refused to accept the judgement, which prompted the judges to resign. Polycarpos Yiorkadjis, Minister of the Interior, a former EOKA gunman, controller of the islands security forces announced: 'There is no place in Cyprus for anyone who is not Greek.'[16] Even Makarios declared: 'Unless this small Turkish community, forming part of the Turkish race which has been the terrible enemy of Hellenism, is expelled, the duty of the heroes of EOKA can never be considered as terminated.'[17]

Toward the end of the year Makarios announced proposals to change the Constitution and remove the Turkish Cypriots' right of veto. The armed groups of both sides prepared for war. It was apparent that both sides had not gone into Government to try to make the Constitution work.[18]

On 21 December fighting between the two communities broke out. EOKA and the TMT were both openly on the streets shooting at each other. Throughout Cyprus the Turks began to erect barricades preparing for a siege. Although Makarios and Dr Kuchuk met in the presidential palace, the old governor's mansion for talks, and invited to the meeting representatives from the USA and the UK, it was all too late, for the leaders had lost control of their followers. Nicos Sampson was already broadcasting on the Government radio, CBC, to his supporters to collect weapons from police stations and attack their Turkish neighbours.[19]

The EOKA men were soon joined by the 950 Greek Army soldiers on the island using mortars and heavy machine guns against the Turkish enclaves. The 650 Turkish soldiers in Cyprus soon blocked the main road from Nicosia to Kyrenia. Turkey now directly took a hand, sending jet fighter aircraft to support Turkish ground forces with massive fire power. Appeals for a ceasefire from the island's guarantor powers, Britain, Greece, and Turkey was accepted by Makarios. Just over three years from giving up power British troops, from the SBAs, took up positions between the warring factions, under the command of Major General Peter Young.[20]

By New Year's Day 1964 a 'Green Line' had been established between the two sides in Nicosia. The British troops had no powers other than their own common sense and verbal persuasion and could only use their arms in self-defence. The result of the fighting was that 30,000 Turkish

Cypriots had fled from 103 villages in the four days of fighting. It was to this situation Colin Robinson returned in 1964:

> In late 1963 I volunteered for service with the Airborne forces and started my pre-parachute course in December 1963. I and the others on the course were sent home on Christmas leave as usual. On New Year's Day we received telegrams ordering us to report back to our units, the reason being the breakout of fighting on Cyprus. As I had only left Cyprus twelve months before, after a two and a half year tour, I was keen to finish my Para training. I opted with others to remain on P Company. The Brigade, with 1 Para deployed to Cyprus in early January 1964.[21]

1 Para, commanded by Lieutenant Colonel Pat Thursby initially moved to Dhekelia. It spent two weeks there, patrolling Paphos and Nicosia. Late in February it took over Nicosia from battalions of the Gloucestershire Regiment and the Rifle Brigade. D Company took over the Neapolis area while C Company had responsibility for Trakonas. Support Company took over a flour mill in the Turkish District. A Company took over the area of Kokkina Tremeloix, a Turkish enclave.[22]

Soon after this, C Company had to rush to the aid of British civilians working in the tin mine at Limni near Paphos who were trapped there by another flare-up in the fighting. RAF Whirlwind helicopters evacuated the civilians once the Paras were there. Shortly after C Company withdrew to Nicosia taking over the area of Ayios Nicholaos which had largely been deserted by Greeks and Turks, but the day the company arrived there was an outbreak of heavy fighting which left many bodies in the streets.

Support Company was rushed to Limassol in another incident where some British families were trapped in their homes between the warring factions. Here the Paras threatened to open fire on both sides which did have the desired effect of stopping the fighting.[23] Colin Robinson continues:

> By the time I arrived in Cyprus the situation was quieter but there was still huge tension between the Greeks and Turks and still some killing by both sides. I was serving with the HQ 16 Parachute Brigade. The HQ had taken over the Nicosia Club for expatriates living in Nicosia. The Club was on

the Green Line, the line which was deemed to be the border separating the Greek and Turkish communities.

On a number of occasions during the next two months we stood-to as the Greeks and Turks attacked each other, with ourselves in our trenches taking cover, helpless spectators as the shots went over our heads.

On one occasion half a dozen of us, off duty, were playing cricket in the grounds of the Nicosia Club, when we came under fire from the second floor of a building overlooking the club. We took cover, two of us behind the large cricket pitch roller, until we were sure that the firing, which was only a few shots, had ceased.

A patrol of the HQ defence platoon, with Para Royal Military Police deployed to the incident. They discovered several Greek males with automatic weapons in the building. They stated the shooting had been an 'accident'. It was almost certainly not an 'accident' but an attempt to frighten us, which to a large extent succeeded.[24]

While the British squaddies did their best in another thankless task, the NATO Allies tried to find a solution. Turkey and Greece were both members and their constant feuding over Cyprus was not good for unity. Britain recommended a NATO 'Peace Keeping Force' with the USA committing troops to it. Makarios rejected the plan, wanting Cyprus to remain non-aligned, while Russia's Nikita Khrushchev accused the West of attempting 'occupation by NATO armed forces'.[25]

In February 1964, the British, not wishing to remain in the middle, having had enough of the situation in the 1950s, handed 'the Cyprus problem' to the United Nations. John Reddaway thought the reaction was:

not surprising that Ministers in London quailed before the prospect of being drawn back into the morass of a renewed armed conflict in Cyprus. Perhaps they ought nevertheless to have had the courage to act and, by re-imposing the 1960 settlement, so rashly thrown aside, to have saved the Greek Cypriots from themselves and the Island from eventual partition.[26]

Early in March the 'United Nations Force in Cyprus' UNFICYP was founded under the command of Lieutenant General Prem Singh Gyani from India, who was appointed on 6 March 1964.[27] Because of political and financial problems of the troop contributing countries the force did not come into operation until 27 March when the UNFICYP began its three-month ongoing mandate. However, in the near forty years of UNFICYP the British have supplied the majority of the troops to it.[28]

Colin Robinson joined the UNFICYP force in April 1964:

> When we came under the command of the UN, much to our disgust and over our strenuous objections, we were forced to give up our hard earned maroon berets to wear the light blue beret of the UN. We were the first British Troops ever to have worn the UN Beret. Because of our strong objections to giving up our beret, a unique concession was given and we were allowed to wear a maroon patch behind the UN cap badge, identifying us as Airborne Soldiers. We remained in Nicosia until July 1964 when we were replaced by a Canadian Regiment and returned to the UK.[29]

On the whole the UNFICYP conducted a difficult task – well, when allowed to do so – for Makarios they became a tool to use against Turkey. As long as the Blue Berets were there Turkey would not exercise its rights under the Zurich Treaty, and he could run Cyprus as he liked with the Turkish Cypriots having no recourse. However, it rather backfired, for the Turkish Cypriots created their own enclaves where the Republic of Cyprus had no power. It was no concern of UNFICYP if the Turkish Cypriots chose to ignore unconstitutional laws after their leaders had been ousted from Government posts.

Only twice in the ten years from 1964 to 1974 were there major outbreaks of fighting between the two sides. In August 1964, 1,500 Greek Cypriots attacked the Turkish enclave of Kokkina on the north coast, under the command of now General George Grivas, who had returned in June to take over the National Guard.[30]

Makarios had reached agreement in 1964 with the Greek Government whereby Greece sent large numbers of troops to Cyprus. The actual number is not known 'but the likely figure was around 10,000'. He denounced the treaty of alliance with Turkey, which allowed the

Turks to station troops on the island, on the pretext those soldiers refused to stay in barracks.[31]

Swedish soldiers of UNFICYP were pushed aside despite bitter protests. Again Turkish aircraft from the mainland supported the Turkish Cypriots, causing heavy casualties in the Greek forces. Both sides once again were forced to accept a UN Security Council ceasefire.

Enosis retained a strong appeal for some Greek Cypriots; however, there were people within that community, a growing number, who felt it unrealistic 'closing doors to other ideas and aspirations'. Many were enjoying economic prosperity and a better life, 'in which abstract ideals such as Enosis had lost its appeal'.[32]

The second came in November 1967 when, after disarming UNFICYP soldiers, the Greek National Guard attacked Turkish Cypriots living in Kofinou and Ayios Theodoros near Larnaca.

Atrocities took place; the operation was again under the direction of Grivas. This time the Ankara Government declared to the world unless the Greek Cypriots withdrew, Turkey would go to war which would 'go beyond the borders of the island'. Within hours the Greek Cypriots were withdrawing, and Grivas was again thrown off the island along with 12,000 mainland Greek soldiers on Cyprus who were recalled to Greece. The Athens Government told Makarios their primary interest was good relations within NATO and with the USA and not Enosis with Cyprus. Makarios was never to trust the Greek Government again, which was just as well given later events.[33]

In 1972 the writer Colin Thubron undertook a 600-mile walk through Cyprus: the result, his acclaimed book *Journey into Cyprus*. The island it describes with its mosaic of Greek and Turkish villages is gone for ever. He also witnessed during that summer the signs of the inexorable slide toward division. Today sadly it would be impossible to undertake such a journey.

Thubron came across many relics of bygone Empires, including the British. On the wild and remote Akamas Peninsula, named after one of Aphrodite's lovers, he found a British military training area, 'abandoned a decade ago', an old rusted sign informed: 'Keep out when red flags are flying as firing is then in progress. Do not touch anything it may … and kill you.'[34]

I too have walked Aphrodite's Trail around the peninsula, now marked by a Forestry Department nature trail. The views in this top left-hand corner of the island are spectacular. Here I literally tripped over some squaddy's long-lost 'hexi cooker' half-buried in the ground, its vicious points, on which you rest a mess tin, like some miniature man-trap.

It was further to the east beyond Lachi, with its sunken ancient break-water, in Polis that Thubron came across signs of impending doom. The village had been strafed by Turkish jets in 1964. Walls were alive with slogans 'Up Enosis', 'Bring back Dighenis'.[35] He asked a Greek Cypriot villager what had happened. 'Nothing', was his reply; the village too was deserted. 'Empty? Yes like a rotten melon, when a man dies his sons go away to Nicosia, abroad, anywhere. Anywhere's better than here.'[36]

In Bellapais he came across Lawrence Durrell's Mr Kollis, who pointed out the gardens in the Gothic abbey he had laid out and looked after. The cypresses he had planted thirty years before. He had found skeletons there when planting the trees; who they were he did not know.[37]

On the Karpas Peninsula, Thubron one day '… crept into Trikomo, the home town of General Grivas slogans for Enosis blazed on every wall, and I noticed that the engraved initials of the British Sovereign had been hacked from the concrete freshwater fountains …' Still then, and now, to be found all over the island.[38]

In the summer of 1973 Vyv Walters visited the island on something of a 'hush hush mission'. 'Prior to the unrest in Cyprus (1974) I was part of a flight of RAF Regiment personnel who were on a detachment on the island testing a system called the Rapier Low Level air Defence system.'[39] It was not such a bad mission to be on, Vyv Walters continues:

> The purpose of our detachment was kept low key at the time so as not to cause any undue incident that could affect the stability and mistrust buoy-ant in the area at the time. We were running the systems for long periods of time to access its capabilities in hot conditions.
>
> We were deployed for up to a week at a time over a three-month period around the higher points of the island demonstrating how highly mobile and versatile the system was. It was far more mobile than its operators because we were burnt to a frazzle being fully exposed to the sun for

fifteen to seventeen hours a day. Some were evacuated from the site due to the dehydration and sunstroke which was unavoidable when you are stuck on the knob of a hill.

One of my favourite memories was picking my own grapefruit from the tree and making a complete pig of myself because they were so pink inside. I ate so many that I cannot stand to even look at them these days.[40]

In 1971 George Grivas, the 'joker in the pack', as US ambassador in Nicosia David Popper called him, slipped back into Cyprus and founded EOKA-B; its aim, as always, and never changing, Enosis Union with Greece. But the old man then in his 70s, remarkable if for nothing else but his tenacity, died in January 1974, still in hiding. He would never see the full fruits of his meddling: when the division of Cyprus came about.[41]

Notes

1. Charles Foley, *Island in Revolt*, p. 240, 'There remained only …'
2. Tabitha Morgan, *Sweet and Bitter Island*, p. 254, 'Negotiations over the precise …'
3. Suha Faiz, *Recollections and Reflections of an Unknown Cyprus Turk*, p. 189, 'Two secretaries …'
4. Ibid., p. 190, 'At these meetings …'
5. Ibid., p. 191, 'And so, at the beginning …'
6. BECM Oral Tape 806 A and B Mary-Pat Lennard
7. Robert Holland, *Britain and the Revolt in Cyprus*, p. 332 and Morgan, p. 254
8. Morgan, p. 254, 'One of the final …'
9. LTA Colonel Colin Robinson 23/11/2000
10. Derrik Mercer (ed.), *Chronicle of the 20th Century*, p. 851, 'The last national …'
11. LTA Robinson
12. Ibid.
13. BECM Oral Tape 370 Lt Colonel Wilde
14. David Matthews, *The Cyprus Tapes*, p. 102, 'Even if the two …'
15. Ibid., p. 102, 'By 1963 several …'
16. Ibid., p. 102, 'Just as a looming …'
17. Ibid., p. 103, 'Minister Yorgadjis …'
18. Ibid., p. 103, 'Against the bodyguard …'
19. Ibid., p. 105, 'Their fears grew …'
20. Ibid., p. 107, 'Because Britain …'
21. LTA Robinson
22. Peter Harclerode, *Para*, p. 236, 'Toward the end …'
23. Ibid., pp. 236–7, 'Further battalions …'

24. LTA Robinson
25. Mercer, p. 911, 'Twenty Turks and one …'
26. John Reddaway, *Burdened with Cyprus*, p. 154, 'It is not …'
27. Mirbagheri Farid, *Cyprus and International Peacemaking*, p. 37, 'On 6 March …'
28. Ibid., pp. 37–8, 'UNFICYP's three month …'
29. LTA Robinson
30. Mirbagheri, p. 45, 'Since the settlement …'
31. Ibid., p. 46, 'As we saw …'
32. Ibid., p. 46, 'For the Greek Cypriots …'
33. Matthews, p. 112, 'Unless this happened …'
34. Colin Thubron, *Journey into Cyprus*, pp. 46–7, 'but the coast kept …'
35. Ibid., p. 51, 'Polis, which means …'
36. Ibid., p. 51, 'Nothing, he said …'
37. Ibid., p. 171, 'Bellapaix nestled in …'
38. Ibid., p. 233, 'Toward noon …'
39. LTA Vyv Walters 24/5/2001
40. Ibid.
41. Mirbagheri, pp. 76–7, 'The authority of Makarios …'

12

UNFINISHED
BUSINESS 1974

Colin Pomeroy, co-pilot of RAF Nimrod XV241 from Malta, had a grandstand view of the Turkish invasion fleet on 20 July 1974:

> It was really like participating in a NATO exercise, except that we were talking on the R/T to the Near East Air Force operations room at Episkopi instead of the air warfare controller aboard a warship. We watched and reported as the Turkish units formed up, with the landing craft in line abreast, and headed for the beaches, then exactly three miles offshore, the whole force turned seaward again, and we thought that it was all bluff and the invasion wasn't going to happen after all.
>
> Clear of the territorial waters limit, the fleet turned through 180 degrees and headed back for the planned landings. We continued to watch and report and then, with radar confirming that no further units were approaching from the Turkish mainland or offshore islands we were withdrawn and flew around the island to land at RAF Akrotiri.
>
> After de-briefing and resting we were kept at readiness for the rest of 20 July and the 21st. We were aware of the gunfire and explosions in nearby Limassol but feeling quite safe and protected behind the well guarded Akrotiri perimeter. On the 22nd, we flew a second surveillance sortie off Kyrenia to update the plot after which we returned to Malta. It was a sortie I wouldn't have missed for anything – history in the making.[1]

The events that culminated with the Turkish invasion started with the Greek junta of colonels in power in Athens. By early 1974 this repressive regime was tottering and hated at home. To stay in power they tried to gain popular support with an overseas adventure. Their plan was to bring Cyprus into union with Greece by overthrowing Archbishop Makarios's Government. By this time Makarios was well aware of the extent to which the island's defence force, the National Guard, was playing to the colonels' tune, having a majority of mainland Greek officers in command and being virtually encouraged openly by the EOKA-B. On 2 July Makarios wrote a letter to the Greek President Ghizikis accusing him and the Military Junta of Greece of being behind the activities of EOKA-B. The letter was printed in Cyprus four days later and part read:

> that the tree of evil, the bitter fruits of which the Greek Cypriots are tasting today, is being fed and maintained and helped to grow and spread. In order to be absolutely clear. I say that the cadres of the military regime of Greece support and direct the activities of the EOKA-B terrorists ...[2]

He went on to reveal his personal fear. 'I have more than once so far felt, and in some cases I have almost touched a hand invisibly extending from Athens and seeking to liquidate my human existence.'[3]

Instead the Junta ordered the overthrow of the Archbishop and his supporters. On 15 July the National Guard attacked the presidential palace. Word soon spread that the Archbishop was dead. But in fact Makarios had escaped and with the help of the RAF left the island for Britain. The coup leaders proclaimed Nicos Sampson as president. It should have been apparent to the Junta and EOKA-B that their action would give Turkey and Britain the legal right to intervene on the island, under article four of the Treaty of Zurich. However, perhaps American intelligence had told someone in Greece, as they had reported to Washington an opinion that Turkey did not have the military capability to move against Cyprus and Britain nor the political will. Or this is what the Greeks thought, even when warned by their own KYP station (Greek Central Intelligence Service) on Cyprus that invasion was imminent. Athens dismissed the report as incorrect, and it was merely Turkish military manoeuvres, sabre rattling, pointing to secret American assurances. However, the CIA in a report after the coup stated that all they had pointed out was they would not interfere in the coup as long as it 'was intra-Greek'.[4]

On 16–17 July the Turkish Prime Minister Bülent Ecevit flew to London to urge the British Government to fulfil its obligations as a guarantor of the Cyprus Constitution under the 1960 treaties. He warned that if Britain did not so act, in conjunction with Turkey the second guarantor, to stop the coup and Greece trying to bring about Enosis, then Turkey would exercise her treaty right to move unilaterally. The British Government, in office only four months, quickly reached a decision based on two factors. One, for a start there were too few British troops on the island: about 5,000 including RAF personnel. However, this would soon rise to over 8,000 with the arrival of HMS *Hermes* and HMS *Devonshire* and two Royal Marine Commando units.

The second factor was more decisive in that Britain had already tried hard enough and shed enough blood trying to find a solution to the Cyprus problem. Thus Prime Minister Harold Wilson's Labour Government, with only a small majority in the House of Commons, decided not to adhere to, but would renege on, their treaty obligations, arguing instead in favour of a political solution. With the Cold War at its height the proposed Turkish action put Anglo-Greek and Anglo-Turkish relations to a hard test.[5]

Ecevit told Wilson, and British Foreign Secretary James Callaghan, that Turkey would exercise her treaty right. However, without some support the Western Allies still doubted Turkey's ability to mount a large amphibious operation and rather expected some intervention by the Turkish Air Force as had happened in 1964 and 1967. But Admiral Kayracan of the Turkish Navy and his staff had been planning for years for intervention on Cyprus.[6]

At about 4 a.m. on 20 July Ecevit ordered Operation Attila to go ahead. By that time thirty-one ships were in position. Landing craft were soon running onto Five-Mile beach west of Kyrenia landing the first waves of infantry. Although planned for years the landings were initially disastrous. The landing troops were inexperienced and poorly equipped conscripts. Tanks went ashore without fuel or ammunition. The general in charge of the landings was killed as he came ashore. Turkish jets managed to sink two of their own landing craft. The Greeks, although outnumbered and out-gunned, fought back strongly and confined the Turks to a bridgehead straddling the Nicosia–Kyrenia road. But by 22 July Turkish troops had completed the occupation of Kyrenia.[7]

About this time HMS *Hermes* arrived off the north coast. Corporal Harnant, part of the ship's Royal Marine detachment, tells the story:

> The situation ashore started to deteriorate so the ship got the order to sail around to the northern side of the island and evacuate British subjects from the town of Kyrenia and bring them back to RAF Akrotiri. The original plan to evacuate the refugees was to use the ship's boats, including the LCVP's (landing craft vehicle and personnel) and the rig for the LCVP crews was to be 'white overalls'. After all the preparation of getting the boats ready, the weather was too rough and we were told later the beach we were to have used was mined, so the ship used her helicopters instead. However we helped to evacuate 900 people on the ship in twenty-four hours. We then took them round to Akrotiri and disembarked them again by helicopter.[8]

One refugee who had been caught up in fierce fighting said of *Hermes*: 'When I drove down the hill and saw that ship sitting in the bay, it was as much as I could do to stop myself crying, I was so relieved to feel secure again.'[9] Norman Rose, an RAF Britannia captain, was also helping refugees off the island. Before that, on 20 July, he had been waiting to take off with a regular flight heading to Masirah, Gan and Singapore:

> Early on the morning of the 20th I taxied out to the runway to be told to 'hold' before take-off. After about ten minutes I enquired to know what the problem was.
>
> At that air traffic told me to line up on the runway, but again to 'hold'. The Tower said they were unable to obtain clearance from Nicosia Centre for us to proceed north over Turkey. Five minutes later they suddenly said 'return to dispersal we have heard a rumour that paratroops are descending over Nicosia'.

The routing to Masirah and the Far East involved flying north from Akrotiri over Nicosia and southern Turkey then turning east avoiding Syria. Subsequently when I got back to operations I learned of the full scale invasion.

I went back to our transit quarters with my crew wondering what was going to happen. We listened intently to the Cyprus Forces Broadcasting Service; they were doing a really magnificent job keeping everyone apprised of events as they happened minute by minute. The CFBS gave out detailed instructions to families in Limassol Larnaca, and Famagusta on what to do and where to assemble for the rescue convoys. At this stage we did not know whether the Turks were advancing south into the predominately Greek half of the island but Akrotiri was most certainly gearing itself for the worst. [10]

At Akrotiri the base commander Air Marshal Donald Hall soon had the base at a high state of readiness, to assist service families and foreign tourists or anybody who required sanctuary within the SBA.

The resident infantry battalion, the 1st Royal Scots, deployed in trucks to bring in service families. Meanwhile at Dhekelia the Somerset and Cornwall Light Infantry took up defensive positions on the perimeter.

Norman Rose continues:

As we listened (to CFBS) at one point I well remember an astonishing announcement over the radio to families in Famagusta to 'Keep your heads down and stay away from the windows, Turkish Jets are running in from the sea and strafing'. As we sat in the sunshine it was as though we were hearing a radio play.

Families living outside the base were ferried in and were hosted by the residents of Akrotiri married quarters. No2 officers mess was opened to receive and accommodate the hundreds of incoming tourists, no matter their nationality most of them had only what they stood up in. They were given drinks, food and blankets hastily found and distributed. These distraught and distressed women and children had to sit or lay on the floor as there was no furniture in the mess. Later the ever popular camp beds came into play. [11]

Jan Bradley, in 1974 Janet Dawe, was one of those ex-pats evacuated from the island. Jan and her parents were in partnership with a Greek Cypriot friend running the cafe called 'Escurial' in Famagusta. They, like many others, lost much of their investment. She recalls one lucky escape:

> After the invasion by Turkey, military wives and children had to leave the island immediately with just what they could carry. One little girl had been quite poorly and during her illness her one comfort was a pet canary. All pets obviously had to be left but one mum came up with the idea, as she had an ample bosom she volunteered to hide the bird in her bra. Brilliant, until the canary began to sing as they entered the plane, unperturbed, all the women began to sing too at the top of their voices for the whole of the four hour journey, making the crew believe they were just happy to be going home.[12]

At RAF Episkopi a large tented refugee camp was built by all arms called Happy Valley. At its height there would be some 8,000 Turkish Cypriots accommodated in the SBA's refugee camps.

Norman Rose continues:

> That evening a savage rumour spread through Akrotiri that the Keo Brewery had been bombed. However when this malicious tale proved untrue morale rocketed and as it happened, beer supplies fortuitously never faltered throughout the whole emergency.
>
> By the morning of 21 July news spread that the Britannia Fleet was being launched from the UK to start a mass evacuation. I was alerted to stand by to take the first load of tourists out as soon as possible so I departed Akrotiri with twenty-three French, two Belgian and seventy-five British women and children, some still in their bikinis.
>
> News of the invasion and the evacuation by the RAF had spread worldwide for when we reached the south coast of France the air traffic controller wanted to know if we had any French Nationals on board so I let one or two have a little chat over the radio. We received profuse thanks from the controller for what we, and the RAF were doing and were given a priority clearance to fly direct to Abbeville without having to navigate along the French airway system, quite an accolade.[13]

As the tourists left Akrotiri 40 Commando Group began to arrive. The Commando had had a 'clear lower deck' at Seaton Barracks before they left, where they were told by a general that they might be 'bombed, strafed or napalmed, attacked by tanks and waves of fanatical infantry' but everybody at HQ was confident we would maintain the highest traditions of the Corps. One voice was heard to mutter: 'We'll die with our boots on whistling Land of Hope and Glory.'[14]

41 Commando landed from HMS *Hermes*. The rifle companies deployed to defend the eastern SBA, while F Company in reserve began receiving refugees. OPs observed the ground between the Greek village of Xylotymbou and the Turkish village of Pergamous. In conjunction with B Squadron 16/5 Lancers, Reece Troop conducted mobile patrols on the Famagusta side of the SBA. While this was going on Turkish jets could be heard bombing near Famagusta while refugees continued to pour into the SBA.[15] From the north a large convoy of civilian vehicles left for Nicosia escorted by troops from the UNFICYP. The actor Edward Woodward came south in one of these convoys with his family: 'I can only say having travelled in a dicey civilian convoy across the Mesaoria Plain away from the invasion, I was so happy to see the Union Jack flying on an armoured car which escorted us into the SBA.'[16]

Much political and diplomatic manoeuvring had been going on behind the scenes. On 17 July Prime Minister Harold Wilson met Makarios in London. The Archbishop admitted his mistake in not giving credence to rumours of the Junta and Greek Military on Cyprus staging a coup.[17]

James Callaghan asked the MOD to put together a plan to restore Makarios by force. There were probably only about 10,000 Greek Cypriot fighters led by Greek officers on the island, supported by reservists and militia, and two Greek Infantry battalions with some heavy weapons. He was warned: 'We might well end up by facing an open-ended and expensive situation; similar to Northern Ireland … it is of interest to recall that our previous experience of an insurgency situation on the island tied up the equivalent of three divisions.'[18] The same day the Turkish Prime Minister Bülent Ecevit was pressing for a joint Anglo-Turkish intervention under the 1960 treaty, he also asked for the use of the SBAs by Turkish troops. This was rejected.

On 18 July Wilson was warned by the MOD that Turkish direct 'intervention in Cyprus' was imminent. The Chiefs of Staff recommended bringing additional forces to a state of readiness to move to defend the SBAs.[19]

At 2.20 a.m. on Saturday 20 July Callaghan was told an RAF Nimrod on patrol had spotted the Turkish invasion force. Wilson gave orders for a UK task force to sail to Cyprus with 40 and 41 Royal Marine Commandos; HMS *Hermes* the Commando carrier would be joined by the destroyer *Devonshire* and the frigates *Rhyl* and *Andromeda*.[20]

For the Turks their invasion did not run smoothly. The resistance of the Greek forces and Greek Cypriots, albeit only lightly armed, was fierce. The MOD–FCO assessment on 22 July said:

> It seems clear that the Turks badly misjudged both the potential extent of the National Guard resistance and the ability of outlying Turkish Cypriot enclaves to hold out until relieved. They made no attempt to secure the deep-water port of Famagusta and their failure to gain control of Nicosia Airport prevented the rapid build-up essential for a successful operation. If the conflict continues the Turks would probably be able gradually to gain the initiative if they succeeded in reinforcing quickly …[21]

Two days before in Athens a general military mobilisation was ordered and the 10th Division moved east toward the Greek–Turkish border in Thrace. On 23 July the Junta in Athens ordered the Greek Army to attack Turkey. Its officers refused, its men stayed in barracks and 100,000 Athenians took to the streets demonstrating for a return to democracy. Within days the colonels had fallen from power and ex-Premier Constantine Karamanlis returned from exile in France to form a new Government.

On 24 July the Turks were still apprehensive that Greek reinforcements would reach Cyprus. That day Turkish Air Force bombers sank their own destroyer the *Kocatepe* by mistake. HMS *Andromeda* and Sea King helicopters from a Royal Fleet Auxiliary saved a total of seventy-two crew members; fifty-four men were lost. It was one of the worst Turkish blunders of the invasion.[22]

The sinking of the *Kocatepe* alarmed the British, thus RAF Phantom F-4 fighter bombers were deployed to Akrotiri. Callaghan, the Foreign

Secretary, instructed the UK ambassador in Athens, Sir Robin Hooper, that this was 'a precautionary measure in view of the possible need to support UN Forces particularly at Nicosia Airport'. And no doubt more important to support Royal Navy ships.[23]

In Cyprus the week-long reign of Nicos Sampson came to an end. The moderate Glafkos Clerides took over. Sampson at his trial in 1976 pleaded that he only accepted the presidency under the pressure of Brigadier Ioannides, head of the feared Greek military police, but he was still sentenced to twenty years in prison.[24]

By this time Turkish forces had pushed back the Greeks east and west of Kyrenia. The Greeks, although brave, were out-gunned and hopelessly divided as it was only days since they had been fighting each other. Armoured columns were closing in on Nicosia, while in Famagusta some 12,000 Turkish Cypriots were holed up in the old city being pounded by GNG artillery and mortars. They were unwilling to surrender, even under UN supervision, having heard about, and some of them having witnessed, the atrocities of EOKA-B.[25]

On 30 July in Geneva, James Callaghan got the Turkish and Greek foreign ministers to agree to a ceasefire. It took a considerable amount of 'transatlantic arm twisting' but resulted in a plan for the withdrawal of forces, and the island would be divided into two administrative areas and a buffer zone policed by the UN. On 8 August talks resumed with the Cypriot leaders Clerides and Denktash present.[26]

On the 10 August Callaghan received a secret report claiming the Turks had plans to increase the zone they occupied. Three days later the Turks gave the Greek Cypriots an ultimatum either to accept their plans or hostilities would be renewed. Clerides tried to delay, with the result that at dawn 14 August the Turkish Army resumed its offensive, phase two of Attila.[27]

With massive reinforcements of better quality and with the Greek Cypriots reaching the end of their endurance, and with no hope of help from any quarter, the Turkish advance was rapid. Some 150,000 Greek Cypriots fled south away from the Turkish Army, who were reported to be committing widespread atrocities including rape, murder and looting.

For twenty-one days the Turkish Cypriots had held out in Famagusta for much of the time with very little water. However, on 15 August they were relieved by the Turkish Army. The Greek Cypriot inhabitants streamed south out of the city in a 7-mile-long convoy into the British SBA of Dhekelia.

On 16 August a second ceasefire came into effect, by which time the Turkish Army had occupied some 38 per cent of the island's area. The Attila Line extended from Kato Pyrgos in the west through Nicosia to Famagusta on the east coast. Karamanlis felt Greece had no option but to leave NATO in protest as in their view the Western Allies had failed to back a traditional friend. The CIA found Karamanlis was 'genuinely upset with US Cyprus policy'.[28]

Three days later anti-American riots broke out in Nicosia and the US ambassador Roger Davies and a Cypriot employed at the embassy were shot dead by EOKA-B gunmen, for a belief that the United States had favoured Turkey above Greece and the integrity of Cyprus.[29]

In the months after the invasion top priority by the British was given to the plight of the refugees from both communities. In September 1974 Gary Spencer was serving with 19 Field Ambulance RAMC:

My section was on standby duty with the spearhead battalion, we were told we were going to Cyprus in two days time. We flew from Brize Norton by VC10. After landing we were bussed to the British Military Hospital in Dhekelia. There we were bunked in an empty ward of the hospital. For the rest of our time there we travelled daily to the Athna Forest Refugee Camp by Land Rover. The camp was a short journey north of the base. We set up a tented area in the middle of the camp where we dealt with any injuries or illnesses among the refugees. Our main job daily was to issue all the mothers baby food and milk.

We were welcomed all over the camp and were helped with our Greek and translation by the family who were tented next to us. In the evenings we were invited into many tents for coffee and in this way got to know many of the refugees well. It was sad to hear how they had lost everything, when they fled their homes in Famagusta after the invasion.[30]

In January 1975, in the face of Greek Cypriot anti-British demonstrations, thousands of Turkish Cypriot refugees left RAF Akrotiri in civilian aircraft for Turkey. The vast majority would come back to Cyprus to be re-settled in the north of the island. Greek Cypriots in the north under Turkish occupation were simply expelled to the south. In February 1975 the Turkish Cypriots in the north proclaimed themselves the Turkish Federated State of Cyprus. In November 1983 the North became the independent Turkish Republic of Northern Cyprus. To date no other state but Turkey has recognised the TRNC.

Notes

1. LTA Colin Pomeroy 10/6/2000
2. FO, Policy No. 19 summer 1975 and Mirbagheri Farid, *Cyprus and International Peacemaking*, p. 87, 'On 2 July …'
3. Mirbagheri, p. 88, 'Makarios was also …'
4. Memorandum from Director of the Bureau of Intelligence to Secretary of State Kissinger 10/9/1974 and Dimitrakis Panagiotis, *Military Intelligence in Cyprus*, pp. 133–4, 'Athens reacted strangely …'
5. Dimitrakis, p. 131, 'The Turkish invasion …'
6. David Matthews, *The Cyprus Tapes*, p. 17, 'As only four days …'
7. Ibid., pp. 16–17, 'Although the Turkish forces …'
8. Corporal T.A. Hannant, *The Globe and Laurel*, Journal of the Royal Marines, August 1974, 'There we were …'
9. Matthews, pp. 163–4, 'Yesterday he announced …'
10. LTA Squadron Leader N.E. Rose 27/5/2000
11. Ibid.
12. LTA Janet Bradley 26/7/2014
13. LTA Squadron Leader N.E. Rose 27/5/2000
14. *The Globe and Laurel*, August 1974, '40 Commando in Cyprus'
15. Ibid.
16. LTA Edward Woodward 31/5/2000
17. Dimitrakis, p. 134, 'Three days ealier …'
18. Ibid., p. 135, 'Callaghan asked …'
19. Ibid., p. 138, 'On 18 July …'
20. Ibid., pp. 139–40, 'In Whitehall …'
21. Ibid., pp. 142–3, 'Turkish Paratroops …'
22. ADM-(PRO) DEFE-Navy 69/210
23. FCO-(PRO) 25/7/1974 and Dimitrakis, p. 144, 'Next day Callaghan …'
24. *The Times* 11/5/2001
25. Matthews, p. 164, 'We were at home …'
26. Dimitrakis, p. 147, 'On 30 July …'
27. Ibid., p. 148, 'On 10 August …'
28. CIA Paper 29/8/1974, p. 87
29. Dimitrakis, p. 153, 'At the UN Security Council …'
30. LTA Gary Spencer 7/6/2000

13

BELLAPAIS 2000 AND WAYNES KEEP 2004

'Nescafe, lager beer, coke, come sit,' cried the owner of the Ulusoglu Cafe at us, or anybody else in the square who would take notice. The greeting was warmer than that received by Lawrence Durrell on his last lonely walk across Bellapais Square. The cafe is under and surrounds what we take to be the 'Tree of Idleness', a mulberry tree that hardly seems big enough to throw enough shadow over the tables even when in full flower. There seemed some little doubt if indeed this was the cafe, for a restaurant, the Huzur Agac, had some sort of claim. But on further examination it fell flat. The restaurant has only a few tables outside, and is across the road from the abbey and it has a poor excuse for a tree even compared to the cafe. No, this must have been the place where Durrell used to pass the time of day with the villagers.[1]

My wife and I did stop for a coffee at the cafe. I suppose most people do. Other tables were occupied by old men playing cards and draughts, reading papers or just gossiping. There were eight or so, none wearing the traditional baggy black trousers and white cotton shirts of Durrell's time, apart, that is, from the owner and that was playing a part for the tourists.

A narrow winding street past the post office-cum-shop heading south leads to Durrell's house, Bitter Lemons. The door is now heavy and dark with a high knocker and its huge lock which Durrell likened to those used in 'medieval English Houses'. It took three of them to

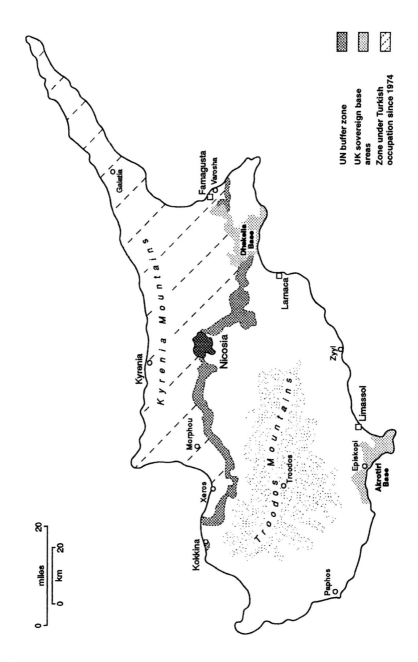

Cyprus since 1974

turn the great key 'screeching' in the lock. A small circular plate above the door has the name Bitter Lemons on it and 'Lawrence Durrell lived here 1953–1956'.[2]

When Lawrence Durrell left, taking with him his manuscripts for *Bitter Lemons of Cyprus* and the first volume of the Alexandria quartet *Justine*, Penelope Tremayne took over the house Bitter Lemons. Since Penelope arrived the two became friends in 'fairly continuous touch until the time of my departure'.[3]

Directly opposite Bitter Lemons was a derelict house. Its ground-floor windows, the glass long since gone, were masked by chicken wire to keep its present feathered occupants off the streets. They took little notice of our passing which only briefly disturbed their chicken-like habits. This, in perhaps Northern Cyprus's most famous village, demonstrates the chronic under-population of many of the villages.

We stayed in a small hotel in Bellapais. The lady owner, a Turkish Cypriot, spent as much time in London with her Cypriot family there as in Northern Cyprus. Sheila Mullins, a head teacher for much of her working life, had taught large numbers of Greek Cypriot children at Islington Primary School in London:

> Always we had to deal with men not the mothers. A lot of the women did not speak English. The older women still wore black. The families ran small clothing factories. The men were not above using bribery to try and obtain places in the school. However, it was not sinister in any way; it was their way of life, their 'coffee shop' culture.

Sheila spent many happy holidays on Cyprus and came across no anti-British feeling; in fact in her view if anything the Cypriots 'were pro British'.[4] In Bellapais we suffered with the rest of the village the odd power cut and the shortages of water.

We were sympathetic, imagining the hotel at the mercy of some bureaucratic water authority, until we learnt the hotel had a tank and they had forgotten to order the water. 'Order the water?' Why were they doing that?

That same day an old Bedford MK bowser arrived, looking like it needed the water more than we did, to fill the tank. Now if you take the Crusader Path down to the lower village of Ozankoy you cross a small ravine on a bridge. At the head of the ravine was a defaced British drinking trough dated 1953. Bellapais had had running water then, courtesy of the Royal Engineers. Entering Bellapais by the same route you cross behind the abbey near its car park. There, rusting away in one corner, its tyres long gone flat, was another British marker, a Morris Oxford.

The Rough Guide to Cyprus says of Bellapais that 'there are more attractive villages in the Kyrenia Hills'.[5] True, but none have the abbey, which Colin Thubron called the 'loveliest of Gothic Abbeys'.[6]

The abbey dates from the twelfth century and was originally founded as St Mary of the Mountains by Augustinian followers who had fled from Palestine. Shortly afterward they changed allegiance to the Premonstratensian, Roman Catholic monastic order. Its canons wore white habits and soon the abbey had the nickname the 'White Abbey'. The Lusignan kings were great benefactors of the abbey and in 1246 it benefited from a large legacy left by a knight known only as Roger the Norman and perhaps more importantly it was endowed with a piece of the True Cross. Such a famous sacred relic put the abbey on the wealthy pilgrims' map that were willing to pay top rates to stay there, but it also made it more appealing to invaders.[7]

In 1373 the Genoese overran Cyprus and the abbey was looted and the piece of the True Cross vanished. After this the abbey went into decline both physically and morally. The monks took concubines and only allowed their own sons to become novices. In 1570 the Ottoman forces took over Cyprus and sacked the abbey. The monks then probably became part of the local community, while the building was handed over to the Orthodox Church.

With the coming of the British the buildings declined further, with soldiers using the refectory as a shooting range. You can still see the bullet holes in the east wall. The locals abused the abbey, using it as a source of building stone. However, at the beginning of the twentieth century the new Antiquities Department started by the British began taking an interest in the abbey, what Sir Harry Luke called the 'most beautiful monument of the Latin east'.[8] In 1974 the abbey was used as a hospital by the Greek National Guard. The Greeks had positions above Bellapais that were napalmed by Turkish aircraft, after which the village was occupied.

We watched a full moon rise above the cloisters and the giant cypresses which Kollis, friend of Lawrence Durrell, had planted over fifty years before. It may well be the cypresses grew here in classical times and were worshipped; it may even be the case the tree takes its name from the island. Yet for all the appeal of the abbey the place was tinged with sadness. Where was Mr Kollis, who now wanted nothing more than to die here tending the garden he had for a brief time made his own? Of course he is long gone now and I imagined him watching us with his 'round good-natured face of Friar Tuck'.[9] And where was Hugh Grant's teacher who had hopes for an independent Cyprus if EOKA had been kept out of power?[10] Perhaps they may have come back as abbey cats. It's another strange thing about the place.

We dined in several restaurants around the abbey square where stray cats come and go of every shape and size and colour. However, inside the abbey grounds they were always white. We studied this on several occasions and never saw any but white. Were these reincarnated monks, or the vanished Greeks come to haunt the grounds? Which brought me back to the question I had come hopefully to put to rest: had the British somehow let Cyprus down? Could we have saved Mr Kollis and the other Greeks of Bellapais being expelled to the south, or saved the Turks moving from their ancient villages? Many of the Turks in Bellapais today had come from the village of Mari near Limassol in the south.[11]

In 1959 Harold Macmillan summed it up thus: 'Why do they hold Cyprus against us? It was nothing but a quarrel between the Greeks and Turks and we settled it.' I think perhaps this is going too far. I did find an answer of sorts on a walk to St Hilarion Castle.[12]

One early morning we set out from the village of Karaman to walk to St Hilarion Castle, the western-most of the three Kyrenian mountain fortifications started in the seventh century as lookout posts. They were improved by the Crusaders and Byzantines. When the Venetians came they largely dismantled the castle and left it abandoned to crumble away, for it was not proof against cannon.

We breakfasted high up in the saw-tooth-like mountains, with the whole north coast laid out before us. Our arrival at the castle entrance was

early, before the caretaker had arrived to open up. When open we scram-
bled over its ruins and climbed its towers. Its appearance belies its past
for the castle does not look, at first sight, hugely formidable, nothing like
the one in Kyrenia Harbour. But in 1964 it became a Turkish stronghold,
able to withstand EOKA attacks with a small garrison of TMT. Today it
remains near to Turkish Army facilities. From its heights we could hear
firing and watch the fall of shot on the Army rifle range far below.

Some 35,000 Turkish troops are stationed in Northern Cyprus. The vast
majority are mainland conscripts, who pass some of their time waving
to tourists, perhaps to relieve boredom. However, I suspect there might
be something on 'Standing Orders' to help encourage tourism and the
economy: 'All tourists are to be assisted and greeted in a friendly manner.'

We were soon on our way back to Karaman, but by a different route,
the blue route, while we had climbed up to the castle by the orange route.
All these routes mean that the routes are marked for walkers on rocks
or trees with paint. Early on were views inland across the shimmering
Mesaoria Plain toward the distant Nicosia, which looked like an Arabian
city looming out of the desert. It was barely past ten in the morning but
the temperature was already in the nineties.[13]

However, our troubles began when we left the road for the track down
to Karaman for a forest fire had obliterated many of the blue markers,
little more than a dab of paint at best. The track follows a ridge line down
but we missed it and got lost in a ravine that there was no way down
from. Luckily, for it was now well past noon, we came across the former
dentist of 45 Commando who was staying in Karaman and knew the
route down well. He told us it had been well trod by the EOKA terrorists
years ago, whom I had to admit must have been like mountain goats. But
it was what the dentist said about Cyprus that stuck in my mind as we sat
upon some rocks having a drink of water having at last emerged from the
ravine: 'The division of the island is an answer of sorts. Not perfect. And
anyway it stops them killing each other, not that they talk much about it
in the North. Whereas to the Greeks it's their favourite subject, mind you
of course they lost the most.' I asked him what about the British? Could
we have done more, had we let Cyprus down in some way? I could see by
his face he thought this a strange question:

I don't think so. In 1974 we could have come to the rescue but it would have been a massive operation. But then we tried that before, we had over 40,000 troops on this island at one stage, we stood between them then and it did no good. Even then with the SBA's down south we probably saved that for the Greeks by just being there.

He was right about the last point. Indeed Mr Erbakan, Prime Minister of Turkey and part of the Ankara Government in 1974, has expressed the view that it was a mistake for Turkey not to have taken over the whole island. Part of the Turkish thinking at the time must have revolved around a possible clash, no matter how remote, with Britain.[14] And then think how much revenue the SBAs pump into the Southern economy and how many jobs they provide for the Greeks. And then there's the tourist industry; the majority of visitors are Brits, both north and south.

So there we have it. Who would doubt the word of a dentist? But who knows what history will say in the long run? Now it seems Cyprus has on the whole done well out of its relationship with Britain. Its ills have been largely self-inflicted.

Penelope Tremayne, friend of Lawrence Durrell who lived on Cyprus during the 1950s, thought the opportunity of the Republic of Cyprus had been wasted: 'They had the opportunity to become Cypriots and have thrown it away. The Turks probably didn't realise it, the Greeks did and know what they have thrown away. It's a sort of poetic justice both sides have got what they asked for.'[15]

After a hearty breakfast we set off from the village of Platres high in the Troodos Mountains early one September morning in 2004, for Waynes Keep. It was curious, for in a manner of speaking, we had set off on this road to the cemetery in this book and on the ground long ago. The Military Cemetery of Waynes Keep in Nicosia is where most of the British personnel who died on active service during the Cyprus Emergency are buried. Although it was originally established during the Second World War, today, the cemetery, some 2 miles west of the centre of the divided capital on the Myrtou Road, lies within the United Nations Buffer Zone, which separates the Greek Cypriot- and Turkish-controlled sections. This is also referred to as the Green Line, so called because the UN official who drew the line on the map in 1974 used a green pen.[16]

Our visit to Waynes Keep had been arranged with the UNFICYP, the only force able to arrange such a visit. However they are more than happy to do this and actively encourage visits. My letter of enquiry was promptly replied to from 'Troop Sergeant Major, Bengal Troop RA, Sector 2 West, UNFICYP, Ypenburg', informing us we would be met at Sector 2 checkpoint Ledra Palace Hotel in Nicosia at 10 a.m. on the allotted day. The checkpoint lies beside the (Turkish Zone) old city walls and the Roccas Bastion now forming part of the Buffer Zone. Sergeant Mark Williams of Bengal Troop met us at the checkpoint, dressed in his desert combats and UN blue beret; we left our car in the hotel car park and transferred to a white UN vehicle for our visit to the cemetery. On entering the zone the vehicle is stopped and the UN flag raised on the vehicle before proceeding.

Waynes Keep Cemetery, to the north and west, is overlooked by the posts of the Turkish Army and to the south by the Greek Cypriot National Guard; both are watched to the east by a UN Observation Post. A narrow road running through a narrow shallow valley takes you to the cemetery while all these eyes follow you. The actual cemetery is directly overlooked by a Turkish OP.

The cemetery was founded in the 1930s for servicemen and their dependants. Three Turkish Cypriot gardeners are employed to maintain the cemetery. However, Sergeant Williams told us water was a problem. A small well was adequate in spring and autumn to keep the grass and flowers alive but during the long summer it dries up. So water is then brought in by military bowsers from the Turkish side. So arriving toward the end of summer the cemetery did look barren, not like the usual lush grass of most CWGC sites. The Turks during the summer months would only allow a limited number of deliveries. However, all the plants and shrubs beside the headstones appeared in good shape.

Some of the headstones were showing signs of weathering. Sergeant Williams told us replacement stones in more durable granite have been made and were even on site. Greek Cypriot builders had been contracted to erect the new stones. But up to then the Turkish Army had refused permission for the work to be carried out. He felt for sure if Turkish builders had got the job the Greeks would have objected. And so the old tit for tat continues, even over the graves of many people who died trying to keep the warring factions apart.

There are 582 graves at Waynes Keep. The Cross of Sacrifice found in all Commonwealth war cemeteries is in the centre. Another memorial commemorates the officers and men of the Cyprus Regiment and the Cyprus Volunteer Force who were laid to rest generally elsewhere. The Cremation Memorial honours Hindu soldiers of the Indian Army, whose remains were cremated as required by their religion.

So many names on headstones I recognised. There was Quartermaster Sergeant Graham Casey, 45 Commando, who died in the tragic helicopter accident of May 1957, and Catherine Cutliffe. Sergeant Williams took a special interest in Catherine, being the wife of a Royal Artillery sergeant; her grave was often visited by members of the regiment and civilians.

Lance Corporal J.B. Morum, Royal Engineers, who died in an EOKA ambush where Captain Brian Coombe won the George Medal for his action against a four-man terrorist group, and who had read the lesson at his driver's funeral service:

> And God shall wipe away all tears from their eyes, and there shall be no more death, neither sorrow, nor crying, neither shall there be any more pain; for the former things are passed away.[17]

And all those graves of the 1st Battalion Gordon Highlanders and 1st Battalion Royal Norfolk Regiment, around 17 June 1956 caught in the forest fire on Operation Lucky Alphonse, were mostly in their teens or early 20s.

It was only a matter of weeks before we came to Cyprus in 2004 that the story of Private David Morrison, 1st Battalion Argyll and Sutherland Highlanders, turned up, who died on 13 September 1958 age 22, and here I was standing before his headstone. An anonymous poem called 'An Argyll's Farewell' had been written about him and forwarded to *The Thin Red Line* magazine of the Argylls in 1992.[18] Private Morrison of C Company was among a party of soldiers returning from rest and recreation to Polemi Camp, between Paphos and Kannaviou amid vineyards and wild country in the foothills of the Troodos Mountains. The truck the party was travelling in was ambushed by EOKA at 7.30 p.m. Morrison died of his wounds shortly afterwards:

'An Argyll's Farewell'
It was on a Saturday evening
An Argyll passed away
Ne'er to see another day
Oh! My heart went cold within me
When I heard the awful news
That he had been killed in action
By the Greek EOKA crews
It was from the dark the shots came
As the truck came down the track
Two light machine gun bullets
Struck him in the back
He left this world without a sound
As all brave men should die
To take his place amongst the host
Of Angels in the sky
Many years may pass before I die
If the good Lord wills it so
But as long as breath's left in me
His memory cannot go
And before we leave this island
EOKA shall regret
The wakening of our motto
We shall never forget.[19]

The Argylls' reaction to this has been mentioned and was perhaps severe on the local population. While the official report stated 'not only were the soldiers searching for the killers of one of their comrades, but the villagers were unco-operative to the point of serious resistance in one case'.[20]

After our visit Sergeant Williams drove us to the Ypenburg HQ, still within the Buffer Zone, the building still pock-marked with bullet holes from 1974. We took welcome refreshment there and signed the visitors' book. For thirty years British troops have been patrolling part of the 180km Buffer Zone, under the auspices of the UN, maintaining the curious link with the island's troubles. At present the British contingent of UNFICYP control 29km, mostly running through the heart of old Nicosia and its sub-urbs east and west. Nicosia at present is the world's only divided city. Bengal Troop's tour of duty was shortly coming to an end. It had been eventful falling at the time of the UN referendum on unification.

In April 2004 three border crossing points had been opened and since some 3 million people had crossed the divide without major incident.

Our visit had lasted just over an hour. 'Most of the lads,' said Sergeant Williams, 'would be glad to get home.' But he would not have minded staying a bit longer, perhaps, to see the new headstones erected. He had enjoyed looking after Waynes Keep and was pleased to promote visits to the cemetery. That month there had been twenty-eight visits.

Notes

1. Lawrence Durrell, *Bitter Lemons of Cyprus*, p. 247, 'It was a beautiful ringing day …'
2. Ibid., pp. 56–7, 'The owner swung …'
3. Penelope Tremayne, *Below the Tide*, Preface by Lawrence Durrell, 'A preface to a good book.'
4. ITA Sheila Mullins 13/2/2014
5. Marc Dubin, *The Rough Guide to Cyprus*, p. 293, 'A couple of kilometres …'
6. Colin Thubron, *Journey into Cyprus*, p. 171, 'Bellapaix, nested in orchards …'
7. Gordon Home, *Cyprus Then and Now*, p. 170, 'It was not unusual …'
8. Sir Harry Luke, *Cyprus*, p. 104, 'Below Hilarion lies …'
9. Durrell, p. 77, 'They gave us …'
10. Hugh Grant, *A Game of Soldiers*, p. 107, 'We walked on and once …'
11. Oliver Burch, *The Infidel Sea*, p. 73, 'There was no Greek …'
12. Charles Foley, *Island in Revolt*, p. 228, 'Harold Macmillan 26 September 1959 …'
13. *Walks in North Cyprus*, p. 23, 'Hilarion Castle walk No. 10 …'
14. James Pettifer, *The Turkish Labyrinth*, p. 196, 'Another important factor …'
15. David Matthews, *The Cyprus Tapes*, p. 99, 'Durrell, although prepared …'
16. LTA UNFICYP 15/5/2004
17. Foley, p. 51, 'Coombe replied …'
18. *The Thin Red Line*, Journal of the Argyle and Southern Highlanders, Summer 1992
19. Ibid.
20. Ibid.

AFTERWORD

In 1957, when the EOKA crisis was at its height, on 25 March six nations – France, West Germany, Italy, Belgium, Holland and Luxembourg – signed the Treaty of Rome, creating the European Common Market. It was hailed as a European Renaissance from the ashes of the Second World War. Britain stayed out worrying about the surrender of sovereignty, Prime Minister Macmillan conceding 'great risks in this policy'.[1] In January 1972 Britain joined what was then called the European Economic Community along with Ireland, Denmark and Norway; thus the six became ten. It was a personal triumph for Prime Minister Edward Heath, who was active throughout Britain's ten-year struggle for membership. In 1981 Greece became a full member of the EEC.

In 2004 Greece was the Community President and was keen to focus on two main policies which it wished the EU would take more responsibility over: the Balkans and the ending of the twenty-eight-year division of Cyprus, both linked by the age-old fault line between Muslims and Christians.[2] Southern Greek Cypriot membership of the EU in 2004 was guaranteed, but the other members have made it clear they would rather welcome to their ranks a united Cyprus, as outlined in the UN Mandate 1442 for a federal bizonal island.

The story of the divided island since the declaration in 1983 of the Turkish Republic of Northern Cyprus has revolved around the UN trying to find some sort of solution to its original intervention in March 1964 under resolution 186.[3] That mandate had been 'in the interest of preserving international peace and security, to use its best efforts to prevent a recurrence of fighting and, as necessary, to contribute to the maintenance and restoration of law and order and a return to normal condition'.[4]

In 1985 UN Secretary-General Pérez de Cuallar came close to a solution. He had the leaders of both sides, President Rauf Denktash and President Spyros Kyprianou, in New York. For six months the Secretary-General had conducted talks with both leaders, a 'draft agreement' was ready to sign, and then Mr Kyprianou refused, wanting further concessions. After three days the summit broke up and the leaders returned home – Mr Kyprianou into a political storm, for many in the south had wanted a settlement. Mr Denktash was welcomed home by his people glad that he had stood his ground.[5]

In March 1986 Pérez de Cuallar again pressed both sides to make concessions and once again submitted a draft agreement to them. Pressure groups within the British House of Commons tried to bring both sides closer. In May the Foreign Affairs Committee of the House of Commons announced an inquiry into the Cyprus problem. In November President Denktash was invited to give evidence before the Committee. Greek Cypriots soon arranged demonstrations in London demanding Denktash should not be allowed to speak for 'violating justice' on Cyprus. Denktash did speak, making an opening statement which was followed by the committee chairman Sir Anthony Kershaw MP reminding the other members that the TRNC had accepted the UN Secretary-General's latest 'draft agreement' as a 'compromise solution for the good of Cyprus' which Denktash thought 'reasonable Greeks' would accept.[6]

In December the Committee members toured Athens, Cyprus and Ankara. While this took place the island was debated in the House of Lords. The House was split. Lord Caradon, the last colonial governor, spoke, blaming both communities and saying Britain should not take sides nor should she recognise the independence of the TRNC, which would seem like taking sides. The debate ended with Baroness Young for the Government, as Minister of State for the Foreign and Commonwealth Office, pointing out Britain's continuing support for the island, and that Britain was the largest single contributor to UNFICYP, and she expressed regret that 'one side' could not accept the UN Plan for a united federal Cyprus.

In 1992 Boutros-Ghali, the then UN Secretary-General, got both sides together again for his 'set of ideas' for the Cyprus problem, another bizonal set of proposals. In this, Varosha and much of the Marfou plain would revert to the Greek Cypriots and Greek refugees would be able to return to the north. Both sides would be represented equally rather than proportionally in a higher house.

George Vassiliou, the new Greek Cypriot President, and Denktash met at the UN in July and October but achieved little. In November a new resolution laid most of the blame for failure of the Boutros-Ghali plan on Denktash. It seems by this time the ageing Turkish Cypriot President was more interested in protecting the status quo.

Since the 1992 attempt by Boutros-Ghali, when he declared Cyprus 'a labyrinth with no exit', the UN position has been to try to scale down the UNFICYP operation and try to leave the islanders to themselves. However, this has resulted in various border incidents or demonstrations by both sides at the Buffer Zone, resulting in deaths on both sides, thus forcing the UN to maintain large numbers of troops on Cyprus; indeed it is estimated there are about 80,000 soldiers on the island including Turkish, GMG, UN and British.[7]

The British SBAs have not been the focus of trouble over the years apart from odd demonstrations by the farming community and more significantly the riots of July 2001, when the base of Akrotiri came under attack by over 1,000 Greek Cypriots. The riot was orchestrated by the opposition MP for Limassol, Marios Matsakis, against the building of additional telecommunication masts at the base. Matsakis, who was a former captain in the Territorial Army and lived in Britain for over twenty years, has over the years been one of the main opponents of the SBAs. In the July riot forty police and soldiers were injured and MOD vehicles set on fire; damage was estimated at £300,000.[8]

Since the independence of Cyprus in 1960 the SBAs have been vital to Britain's global reach. The garrison strength has fallen from 6,000 in 1970 to around 3,500. The bases serve as a forward listening post for the volatile

Middle East, not just for Britain but the Western alliance. During the Gulf War some 10,000 sorties were flown from the island. US spy planes use the bases to monitor the region, U-2 spy planes being based at RAF Akrotiri. The SBAs seem even more important today as one of the world's most important listening posts.

The RAF radar station on Mount Olympus continues to monitor civil air traffic and military air movements extending over Syria, Lebanon, Israel, Turkey and parts of Egypt. The Troodos station was founded in 1878 and is the oldest British site on the island. It provides the British military and her allies with invaluable radio intelligence collected with a variety of sensors. The addition of the Starbrook system in 2006 allows Britain to scan the skies for objects as small as 1.5m.[9] Successive Greek Cypriot Governments have had little opposition to the bases or sought to reclaim them and terminate the treaties with Britain. The direct and indirect benefits for the economy and security far outweigh the mere sovereignty of less than 100 sq. miles. President Clerides has seen the bases as useful in the pursuit of entry of Southern Cyprus into the EU.

Which brings us up to date with the Greek Foreign Minister George Papandreou having the unique carrot of EU membership to tempt the Turkish Cypriots and perhaps even Turkey in the long run. In a way Cyprus will, with membership of the EU, have gained a sort of Enosis with Greece and for that matter with Britain as well and maybe in the future with Turkey. Even Rauf Denktash is in danger of being left behind by the wishes of his own people, and Turkey's leader Recep Tayyip Erdogan revealed on television a wish to solve the Cyprus problem: 'we will do whatever falls on us. This is not Mr Denktash's private matter.'[10]

Demonstrations in Northern Cyprus called for the veteran president to resign, after he refused to approve the UN Plan of Secretary-General Kofi Annan. Whether the Turkish Army will go along with Mr Erdogan is another matter, for it is they who have had the final say for years. It may be the Army who could be the obstacle to Turkey's membership of the EU, for the Army have been the guardians of the secular state since Ataturk; membership would curb the power of the generals to interfere in politics.

In February 2003 UN Secretary-General Kofi Annan arrived in Cyprus with his revised UN Plan 3. According to this the Karpas Peninsula will remain under Turkish Cypriot administration. Under Plan 2, the Karpas was to have reverted to Greek Cypriot control. To compensate the Greeks, additional areas west of Famagusta and around the Gulf of Morphou would come under their control. This would allow for the return of 2,700 more refugees, with fifteen villages coming under Greek Cypriot administration.

Twenty-one per cent of refugees will have the right to return to homes remaining under Turkish Cypriot control; this is a drop from the previous quota of 28 per cent. A postponement of six years will apply for the return of refugees, increased from four years in Plan 2.[11] However, there are some exceptions for the elderly who can return straight away. The return of most refugees will take place over a twenty-one-year period from the moment of signing, with a sliding scale from 7 per cent to 21 per cent over the time period. However, will all these quotas be abolished if Turkey becomes a full member of the European Union? At present the number of settlers from mainland Turkey remaining in Cyprus will range between 45,000 to 60,000, pending finalised arrangements.

A controversial point has been military contingents from Greece and Turkey; the figure most likely seems to be about 6,000 for each contingent, while all troops will be removed from the island again once Turkey joins the EU. The new state will be called the 'United Cyprus Republic', based on a federal Government comprising two 'constituent states'.

The British have tried to facilitate the negotiations by offering in a proposal, presented by the British special envoy Lord David Hannay, the return of some 45 sq. miles of the SBAs to the new republic. Ninety per cent of the territory returned would come under Greek Cypriot control; the rest would go to the Turkish community. The offer is only valid provided both sides agree to the UN Plan. Britain could have handed back, and some say should have, the territory under the 1960 treaty to the present Republic of Cyprus. However, although Britain admits to not needing the land in question for military operations or training, it was reluctant to give up the land on which many Turkish Cypriots live until a settlement had been reached. Marios Matsakis was soon quoted in the *Cyprus Mail* saying 'if they don't need it, they should give it back immediately and it shouldn't be part of a solution'. But the Greek Cypriot Attorney-General said:

'They want to make a gesture for the purpose of facilitating a solution to the Cyprus problem. The bottom line is they want to make a gesture, nothing less, nothing more.'[12]

With Kofi Annan in Cyprus mass demonstrations took place in Nicosia by Turkish Cypriots. Depending on which news agency you follow the crowd was estimated at between 40,000 and 70,000. Protestors carried banners with 'Save us Mr Annan' and others calling on Mr Denktash to sign the UN deal or resign. It was one of the largest ever demonstrations to be held in the north. Speaking to the Cypriot leaders it must have been apparent to the Secretary-General they would keep objecting for evermore. So Mr Annan put it simply; he did not want the leaders to sign the plan; instead he asked them to put the plan to a referendum of all the Cypriot people on 30 March. They had a week to come to The Hague with their answer, either 'yes' or 'no', and at the meeting would be representatives of the Greek, Turkish and British Governments.[13] If either Cypriot side says 'no' on 10 March that will be the end of the process, and there will be no other UN peace initiative during Annan's three remaining years as Secretary-General.

As Loucas Charalambous wrote in the *Cyprus Sunday Mail* about Annan's 'brilliant move to bypass the leadership of the two communities', taking away power from the politicians and giving it to the people reverting in a way to the democracy of ancient Athens 'has been enthusiastically welcomed by all those on both sides of the dividing line who genuinely want a settlement'. Indeed is it not a trait of most politicians to be more interested in power and their own views rather than in the will of the people? Charalambous went on to say, here we have:

> a UN Secretary-General who has decided that the lies must stop. A few weeks ago I wrote that our leaders were capable of 'negotiating' a solution for the next 300 years … At last there is hope. Now that the burden of responsibility for the major decisions is being transferred from the shoulders of incompetent leaders to the shoulders of ordinary citizens there is hope.[14]

Yes, there is always hope. But my mind wanders back to Michael at Pissouri Bay in 1992 and his resignation to the Cypriot burden of history. Have we not seen the same thing in Northern Ireland? Will the people get their chance and will they be able to overcome the burden of their history?

Jan Bradley recalls a story of hope and reconciliation:

> John Hercules was a successful business man in Famagusta, he lost everything during the 1974 invasion, apart from his car in which he escaped to the Troodos Mountains. John had fought with Grivas against the British during the EOKA conflict, so he knew the area well. He used to bundle his possessions under a bush during the day and used his car as a taxi, sleeping in it at night. Returning to the island in 1992 Geoff my husband and I met him; he was a millionaire once more. I lost contact with him several years later. John taught me not to hold grudges when the peace came after the EOKA troubles. John took the hand of a British soldier and offered to buy him a drink, when we first met John in 1969 and were told this story the retired soldier was there on holiday.[15]

At the 10 March 2003 meeting in The Hague on the Cyprus question, between UN Secretary-General Kofi Annan, President Tassos Papadopoulos for the Greek Cypriots and Rauf Denktash the Turkish Cypriot leader, also present were representatives of the guarantor powers, Greece, Turkey and Britain. The meeting failed to reach agreement on the referendum to have been put before the people of Cyprus on the UN Plan for a reunited Cyprus. The Greek Cypriot side agreed in principle but wished to continue negotiations on the Annan plan, while the Turkish Cypriot side and Turkey opposed the referendum on the UN Plan.

Kofi Annan had engaged in twenty hours of further talks overnight with both Cypriot leaders when they should have come to The Hague with a simple 'yes' or 'no' to the planned referendum. Annan announced at the end of the meeting: 'Regrettably, these efforts were not a success. We have reached the end of the road and I am not sure another opportunity like this will present itself any time soon.' But the people were not to be denied, the EU Commissioners thought they had agreement to a referendum and wanted the whole island to join and not to be lumbered with the Cypriot problem and insisted it be held. Perhaps they should have further insisted that only a united Cyprus could join the EU; thus both sides would have had something to gain.

Thus the people north and south had the chance on the 24 April 2004 to vote for the Annan UN Plan and put history behind them, before the south was due to join the EU on 1 May. But the Greek Cypriot leaders soon started backtracking on the understanding they had given the EU Commissioners to back the settlement. Papadopoulos appeared on TV, in tears, casting the Annan plan as the worst plan ever. Yet when talking to the EU he had backed it.

The 'yes' campaigners in Southern Cyprus came under increasing intimidation from the 'no' camp. Students were on the streets hectoring them and destroying their campaign aids. Former Attorney-General Alecos Markides said the 'unacceptable atmosphere' reminded him of the fanaticism of 1973. Then there were the priests whom Lawrence Durrell, years before, had witnessed meddling. The Bishop of Kyrenia was saying anybody voting 'yes' for the plan would go to hell. The Bishop of Paphos was ready to celebrate on 1 May with 'all freedom fighters of the 1955–59 period' with champagne the 'Cyprus enosis with Greece'.[16]

Given the atmosphere the vote was hardly surprising: 76 per cent in the Greek Cypriot South voted against the plan put forward by Kofi Annan, the UN Secretary-General, which had been backed by the EU and the United States, while people in the Turkish Cypriot north had voted 64.9 per cent in favour. Chris Patten, the European Union's External Relations Commissioner, speaking on BBC Radio felt the Greek Cypriots were 'not going to be a very popular addition to the family' of the EU. Gunter Verheugen, the EU's Commissioner for Expansion, felt: 'The political damage is large. There is now a shadow over the accession of Cyprus.' Alvaro de Soto, the UN envoy who had worked so hard on the plan for nearly five years said: 'A unique and historic chance to resolve the Cyprus problem has been missed', and his office on the island would close.[17] However, it appears the EU will go ahead with an aid package for Northern Cyprus and will consider the possibility of lifting the flight ban to the North. Thus, it is hoped, the Turkish Cypriots will reap the rewards for their courage of defying their politicians and voting to accept the plan.

In 2008 I was able to travel to Northern Cyprus via a flight to Larnaca in the South. Margaret, my wife, and I were met at Larnaca Airport by a taxi from the North which duly took us to Bellapais. It took only a few minutes to cross the border after showing our passports. Returning, the Greek Cypriot authorities only wanted to know if we had brought with us any cigarettes from the North.

As for the Greek Cypriots, their attempt to try to barter with the UN and mislead the EU is likely to cost them and renegotiating the plan is unlikely. Perhaps it will be to Britain again that both sides turn, with their bases on the island and their close ethnic links in the North and South, to try to calm emotions. But sadly it now seems like de facto partition. Indeed this is what Sergeant Williams at Waynes Keep thought might be the eventual outcome: 'Oh the UN might try again but after that, if the Greeks keep turning it down, there can be only one outcome, Northern Cyprus will become a country in its own right.'

For is it not so, as the great American novelist William Faulkner wrote, 'The past is never dead. It's not even past.'[18]

Notes

1. Harold Macmillan, *Riding the Storm*, p. 68, 'Although the resolution …'
2. *The Times* 1/1/2003
3. Farid Mirbagheri, *Cyprus and International Peacemaking*, p. 182, 'Resolution 186 …'
4. Ibid., p. 182, 'Article 2, paragraph 4 …'
5. Ibid., p. 128, 'On 11 January …'
6. Ibid., p. 128, 'A Greek-Cypriot President …'
7. Cyprus UNFICYP Background UN Documents 19/2/2003 p. 3
8. *Daily Telegraph* 5/7/2001
9. Giorgos Georgiou, Article, *British Bases in Cyprus and Signals Intelligence*, p. 5
10. *Guardian*, 20/2/2003, Behind the barbed wire of despair
11. *Cyprus Mail*, 25/2/2003, Annan III the key points
12. Ibid., 26/2/2003, Bases Offer
13. Ibid., 2/3/2003, At long last the people will decide
14. Ibid.
15. Janet Bradley LTA 26/7/2014
16. *Cyprus Mail*, 11/3/2003, so much for a simple 'yes' or 'no'
17. *The Times*, 26/4/2004, The cost of saying no
18. William Faulkner, *Requiem for a Nun*

BIBLIOGRAPHY

Andrew, Christopher, *The Defence of the Realm* (Allen Lane 2009).

Andrew, Christopher, *Secret Service* (Heinemann 1985).

Aristidou, Ekaterinich, *Kolossi Castle through the Centuries* (Nicosia 1983).

Attard, Joseph, *Britain and Malta* (Enterprises Group 1988).

Ballantyne, Iain, *HMS London* (Pen & Sword Books 2003).

Beadle, Jeffrey, *The Light Blue Lanyard* (Square One Publications 1992).

Bradford, Ernle, *Mediterranean Portrait of a Sea* (Penguin Books 1971).

Buckley, Christopher, *Greece and Crete 1941* (HMSO 1952).

Burch, Oliver, *The Infidel Sea* (Ashford, Buchan & Enright 1990).

Cavenagh, Sandy, *Airborne to Suez* (William Kimber 1965).

Cavendish, Anne (ed.), *The Journal of Sir Garnet Wolseley Cyprus 1878* (Cyprus Popular Bank Cultural Centre 1991).

Cunningham, Andrew, *A Sailor's Odyssey* (Hutchinson 1951).

Denham, H.M., *Southern Turkey, the Levant and Cyprus* (John Murray 1973).

Dimitrakis, Panagiotis, *Military Intelligence in Cyprus* (I.B. Tauris 2010).

Dubin, Marc, *The Cyprus the Rough Guide* (Rough Guides 1999).

Durrell, Lawrence, *Bitter Lemons of Cyprus* (Faber & Faber 1957).

Durrell, Lawrence, *Justine* (Faber & Faber 1957).

Ellis, Peter Berresford, *H. Rider Haggard: A Voice from the Infinite* (Routledge & Kegan 1987).

Faiz, Suha, *Recollections and Reflections of an Unknown Cyprus Turk* (Avon Books 1998).

Farid, Mirbagheri, *Cyprus and International Peacemaking* (Hurst & Company 1998).

Foley, Charles, *Island in Revolt* (Longman 1962).

Foley, Charles, *Legacy of Strife* (Penguin 1964).

Foley, Charles (ed.), *The Memoirs of General Grivas* (Frederick A. Praeger 1965).

Grant, Hugh, *A Game of Soldiers* (Beaulieu Books 2001).

Grove, Valerie, *Laurie Lee: The Well-Loved Stranger* (Viking 1999).

Haggard, H. Rider, *A Winter in Palestine, Italy, and Cyprus* (Langman 1901).

Handel, Paul D. *Australian Armour in Cyprus* (Anzac Steel 2000).

Holland, Robert, *Britain and the Revolt in Cyprus 1954–59* (Oxford University Press 1998).

Home, Gordon, *Cyprus Then and Now* (J.M. Dent & Sons 1960).

Jansen, Michael, *The Aphrodite Plot* (Kyriakou Books 1988).

Kelling, George Horton, *Countdown to Rebellion* (Greenwood Press 1990).

Lake, Carney, *Reflected Glory* (Pen & Sword Books 1994).

Leigh Fermor, Patrick, *Mani: Travels in the Southern Peloponnese* (John Murray 1958).

Lloyd George, David, *The Truth about the Peace Treaties* (Gollancz 1938).

Luke, Harry, *Cyprus under the Turks 1571–1878* (Coup 1921).

Luke, Harry, *Cyprus: A Portrait and an Appreciation* (George G. Harrap 1957).

Macmillan, Harold, *Riding the Storm 1956–1959* (Macmillan & Co 1971).

Macmillan, Margaret, *Peacemakers* (John Murray 2001).

Matthews, David, *The Cyprus Tapes* (Kemel Rustem & Brother 1987).

Matthews, John and Stewart, Bob, *Warriors of Christendom* (Firebird Books 1988).

Max, Arthur, *Men of the Red Beret* (Hutchinson 1990).

Morgan, Tabitha, *Sweet and Bitter Island* (I.B. Tauris 2010).

Morris, Jan, *Pax Britannica* (Faber & Faber 1968).

Morris, Jan, *Heaven's Command* (Faber & Faber 1973).

Morris, Jan, *Farewell the Trumpets* (Faber & Faber 1978).

Neillands, Robin, *By Sea By Land: The Story of the Royal Marine Commandos* (Weidenfeld & Nicolson 1987).

Neillands, Robin, *A Fighting Retreat* (Hodder & Stoughton 1996).

Orr, C.W.J., *Cyprus under British Rule* (Zeno 1972).

Panteli, Stavros, *A New History of Cyprus* (East West Publications 1988).

Panteli, Stavros, *The Making of Modern Cyprus* (International Publications Ltd 1990).

Parker, John, *The Paras* (Metro Books 2000).

Pettifer, John, *The Turkish Labyrinth: Ataturk and the New Islam* (Viking 1997).

Playfair, Major General I.S.O., *The Mediterranean & Middle East*, Volume 1 (HMSO 1954).

Playfair, Major General I.S.O., *The Mediterranean & Middle East*, Volume 2 (HMSO 1956).

Reddaway, John, *Burdened with Cyprus* (Weidenfeld & Nicolson 1986).

Rogers, Anthony, *Churchill's Folly* (Cassell 2003).

Stark, Freya, *Dust in the Lion's Paw* (John Murray 1962).

Stiles, G.M.L., *Mayhem in the Med* (Savannah 2005).

Taylor, Jack, *A Copper in Kypriou* (National Ex-Service Newspaper 2001).

Thompson, Julian, *The Royal Marines: From Sea Soldiers to Special Forces* (Sidgwick & Jackson 2000).

Thubron, Colin, *Journey into Cyprus* (William Heinemann 1975).

Tremayne, Penelope, *Below the Tide* (Hutchinson 1958).

Walker, Adrian, *Six Campaigns* (Leo Cooper 1993).

Waugh, Auberon, *Will This Do?* (Century 1991).

Winward, Walter, *The Conscripts* (Cassell 1968).

Wright, Peter, *Spycatcher* (Viking 1987).

Young, David, *Four Five: The Story of 45 Commando Royal Marines* (Leo Cooper 1972).

Archives

Central Intelligence Agency Centre for the Study of Intelligence
Imperial War Museum
Museum of the Royal Marines
Public Records Office, Kew
United Nations Security Council Official Records

Internet

Anzac Steel –   www.anzacsteel.hobbyvista.com
Britain's Small Wars –   www.britains-smallwars.com
UN News Centre –   www.un.org

Journals and Newspapers

Cyprus Mail
Cyprus Times
Daily Telegraph
Guardian
Illustrated London News
Medal News
The Sunday Times
The Times
Warships International Fleet Review Magazine

INDEX

Visit our website and discover thousands of other History Press books.

www.thehistorypress.co.uk